Thomas Wilson Sir Robert

Narrative of Events During the Invasion of Russia by Napoleon Bonaparte

and the Retreat of the French Army. 1812, Second Edition

Thomas Wilson Sir Robert

Narrative of Events During the Invasion of Russia by Napoleon Bonaparte
and the Retreat of the French Army. 1812, Second Edition

ISBN/EAN: 9783337350673

Printed in Europe, USA, Canada, Australia, Japan

Cover: Foto ©ninafisch / pixelio.de

More available books at **www.hansebooks.com**

NARRATIVE OF EVENTS

DURING

THE INVASION OF RUSSIA

BY NAPOLEON BONAPARTE,

AND

THE RETREAT OF THE FRENCH ARMY.

1812.

BY

GENERAL SIR ROBERT WILSON, K.M.T.,

BARON OF AUSTRIA AND OF THE HOLY ROMAN EMPIRE; G.C.ST.A. OF RUSSIA;
K.C.ST.G. OF RUSSIA, ETC., ETC.

BRITISH COMMISSIONER AT THE HEAD-QUARTERS OF THE RUSSIAN ARMY.

EDITED BY HIS NEPHEW AND SON-IN-LAW,

THE REV. HERBERT RANDOLPH, M.A.,

OF BALLIOL COLLEGE, OXFORD.

SECOND EDITION.

LONDON:
JOHN MURRAY, ALBEMARLE STREET.
1860.

LONDON: PRINTED BY W. CLOWES AND SONS, STAMFORD STREET,
AND CHARING CROSS.

CONTENTS.

	Page
Introduction	xiii
Preliminary Remarks	1
Commencement of Hostilities	8
Composition of the Confederated Army	10
Napoleon's Proclamation	14
Composition of the Russian Armies	16
Passage of the Niemen	22
Alexander's Proclamation, &c.	23
Advance of Napoleon and Retreat of the Russians	25
Positions of the Armies	28
Question of the Nationality of Poland	30
Movements of the Second Army under Prince Bagrathion	37
Camp of Drissa	41
Alexander's Proclamation to Russia	46
" " Moscow	49
Action near Ostrowno	52
" Peczouka	53
Retreat on Smolensk	55
Napoleon at Witepsk	56
Second Army	58
Secession of the King of Westphalia	59
French at Mohilew	60
Davoust attacked at Saltanowka	63
Operations of the First Army under Tormanssow	66
Tormanssow attacked at Gorodeczna	68
Wittgenstein—Essen—Extreme Right Wing of the Russians	73

CONTENTS.

	Page
Action with Oudinot	74
Alexander at Moscow	78
,, S. Petersburg and Abo	79
Junction of Barclay and Bagrathion	80
Napoleon concentrates his troops to move on Moscow	81
Battle of Smolensk	87
Evacuation of Smolensk and Retreat of Russians	89
Operations of Ney and Junot	92
Battle of Loubino	94
Operations of Barclay and Bagrathion	97
Mission of Sir Robert Wilson	98
Despatch of Sir Robert Wilson relative to Smolensk and Loubino	100
Mission of Sir Robert Wilson to the Emperor — Message from the Army	111
Interview of Sir Robert Wilson with Alexander at S. Petersburg — Delivery of the Message — Affairs of Turkey (See Appendix No. 9)	114
Confederate Army — Impatience of the Poles	120
Army of Wittgenstein — Attack on S. Cyr at Polotzk	122
Napoleon quits Smolensk	128
Imperial Russian Army — Barclay superseded by Kutusow	129
Battle of Borodino	136
Borodino and Eylau compared	154
Death of Bagrathion	156
Uncandid Despatch of Kutusow	157
Russians retreat on Moscow — attacked by Murat	158
Rostopchin's proposal to fire Moscow	162
Evacuation of Moscow	164
French enter Moscow	166
Burning of Moscow	168
Position of the Russian Army on the road to Kalouga	170
Sir Robert Wilson communicates his view of the capture of Moscow to the Courts of Constantinople, Vienna, and London	174
Manœuvres of the hostile Armies	176
Patriotism of Rostopchin	178
Contemplated treachery of Kutusow	181

CONTENTS.

	Page
Conference of Sir Robert Wilson with Kutusow, and result	184
Lauriston in the Russian Camp	189
Alexander's Proclamation on the occupation of Moscow	191
Alexander's Instructions to the Russian Generals	196
Movements of Steingell	198
Russian main Army—Unauthorised interviews between the Generals of the hostile Armies	200
Letter of reproof from Alexander to Kutusow	203
Czernicznia — Dispositions for the attack	207
Combat of Czernicznia and brilliant conduct of Murat	208
Evacuation of Moscow	213
Berthier's Letter to Kutusow and reply	214
Destruction of the Kremlin	216
Particulars of the Retreat	218
Russian Council of War — Sir Robert Wilson's advice to the Council	220
Battle of Malo-Jaroslavets	223
Vacillating conduct of Kutusow	231
Remonstrances of Sir Robert Wilson	234
Inaction of the French	235
Napoleon holds a Council of War	236
Napoleon retreats on Smolensk, favoured by Kutusow	238
Milaradowitch attacks Davoust	242
Davoust assisted by the Viceroy	243
Reconnoissance by Sir Robert Wilson	245
French fire Wiazma	247
French order of march from Wiazma	249
Napoleon re-enters Smolensk	250
Passage of the Vop	251
First appearance of snow	253
Horrors of the Retreat	254
Milaradowitch pursues the French	261
Napoleon re-organises his Army	262
Napoleon quits Smolensk	264
March Routes of Kutusow	265
Napoleon enters Krasnoi	266
Davoust effects a junction with the Viceroy at Krasnoi	270

viii   CONTENTS.

	Page
Continued vacillation of Kutusow	271
Boutourlin's futile vindication of Kutusow	275
Ney evacuates Smolensk	277
Desperate situation of Ney	279
Ney attacked by Platow and his Cossacks	280
Ney's retreat and junction with the Viceroy	282
Napoleon re-organises his forces and is pursued across the Beresina	284
Suspension of the Narrative — Operations of the Russian Flank Armies — Movements of the Army of Tchichagow	286
Capture of Minsk	292
Regnier surprised at Wolkowich — escape of Sacken	295
Cossacks surprised by Austrians	297
Borisow attacked and taken by the French	299
Army of Wittgenstein	303
Wittgenstein attacks S. Cyr at Polotzk	304
The French abandon Polotzk	307
Junction of Steingell and Wittgenstein at Lepel	309
French surprised — Victor attacks Wittgenstein	310
Victor retires to Ratuliczi, and forms the rearguard of the French Army	312
Retrospect of the Campaign	313
Passage of the Beresina — particulars of the retreat	319
Napoleon crosses the Beresina	328
Tchichagow pursues the fugitives	337
Condition of the remnant of the French Army	338
"The 29th Bulletin"	339
Napoleon quits the Army for Paris	340
Faults of the Commanders	341
Napoleon arrives at Warsaw	344
Napoleon reaches Paris	345
Retreat of the French on the Niemen	347
Platow attacks Ney at Kowno	348
Wreck of the French Army	349
Kutusow at Wilna	351

CONTENTS.

	Page
Alexander arrives at Wilna	353
Death of Lord Tyrconnel	355
Interview of Sir Robert Wilson with the Emperor	356
Retreat of Macdonald	358
Defection of Yorck	359
Investment of Dantzic	365
Retreat of Schwarzenberg	366
Capitulation of Warsaw — Alexander crosses the Niemen to Merecz	367
End of the Campaign — Alexander's Declaration to his Army	368
Conclusion	370

APPENDIX.

LETTERS AND DESPATCHES.

	Page
1.—Marquis Wellesley to Sir Robert Wilson	373
2.—Lord Castlereagh to Sir Robert Wilson	ib.
3.—Sir Robert Wilson to the Marquis Wellesley	374
4.—Sir Robert Wilson to Mr. Liston	376
5.—Mr. Liston to Sir Robert Wilson	380
6.—Mr. Liston to Sir Robert Wilson	381
7.—Sir Robert Wilson to Earl Cathcart	382
8.—Sir Robert Wilson to Earl Cathcart	384
9.—Sir Robert Wilson to the Emperor Alexander	387
10.—Lord Castlereagh to Sir Robert Wilson	391
11.—Earl Cathcart to Sir Robert Wilson — Extract	392
12.—Earl Cathcart to Sir Robert Wilson	ib.
13.—Sir Robert Wilson to the Duke of Gloucester	393
14.—Sir Robert Wilson to the Duke of Gloucester	398
15.—Mr. Liston to Sir Robert Wilson	400
16.—Mr. Liston to Sir Robert Wilson — Extract	401
17.—Duke of Wurtemberg to Sir Robert Wilson	402
18.—Count Woronzow to Sir Robert Wilson	403
19.—The Duke of York to Sir Robert Wilson	ib.

CONTENTS.

	Page
20.—Sir Robert Wilson to the Emperor Alexander	404
21.—Lord Dumfermline to Sir Robert Wilson	405
22.—Admiral Tchichagow to Sir Robert Wilson	406
23.—Lord Holland to Sir Robert Wilson	408
24.—Count Ludolf to Sir Robert Wilson	ib.
25.—Translation of Russian Order of the Day	409
26.—Count Italinsky to Sir Robert Wilson	411

INTRODUCTION.

INTRODUCTION.

SIR ROBERT THOMAS WILSON was born in London, in August, 1777.

In the autumn of 1793 he received his first commission in the British army.

Very early in his military career he challenged the notice and won the confidence of men in power; and in successive years, down to the close of the war in 1814, occupied several posts of trust and importance.

From time to time during that period of general convulsion he obtained marks of distinguished approbation for zealous and effective services; and received from all the Sovereigns of the Great Alliance, *except his own*, amidst the acclamation of the armies of Europe and their chiefs, those personal decorations which exhibit the Royal recognition of conspicuous loyalty, pure honour, and foremost heroism in the fields of battle.

The exception was no impeachment of Sir Robert Wilson's deeds and character. He won his title to his Sovereign's favour nobly, and he claimed it proudly. His witnesses are Emperors and Kings, Commanders and Statesmen.*

But this is neither the time nor the place to vindicate that title.

There are in the Editor's hands materials for a full memoir of Sir Robert Wilson's private and political as well as of his military life; and these will be prepared for publication as the only answer to works which from time to time issue from the press, reviving misapprehensions and misrepresentations of bygone years and of the passing day. His defence against such attacks as these will be veracious history.

The fact of Sir Robert Wilson's employment in the mission to Constantinople in the year 1812—his presence and authorized action at S. Petersburg, and at the head-quarters of the Russian army through a large portion of the operations—his well known military capacity and personal energy and intelligence—and, finally, the celebrity of his previous writings—raised a general expectation that he would be the historian of the campaign.†

There were reasons, however, for withholding the narrative at that time with which every generous mind will sympathize. In a private letter, dated "at Plosk on the Vistula, February 5, 1813," he writes, "A letter from England offers me a thousand guineas for my papers relative to this campaign. I answered

* See Appendix, Nos. 11, 12, 17, 18, 22, 23, 24, 26.
† See No. 21.

that 'I was a public servant, and could not publish without the sanction of His Majesty's Government, which I should not ask for, nor deem it expedient to make use of if granted.' I never write from pecuniary stimulants—other feelings must prompt me to undertake any military Work; but the events of this campaign will never be traced by me for the public during my life; a variety of considerations imperatively forbids the communication of my view of the past."

Among these considerations a principal one was that he had been in close personal intimacy with the Emperor Alexander, highly trusted and honoured by him. The disclosure of facts and opinions to which he could only have access through this confidence of a generous friendship would have prejudicially affected the relations of the Emperor with his great nobility; and, moreover, it would have given pain to some with whom he had himself relations of attachment and esteem formed by the fellowship of danger among the moving scenes of military service.

Meanwhile, he recorded with exact care the events of which he was a personal witness. He felt the claims of society; felt that the interests of mankind demand from competent narrators, for enduring example, a record of the actions of men entrusted with the conduct of the affairs of nations. The lapse of years, he knew, removes the obstacles which present themselves in the circumstances of the passing period, and liberates the historian's pen.

It appears to the Editor, and to others who have been consulted, that a sufficient time has now gone by; and that without offence against any of those courtesies which the Author himself was scrupulously careful to respect, his narrative may be given in its integrity.

It is therefore published in the full assurance that truth without exaggeration and without injurious suppression is the characteristic of its pages.

A brief relation of the Author's military and diplomatic services is proper in this place: it is given from a memorandum in his own handwriting.

Sir Robert Thomas Wilson joined the British army on the Continent, at the conclusion of the year 1793, as Cornet in the 15th Light Dragoons, the regiment of his own selection.

His first commission was given to him by the Duke of York, on application for a commission in the Guards or cavalry sanctioned by His Majesty George the Third, as an act of personal favour.

All his other steps were obtained by purchase. On the 24th of April, 1794, he was present with his corps in the action of Villars en Couché. For conduct in this action the Emperor Francis I. conferred on each officer a gold medal struck for the occasion, with the inscription, "Forti Britanno in exercitu fœderato ad Cameracum, 24° Aprilis 1794," and further approved the decision of the Aulic Council which gave them the Cross of Maria Theresa and diplomas of Barons of the Austrian States.

INTRODUCTION.

He served with his corps through the campaigns of Flanders and Holland,* and re-embarked with it in the year 1796, having purchased his Lieutenancy, and soon after purchasing a troop.

In the year 1797 he was allowed to quit his corps to go on Major-General St. John's staff to Ireland, where he served as Brigade-Major, and afterwards as Aide-de-camp during the rebellion.

In 1799, on hearing that there was about to be an expedition to the Continent, he rejoined the 15th Light Dragoons, and proceeded to the Helder with his troop, which was engaged in all the affairs. On the convention being signed, he returned with his corps to England.†

Being desirous of joining the British army in the Mediterranean, under the orders of Sir Ralph Abercromby, he bought the Majority of Hompesch's Hussars. His Majesty's Government then despatched him to Lord Minto at Vienna, by whom he was sent to the Austrian army in Italy. Having communicated with General Bellegarde and Lord William Bentinck, then

---

* Sir Robert Wilson was present in all the battles, combats, and operations of these campaigns, the 15th being always engaged; and he was in the famous Peloton, which penetrated through the French army, sixty thousand strong and advancing on Bortel, to General Pichegru's headquarters, where it surprised and put to flight the head-quarters staff, taking one of the aides-de-camp, a secretary, and some gensdarmes; all of whom it brought off safe to the advanced posts of the British army, though pursued by several regiments of cavalry and, for the last league, in view and under their fire. Among the many actions in which the 15th was conspicuous were those of the 17th, 18th, 24th, 26th of April—10th, 17th, 18th, 22nd of May. Sortie of Nimeguen, Duffel, on the Waal, &c.

† In one action, on the 10th of October, the 15th charged and took the two guns that swept the beach.

b

commissioned with the Austrian army, he proceeded to get information for Sir Ralph Abercromby (whose army it was then supposed would act in Italy) at Naples and in Sicily.

Before, however, he reached Malta* the army had sailed; the expedition to Italy having been countermanded, and that to Egypt ordered. He then joined Sir Ralph Abercromby at Marmorice Bay in Asia Minor, and took the command of his corps, with which he landed in Egypt, and served the whole campaign, being attached to the army that moved on Cairo.

After the capture of Alexandria and embarkation of the French forces he joined the expedition destined against Corfu.

The preliminaries of peace being ratified on the passage, the expedition bore up for Malta, when Sir Robert Wilson returned to England by way of France.

On the renewal of the war he was made inspecting field officer, under the orders of General Simcoe, in the counties of Devon and Somerset.

After two years' employment he was allowed to purchase a Lieutenant-Colonelcy in the 19th Light Dragoons, and to exchange into the 20th Light Dragoons.

The effective part of the regiment was in Sicily, but he organized the remaining troops so rapidly that

---

* Sir Robert Wilson was all but lost twice in making the attempt to go from Messina—once in a small boat of the country, which was thrown on shore; and again in a brig that was dismasted, being taken aback just as she was within half cable's length of the breakers.

they were in a short time reported fit fo service; and he was sent with them, and in command of the cavalry detachments proceeding to India, to join the expedition of Sir David Baird then rendezvousing at Cork.

The expedition proceeded to the Brazils,* where he purchased the horses for the cavalry, and thence to the Cape of Good Hope.

He assisted at the capture; and after some time, receiving advice that if he returned to England opportunity might be offered for service on the Continent, he obtained leave to return.

Soon after his arrival he was directed to proceed on the staff of Lord Hutchinson, then going out on a mission to Berlin.

He was in the 'Astræa' frigate with Lord Hutchinson when she struck in the Cattegat on the Anhalt shore and, after remaining there eighteen hours without any hope of safety, was blown off in the gale, everything

---

* On going to the Brazils Sir Robert Wilson was detached in the 'Pique' frigate with half a dozen ships, to precede the fleet at San Salvador. Whilst running at night the 'Pique' found herself embayed in the breakers of the Roccas, and several of the convoy ran ashore. The 'King George' was lost, and General Yorke drowned in an attempt to descend the bowsprit into the surf. The 'Britannia,' a 1200-ton Chinaman, got off and then foundered. The 'Streatham' lost her masts, &c., and the 'Pique' was unaccountably saved, for she got into deep water without her way through the breakers being discovered.

On returning to England he was also nearly lost when in an open boat without water or provisions, and in the midst of the Atlantic. He was at sunset endeavouring to pass from one ship to the other that had not backed sails as supposed. Darkness surprising the boat and the wind rising, there was scarcely a hope, when one of the convoy providentially passed ahead and heard the hail—for the last signal musket shot had been fired in vain.

having been thrown overboard, chests cut away, &c., and carried almost sinking into Copenhagen.

On arrival at Memel he was despatched by Lord Hutchinson to the Russian head-quarters to reside there as British Commissioner.

He continued with the Russian army from the battle of Pultusk to the Peace of Tilsit,* into which town he introduced himself at the conference of the Sovereigns in the disguise of a Cossack, to procure information of what was actually passing.

After the Peace of Tilsit he proceeded to S. Petersburg, and was thence sent to England with despatches. At the end of a week after his arrival there he returned to S. Petersburg,† being charged with a confidential communication by Mr. Canning to the Emperor; and in a short time he was again despatched by Lord Granville to Mr. Canning with the intelligence, *which he was the first to procure*, that the Emperor of Russia was about to invade Swedish Finland and declare war against England.

Notwithstanding that a Russian courier had preceded him thirty-six hours, his passport having been expressly withheld to give the Russian courier that advantage, he pushed from Abo across the Gulf of Bothnia in spite of weather, reached Stockholm before the courier, and

---

* He was present at all the operations of those two memorable and severe campaigns, particularly the Austrian, and which included the great battles of Preiss Eylau, Heilsberg, and Friedland.

† Sir Robert Wilson was ordered to have a frigate at Falmouth, but there being none in the Roads, he volunteered to go in a little cutter, in which he was nearly lost off Gothenburg.

concerted with an English courier a plan to detain him on his arrival, which perfectly succeeded.*

Having communicated to the Government of Stockholm the impending danger, he proceeded to Gothenburg, where he prevailed on the Governor to lay an embargo on all ships for forty-eight hours, and then sailed in a man-of-war brig, but was driven back by a violent gale. Putting to sea again as soon as the weather permitted, he made the English coast, and landing, reached Mr. Canning at four o'clock in the morning with his despatches, and was directed by him to keep out of sight of every one till the telegraph had announced receipt and execution of orders at Portsmouth.

By nine o'clock he was informed by Mr. Canning that, in consequence of his activity, the 'Sperknoi' frigate, with money to pay the Russian fleet, then on the way from the Archipelago, had been secured, and that a vessel had sailed with orders to Sir Sidney Smith to intercept the Russian fleet and conduct it to England.

These orders, unfortunately, from some unavoidable delay, did not reach Sir Sidney Smith till twelve hours too late, as the Russian fleet in sight was just going into the Tagus when he received the communication.

On the following day the Russian courier reached London with orders for the 'Sperknoi' frigate to sail immediately from England, and gain the first port of

---

* The courier arrived about half an hour after Sir Robert Wilson, with whose pre-arrival he was kept quite unacquainted. Snow falling heavily, and the night being very violent, he fell more readily into the snare of delay.

safety she could make; and for the ambassador, Mr. Alopeus, to give notice, by the fastest advice vessel he could despatch, to the Russian admiral, that he must avoid the Tagus and put his ships into some port of France, if he could not reach the Baltic by going north about.

In the year 1808 Sir Robert Wilson was ordered to proceed to Portugal and raise a Portuguese Legion, which service he performed under very difficult circumstances. Having been made Brigadier-General of the army of Portugal, advancing into Spain with his Legion he covered Ciudad Rodrigo, and, by manœuvring on the Tormes, opened a road of retreat for General Romana's army from Galicia, and at the same time checked Marshal Soult's advance from Oporto, which chiefly preserved Lisbon from evacuation* till the arrival of Sir Arthur Wellesley.

He returned into Portugal with his corps when the operations commenced against Marshal Soult, and he was placed in command of the advanced guard of Marshal Beresford's column, in which command he obtained that officer's warmest approbation.

When Sir Arthur Wellesley moved into Spain in January, 1809, Sir Robert Wilson was entrusted with the command of a considerable detached corps, which manœuvred so as to obtain Sir Arthur's most flattering encomium, and which did in fact render essential

* Sir Robert Wilson, notwithstanding repeated directions to leave it and save himself, resolved on maintaining his position; foreseeing and stating the favourable influence which his perseverance would have on the invading enemy.

service by manœuvring on Madrid, and inducing the French army, after the battle of Talavera, to fall back, while the British army effected the passage over the Tagus.

The corps also, by opposing Marshal Ney for eight or nine hours at the pass of Baños, enabled the Spaniards to withdraw from Galicia without loss, and afforded opportunity for other advantages, if circumstances had permitted use to be made of it as proposed.

When the British army entered into winter quarters, he returned to England and sought other employment, as the Legion was absorbed in the new organization of the Portuguese army.

He was then made for his services Aide-de-camp to His Majesty George the Third.

When medals were issued for services in Portugal, Sir Robert Wilson received the medal of a Brigadier-General, according to his rank in the Portuguese army conferred on him at the demand of the British Government under stipulated conditions.

On the 6th of May, 1810, he offered himself for the service to which he was ultimately appointed, in a letter addressed to the Marquis Wellesley.

In August of the same year Lord Wellesley signified his acceptance of this offer of service.

On the 29th of November, 1811,* Sir Robert Wilson received the official notice of his appointment to a special service; but delays still occurred, and the designation of service was not finally communicated and the

* See Appendix, No. 1.

authority given for proceeding upon his mission, until March the 26th, 1812.*

On the 8th of April, 1812, he sailed from England with the embassy (Mr. Liston having been appointed ambassador to Constantinople) in H. M. ship 'Argo,' "under special instructions, and with the rank of Brigadier-General in the British army." Having arrived at Constantinople at the end of June, after various irritating delays he obtained the firman of the Porte for his departure, and on the 27th of July left Pera on a mission from Mr. Liston to the Grand Vizir at Shumla, to the Congress at Bucharest, and to Admiral Tchichagow, to conduct important negotiations. Upon the conclusion of them he was ordered to proceed to the Emperor of Russia at S. Petersburg. He arrived at S. Petersburg on the 27th of August, having been present at the battle of Smolensk on his way; and, having satisfactorily completed all the affairs with which he was entrusted, and received the thanks of Mr. Liston † and Lord Cathcart, he left it again on the 15th of September for the head-quarters of the Russian army.

The Narrative now published is in part the substance of information laboriously collected from credible persons and authentic documents at the time, and carefully compared and digested by himself; in part a record of facts which came under his own observation, and were noted day by day, on journeys, at his

* See Appendix, No. 2.   † Nos. 5, 6.

points of mission, in camp, in quarters, or on battle fields, by his own pen. The whole of these materials he revised, arranged, and cast in their present form for posthumous publication, in the year 1825.

After the passage of the Beresina Sir Robert Wilson accompanied the allied armies through Poland and Germany, and was present with them and engaged during the campaigns of 1813 in the battles of Lutzen, Bautzen, Reichenbach, Dresden, Culm, and Leipsic.

When the allied armies entered France, Sir Robert Wilson was sent as British Commissioner with the rank of Major-General to the Austrian army in Italy, acting latterly in concert with the British army under Lord William Bentinck and the Neapolitan army, and continued with it until the conclusion of the war.

TOLBURY HOUSE, BRUTON,
January 28th, 1860.

TO THE BINDER.

		Page
Plan—Murat's Engagement, Oct. 18th	.. ..	209
,, Malo-Jaroslavets, Oct. 24th	.. ..	223
,, Wiazma, Nov. 3rd	.. ..	247
,, Krasnoi, Nov. 17th	.. ..	271
Outline Map of Part of Russia, &c.	.. ..	*at the end.*

GENERAL SIR ROBERT WILSON'S RUSSIAN JOURNAL.

PRELIMINARY REMARKS.

VARIOUS opinions have been expressed as to the motives which ruled Napoleon's decision to engage in the Russian war of 1812.

This war derived its origin from the war and peace of 1806 and 1807.

When Napoleon quitted Tilsit, he withdrew deeply impressed with a conviction of the vast elementary warlike means possessed by Russia, capable of being cherished into formidable maturity even within a very few years from that epoch of discomfiture and, as it appeared to the world at large, of very long, if not irrecoverable exhaustion.

Napoleon had witnessed the unquailing valour of the Russian soldiery under circumstances the most unpropitious for its display, and had recognized qualities and properties which would render Russian armies, when duly organized, pre-eminent in some respects over all others. He had become acquainted with the no less resolute character of the Russian peasantry, and he had found nothing wanting which art might not supply for the construction of a military power on the most extensive, efficient, and economical basis.*

He was aware that many defects and abuses existed in the internal administrative system of Russia to check the growth of her prosperity, and the development of her innate strength; but he saw that those defects and abuses were only temporary restraints on the vivifying energies of a people that composed a national phalanx of fifty millions of souls, disordered by no religious schisms, enfeebled by no provincial dissensions, but combined and consolidated by a common love of country, and devotional allegiance to the authority of one irresponsible ruler—" Imperator et Pontifex maximus." †

His inquiries into the statistics of Russia had instructed him that, although her inhabitants were distributed over so large a portion of the globe, still dense masses were collected in the provinces in which the principal establishments were situated; and his military information apprised him that, notwithstanding there were nearly eight hundred miles of accessible frontier ‡ from the Baltic to the Dniester, a very few fortresses and têtes du pont, judiciously located, would render an invasion of her integral territory impracticable.

Time and distance did not diminish the fears which grew out of these calculations of Russia's counter-

---

* The Russian soldier's pay was not more than twelve shillings per annum; rye-bread baked like biscuit, and water, his only ration in time of peace.

† The frequent deposition of the sovereigns of Russia by the nobility does not impair the passive obedience of the nation at large to the succeeding sovereign in possession.

‡ 1000 wersts from Polangen on the Baltic, to Zeldcheki on the Dniester.

acting opposition to French dominion and ascendency in Europe; and the rejection by the Grand Duchess Anne of the marriage for which he had intimated his wish, "in order that the alliance between the two empires might be better secured," added personal irritation to his political jealousies, and disposed him to watch with increased suspicion all the transactions of the Russian Ministry.

Controversial discussions soon introduced asperity into the relations which had been established between the two sovereigns on the raft of the Niemen.

At Erfurth, indeed, Napoleon and Alexander met again in apparent amity, and there covenanted that each might pursue his war in Spain and Turkey, with a *carte blanche* as to their respective objects; but they separated without real concord and confidence.*

Alexander's inability or reluctance to prejudice English commerce to the extent he had promised was the cause of new reclamations, and hastened the opportunity which Napoleon had for some time been restlessly coveting, to reduce that power and influence which, as he now found, he had himself essentially and prejudicially contributed to augment by advancing his position in Poland and authorising his acquisition of the island of Aland East, and a part of West Bothnia, as well as of Sweden and Finland; acquisitions not only important for the security of S. Petersburg, but which, by throwing Sweden permanently on a feeble defensive, relieved Russia from the most embarrassing control over her views and operations against the Turkish empire.

* Alexander had required the annexation of Moldavia and Wallachia; Napoleon, the dominion of Spain under his brother.

It is true, there was always a propelling impulse to war, acting on and commanding the subjection of Napoleon to its instigations—an impulse not owing its incentives to his own temperament and habits, but distinctly to the very source and conservative principle of his throne. He felt, and all the world now acknowledges, that he could not *reign in peace.*

Peace was incompatible with his political existence—it was the destroyer of his power, gained by the sword, and which the sword only could maintain.

Under his chieftainship, the martial spirit of the French nation had been excited to the highest and wildest degree. France, always martially disposed, had become a military camp and community; her social as well as her civil system was framed upon a belligerent basis; war was the sole tie between the sovereign and the people; allegiance was demanded and rendered under no other tenure. There was no other shield against the hostility of the Bourbonists, the intrigues of Doctrinaires, and the insurrection of the Republicans, to whom peace would have given active and irresistible animation. There was no other check on the ever changeful, restless spirit of the French nation.

Still Napoleon, although thus unremittingly urged to be always seeking some new battle field, would not have selected Russia as an adversary, whilst the Spanish war was on his hands, but for the reasons and under the considerations stated.

Whilst these feelings and secret causes were bringing about a collision, current public transactions were the subject of mutual incrimination.

Napoleon complained "of the cold support given

after the battle of Essling, of the increasing armaments of Russia, of the projected erection of fortresses on the Dwina and Beresina, and of new commercial restrictions which, although in strict accordance with the treaty, prejudiced French interests."

On the other hand, Russia complained, "that although, by the treaty of October, 1809, she had acquired some additional territory in Gallicia, the hopes of the kingdom of Poland were revived by a considerable aggrandizement of the duchy of Warsaw, which hopes Napoleon refused to extinguish by a declaration in the treaty 'that the throne of Poland should never be re-established;' that Napoleon had incorporated into the French empire, to the prejudice of the balance of power, Holland, the Hanseatic Towns, and the duchy of Oldenburg; and that this last measure was an affront to the dignity and honour of Russia, as on the marriage of the Duke of Oldenburg with the Emperor Alexander's sister the integrity and independence of his state had been guaranteed." So incensed indeed was Alexander at this last act of indecorous as well as violent usurpation, that he made, and transmitted to all the courts of Europe, a formal protest against the seizure; nor would he listen to any terms of composition upon this point of grievance.

The reinforcement of the garrison of Dantzic to twenty thousand men, and the occupation of Hamburgh by the corps of Davoust, under the pretext of counteracting the King of Sweden's connivance with the introduction of English goods and colonial produce, accelerated the rupture, and rendered it manifest to Europe that war was inevitable.

Napoleon, by the magnitude of his preparations, afforded indisputable proofs that he had not been expressing simulated fears of the Russian military power, but that he really did entertain the conviction that the contest in which he was about to engage was one which required for its success the federated aid of all the continental states in alliance with France; and before quitting Paris, he said to Count Lobau, when speaking of the Russian colossus that threatened to bestride Europe, "We must make three campaigns beyond the Vistula to secure our peaceful possession of the Seine;" using a coarse, but expressive illustration of his opinions as to the necessity and probable duration of the struggle.

Napoleon quitted S. Cloud on the 9th of May, and proceeded to Dresden, where he arrived on the 16th. He was met there by the Emperor and Empress of Austria, the Kings of Prussia and Saxony, and a great *cortège* of Archdukes and their consorts, German Princes, and others.

The most brilliant fêtes followed his arrival, and all the crowned heads and assembled potentates strove to do him the most agreeable and obsequious homage as their Suzerain.

It has been said that Napoleon encouraged these adulatory ovations, flattering himself that such evidence of supremacy and subserviency would daunt the resolution of Alexander, dispose him to shrink from the combat, and abjectly yield to conditions that might be imposed to facilitate his own more remote views for the disseverment of the empire, by previous degradation and consequent weakness.

Napoleon certainly was not ignorant of the dissatisfaction created in Russia by the humiliating scenes at Tilsit in the year 1807, and the angry feelings which Alexander's public deference to his pretensions to superiority had engendered amongst his own subjects at that inglorious moment; the lesson had, in fact, been too impressive to permit Napoleon to entertain a reasonable hope that he could induce Alexander to fall again into the same snare.*

On the 25th of April Count Narbonne had been sent to Alexander by Napoleon, with the view of gaining time to carry out the military dispositions in progress. On the 27th of April Prince Kurakin, the Russian Ambassador at Paris, had given in his definitive note, with a declaration "that he must demand his passports if the conditions contained in the note were not forthwith admitted;" but he received no answer till Napoleon had quitted Paris for Dresden, and only then one couched in cold and evasive terms.

In the mean time General Lauriston, who was the French Ambassador at S. Petersburg, had orders "to follow Alexander to Wilna, where he had gone on the 22nd of April, and whilst complaining of the tone and tenor of Prince Kurakin's last note, to keep open negotiations."

The Count de Narbonne, who had executed his previous instructions, had already seen Alexander,

---

* The exasperated state of the Russians was such that Prince Czartorinsky and Count Nowesilsoff stated to Alexander the danger of the course he was pursuing, and after adverting to the secret article of war against England, they ventured to say "that this war would make him as unpopular as his father, and might lead to the same result." "I know it," replied the Emperor, without any emotion; "I believe it to be my destiny; I cannot avert it; I am prepared, and submit."

and reported, on his return upon the 28th of May to Napoleon at Dresden, " that he had found the Emperor inflexible without being arrogant."

Lauriston was not so successful in his mission, for he was prohibited from going to the Imperial head-quarters, and had been referred to the Chancellor, Count Romanzow, for his solicited conference; but Count Narbonne's intelligence " that Alexander had refused to enter into any new negotiations before the French troops had evacuated Swedish Pomerania and the Prussian States, with the exception of the fortress of Dantzic, but which garrison should be reduced to its amount prior to the year 1811," determined Napoleon to commence immediate hostilities; and quitting Dresden on the same day, he arrived at Thorn on the 6th of June, whence he despatched an order for Lauriston " to ask for his passports, and demand that French passports should be given to Prince Kurakin, who had been detained at Paris."

Some hours after Napoleon had left Dresden he received advice " of the King of Sweden's having, on the 24th of March, at Orerebio, entered into offensive and defensive engagements with Alexander;" and he was further disconcerted by the subsequent intelligence, "that under the influence of the British and Swedish envoys a treaty of peace between Turkey and Russia had been signed on the 28th of May."

Foreseeing, though too late, the relief which this peace would afford Russia, and to what a serious degree it might prejudice his operations against her, he immediately directed General Andreossi, who was waiting at Laybach, in Croatia, for his definitive instructions, " to proceed to Constantinople and effect a rupture, by a promise to the Sultan of recovering for him all the lately ceded territory, and even the Crimea." *

The confederated army which passed the Niemen under Napoleon's own immediate orders was composed as follows, according to an official return still extant in the French War Office, and which was framed from the returns sent in by the different commanders, without including the civil employés, servants, and traders who swarmed in every corps.

* Andreossi had arrived at Laybach on the 7th of June, and did not reach Constantinople until the 25th of July. He had been preceded by Mr. Liston the British Ambassador, and Major-general Sir Robert Wilson; and the treaty of peace had been ratified on the 14th of that month.

COMPOSITION OF THE CONFEDERATED ARMY. JUNE, 1812.

CONFEDERATED ARMY.

ETAT MAJOR.

Major-general	..	..	BERTHIER.
Aide Major-general	..	..	MONTBRUN.
Chief of Artillery	..	..	LARIBOISSIÈRE.
Chief of the Engineers	..	..	CHASSELOUP.

General GUILLEMINOT .. ⎫
General JOMINI .. .. ⎬ Extra for Special Services
General TORAZIE .. .. ⎭

Number of Corps	Names of Commanders of Corps	Number of Divisions	Number of Battalions	Nation	Number of Squadrons of Cavalry	Nation	Officers, Non-commissioned Officers and Soldiers of Infantry, Artillery, and Engineers	Officers, Non-commissioned Officers, and Soldiers of Cavalry, and Horse Artillery	Horses of Officers, Non-commissioned Officers, and Soldiers of Cavalry and Train
	Staff, Guard, &c. ..	..	..	..	..	..	3,075	908	1,748
1st.	Marshal Davoust	5	81	French	12	French.	68,627	3,424	11,417
			7	{ Spaniards, Baden, and Wirtembergers.	4	Poles.			
2nd.	Marshal Oudinot	3	88	French.	16	..			
			33	{ Swiss, Portuguese, and Croatians.			34,299	2,840	7,331
			18						
3rd.	Marshal Ney	3	51	French	20	French.			
			27		12	French.	35,755	3,587	8,060
			21	{ Portuguese, Illyrians, and Wirtembergers.	12	Wirtembergers.			
			48	{ French, Spaniards, Italians.	24	..			
	(illegible)	3	8		24	Italians ..	43,460	3,544	10,???
			2						
			47						
			57						

JUNE, 1812. COMPOSITION OF THE CONFEDERATED ARMY. 11

Corps	Commander				Nationality			
5th.	Prince Poniatowski	44	..	..	Poles	32,159	4,152	8,438
6th.	General Gouvion S. Cyr	28	..	..	Bavarians	28,228	1,908	8,699
7th.	General Reynier	17	..	..	Saxons	15,003	2,186	6,682
8th.	(Prince Jerome..) (General Junot..) (General Vandamme..)	16	..	..	Westphalians	15,035	2,050	3,477
9th.	Did not enter Russia until September 3rd.							
10th.	General Macdonald	30	..	16	{French, Germans, and Prussians}	30,023	2,474	6,285
11th.	General Schwarzenberg	27	..	44	Austrians	26,830	7,318	13,126
	Imperial Old and New Guard	54	..	35	..	41,044	6,279	16,322
Cavalry 1st.	General Nansouty	60	..	..	..	..	12,177	13,014
2nd.	General Montbrun	60	..	..	..	..	10,436	11,125
3rd.	General Grouchy	60	..	..	..	..	9,676	10,451
4th.	Latour Maubourg	44	..	..	..	..	7,994	8,765
	Total ..					372,508	79,775	139,877

To this force must be added Victor's Corps, which passed the Niemen on the 3rd of September; Durutte's Division, which joined on the 2nd of November; Loison's, which followed on the 16th; and the troops which were formed by Marshal Augereau, and stationed in the first instance between the Elbe and the Vistula, and sent into Russia by different detachments during the campaign.

Corps	Commander				Nationality			
9th	General Victor ..	3	..	54	{French, Germans, and Poles.}	31,663	1,904	4,081
	Gen. Durutte's Division	..	..	..	..	13,592	..	76
	Gen. Loison's Division	..	..	..	..	13,290	..	422
11th	Marshal Augereau ..	83	..	37	{Composed periodically}	65,000	15,000	20,000
	Total ..					123,545	16,904	24,579

RECAPITULATION.

Infantry	496,053		
Cavalry	96,679	Horses 164,456	
Artillery, engineers, and military equipages ..	21,626	.. 18,265	
Soldiers belonging to the different corps above inserted, and who joined during the campaign	37,100	.. 4,400	
Total ..	651,358	187,121	

	Pieces
Artillery with the Confederated Army	1,146 ex Austria
" " Austrian	60
" " Loison's	16
" " Durutte's	20
Siege artillery for Riga	130
Total ..	1,372

The whole military force of France, and of her vassal states also at the disposal of Napoleon, amounted at this period to 1,187,000 men:—

French troops	850,000
Italian	50,000
Poles	60,000
Bavarian	40,000
Saxony	30,000
Westphalian	30,000
Wurtemberg	15,000
Baden	9,000
Rhine, Confederated	23,000
Prussian	20,000
Austrian	30,000
Neapolitan	30,000
Total	1,187,000

Of which aggregate Spain occupied 250,000.

From this estimate it was presumed that Napoleon could not only apply the force required in the first instance for the invasion of Russia, but that he could command a reserve adequate to its maintenance, according to calculations founded on the usual casualties of war; but to insure this object still more indisputably, he had ordered the establishment of a national guard in France, which included every one between the ages of 20 and 60 capable of bearing arms, and divided this array into three bands or classes.

A hundred thousand Poles, exclusive of the contingent of sixty thousand, also implored permission to raise the standard of independence, and garrison Poland as the advanced bastion and rampart of France against future Russian encroachment in Europe; and there is no doubt that if that wish had been gratified, even a larger force would have been ready to take the field.

Of this mighty mass of six hundred and fifty thousand men which Napoleon destined for the invasion and conquest of Russia, four hundred thousand effective soldiers (of whom one hundred and sixty thousand were native French) and sixty thousand cavalry entered simultaneously into active operations against Russia; but the want of nationality soon began to occasion the most serious evils, for the heterogeneous multitude were actuated by no regard for the honour of the country under whose banner in-chief they were ranked by the inhabitants, without any distinction of uniform or of language. Authority was weakened by the commingled service of troops regulated by no common system; discipline became relaxed; insubordination produced all its disorganizing consequences; confusion and want prevailed; pillage destroyed the resources—for there were no magazines provided—and exasperated the peasantry, who were further infuriated by wanton and outrageous desecrations of their churches and sanctuaries.

The Russian is a religious votary, but not an intolerant bigot. He insults no one for worshipping the God of all according to the practice of his forefathers, or the fashion of his own opinion. He lives on terms of perfect good fellowship with the dissentient from his creed; he arrogates to himself no immunities or advantages founded upon his own profession of faith; but the famished tiger raging for food is not more fierce and bloody in his wrath than a Russian at the sight of his polluted temples and violated altars.

The columns in march were encumbered by an unusual quantity of baggage, an embarrassment which the ancients forcibly and truly designated "impedimenta belli:" it seemed, indeed, as if the different corps were transporting all their movable property with intent to colonize the country they were about to enter, and that the safety of the "*roulage*" had been ensured by the very natives whom they proposed to dispossess of their lands and homes.

On the 12th of June Napoleon arrived at Königsberg. On the 19th of June he proceeded to Gumbinnen, reviewing on his route 160,000 men under Davoust, Oudinot, and Ney, and the divisions of cavalry under Nansouty and Montbrun. He then pushed forward, and established his head-quarters at Wolkowich, two marches from the Niemen, where Lauriston brought him advice "of the continued refusal of Alexander to negotiate until Count Narbonne had complied with the conditions already notified."

Napoleon, highly incensed, announced the commencement of war with the following proclamation :—

"SOLDIERS,

"The second Polish war is begun. The first terminated at Friedland; and at Tilsit Russia vowed an eternal alliance with France, and war *with the English*.

"She now breaks her vows, and refuses to give any explanation of her strange conduct until the French eagles have repassed the Rhine, and left our allies at her mercy.

"Russia is hurried away by a fatality: her destinies will be fulfilled. Does she think us degenerated?

Are we no more the soldiers who fought at Austerlitz? She places us between dishonour and war—our choice cannot be difficult. Let us then march forward; let us cross the Niemen and carry the war into her country.

"This second Polish war will be as glorious for the French arms as the first has been; but the peace we shall conclude shall carry with it its own guarantee, and will terminate the fatal influence which Russia for fifty years past has exercised in Europe."

The Emperor Alexander had not been a passive spectator of these preparations, whose note had vibrated through the most distant regions of his empire, and of which the marshalled array now overshadowed his frontier from the Baltic to the Boug.

After the battle of Friedland, the whole Russian army which had fought that battle, and the preceding ones of Pultusk, Eylau, and Heilsberg, had been reduced to a wreck of thirty-six thousand combatants; and thirty thousand additional troops of the line could not have been collected within three months to cover S. Petersburg and Warsaw.

Five years had scarcely elapsed since that epoch of distress and depression, and yet Alexander, notwithstanding all the demands on his finances to heal the wounds and repair the sacrifices made by the nation, had found means to awe Persia still fretting under her inglorious peace; to control the turbulent and incessantly insurrectionary Caucasus; to carry on a costly, and, in the last campaign, splendidly successful war against Turkey; to force Sweden to sign away at Fredericksham the territorial possessions which she required for her protection against Russia, and for her own independence as a Continental Power; and, moreover, to occupy all the essential military stations of the empire: whilst, foreseeing the life-and-death struggle with France, he had been during the same time unremittingly organizing and collecting a defensive force between the Dnieper and the Niemen, which, on the declaration of hostilities, amounted to two hundred and fifty thousand infantry and cavalry, of which not above twenty-five thousand were irregular.

The whole regular force of the empire at this time amounted to five hundred and eighteen thousand men.

The creation of so large an effective force, with an abundant material and magazines of every kind fully stored during a continuous state of warfare, without any grievous impositions upon the country or the raising of any improvident loans prejudicial to the general welfare, whilst it afforded incontrovertible proof of the immense resources of the empire, entitled Alexander to great credit as an administrator and executive guardian. But the same activity had not been shown in all the departments charged with the completion of a system of artificial defences that would have given much needed support to his armies, secured their lines of communication, and essentially delayed, if they had not altogether baffled, Napoleon's attempts to reach either capital.

Orders had indeed been given to augment the defences of Kiew on the lower Dnieper, and of Riga; to fortify Dunaburg, and to construct an intrenched camp at Drissa on the left of the Dwina, which might cover the high road from Wilna to S. Petersburg and secure the retreat of the army in a retrograde movement, if one should be necessary. Directions were also given to construct a fortress at Bobruisk on the Beresina, and to form a tête du pont of considerable extent and strength at Borisow, also on the Beresina, and on the direct route from Minsk to Orsza; but when the war commenced the works at Dunaburg were little more than traced; those at Drissa were found not to be tenable; and the tête du pont of Borisow was only an imperfect field-work, not closed in any part.

The Russian force destined to resist Napoleon was divided into three operating armies, with reserves distributed at the different points and stations which it was desirable to occupy.

The following was the classification and amount of the different Russian corps at the opening of the campaign of 1812. But it must be recollected that Russian battalions were not eight hundred strong, that a squadron of cavalry did not exceed one hundred and fifty horsemen, and that a company of artillery consisted of only from a hundred and forty to a hundred and fifty men.

It should also be borne in mind, in order that there may not be an erroneous estimate of the relative strength of the combatants during the operations of the campaign, when corps and divisions are mentioned, that a Russian corps and division scarcely amounted to a moiety of the enemy's, according to the original formation of the confederated army.

FIRST ARMY OF THE WEST.

Imperial Head Quarters, Wilna.

GENERAL BARCLAY DE TOLLY, Commander-in-chief.

GENERALS LAWSON, PAULUCCI, AND YERMOLOW, successively .. .. .. } Chiefs of Staff.
GENERAL MUCHIN, COLONEL TOL, successively .. .. } Quartermaster-general

COLONEL KIRIN, General of Service.
GENERAL KOUTAISOV, General of Artillery.
GENERAL TROUSSOU, General of Engineers.

Number of Corps.	Names of Commanders of Corps.	Number of Battalions.	Number of Squadrons of Cavalry.	Number of Cossack Regiments.	Number of Regiments composed of Cossacks, Baskirs, Kalmoucks, and Tartars.	Number of Artillery Companies	Total Number in each Corps.	Remarks
1st	Lt.-general Wittgenstein ..	28	16	3	..	12	23,000	The 5th corps, commanded by the Grand Duke, was composed of the Horse and Foot Guards, and Cuirassiers of the Emperor, Empress, and Astracan. The 7000 Cossacks, Kalmoucks, and Tartars, under Gen. Platow, and the 3rd corps, composed 18 Regiments, and formed 72 squadrons, with one company of flying Artillery.
2nd	„ Bagowath ..	24	8	..	..	7	16,500	
3rd	„ Touchkoff ..	28	6	1	..	7	18,500	
4th	„ Schouwaloff ..	22	8	..	..	6	13,500	
5th	Grand Duke Constantine ..	26	20	..	..	7	20,050	
6th	* Lt.-general Doctorow ..	24	8	..	..	7	20,500	
Reserve. { 1st	„ Ouwarrow ..	..	24	..	..	1	3,000	
2nd	Major-general Korf ..	..	24	..	..	4	4,000	
3rd	* Colonel Pahlen	..	20	..	..	1	3,000	
	General of } Platow, the Hetman .. .. .. Cavalry. }	..	..	..	14	..	7,000	
		150	134	4	14	52	129,050	

The Names of the Generals of Division in this Army were,

1st Corps, GENERAL BERG SACONOFF.
2nd „ PRINCE EUGÈNE OF WURTEMBERG OBSCOURIEFF.
3rd „ GENERALS KONOWNITSYN AND SPIEGOONOFF.
4th Corps, GENERALS TCHOGLOKOFF AND BAKHMITCHEFF.
5th „ „ YERMOLOW AND DEPRERADOWITCH.
6th „ „ KAPTZEWITCH AND SICHACHOFF.

* The corps of Lieut.-general Doctorow, and of Pahlen, were detached to Lida, with the view of preserving a connecting chain between the first and second Armies.

SECOND ARMY OF THE WEST.

Head Quarters, Wolkowick.

Commanded by General of Infantry, PRINCE BAGRATHION.
MAJOR-GENERAL COUNT S. PAHLEN, Chief of the Staff.
MAJOR-GENERAL WISTITSKEY, Quartermaster-general.

COLONEL MORRIAN, General of Service.
MAJOR-GENERAL LOWENSTEIN, Chief of Artillery.
MAJOR-GENERAL FORSTER, Chief of Engineers.

Number of Corps, or Division.	Names of Commanders of Corps.	Number of Battalions.	Number of Squadrons of Cavalry.	Number of Squadrons of Cossack Cavalry.	Number of Artillery Companies.	Total Number in each Corps.	Remarks.
7th Corps	Lt.-general Raeffskoi	24	8	..	7	16,500	The 4 Cossack Regiments may be estimated at 30 Squadrons, 2 Companies of Pioneers, and 4 of Pontoniers, and are included in the list of Companies.
8th Corps	Lt.-general Boroedin	22	20	..	5	15,000	
27th Division	Major-gen. Neverofskoi, (on march to join.)	12	..	..	..	9,000	
4th Corps—Reserve Cavalry	Major-gen. Count Siewers	..	24	..	4	3,500	
	Major-gen. Ilowaiskoi	..	..	9	1	4,000	
	Total	58	52	9	17	48,000	

The Generals of Division in this Army were,

1st Corps, MAJOR-GENERAL PASKEWITCH.
 ,, MAJOR-GENERAL KOLUBAKIN.

2nd Corps, MAJOR-GEN. PRINCE CHARLES OF MECKLENBURG.
 ,, COUNT OURANOW, Division of Grenadiers.
 ,, KNORING, Cuirassiers' Division.

THIRD ARMY OF THE WEST.
Head Quarters, Lutsk.
Commanded by GENERAL COUNT TORMANSSOW.

MAJOR-GENERAL INGOFF .. .. .. Chief of the Staff.
„   „   RENNE .. .. .. Quartermaster-general.
„   „   SIEWERS .. .. .. Chief of Artillery.

Corps.	Number of Battalions.	Number of Squadrons of Cavalry.	Number of Squadrons of Cossack Cavalry.	Number of Artillery Companies.	Artillery, Pontoniers, and Pioneer Companies.	Total number of Officers, Non-commissioned Officers, and Soldiers.	Remarks.
Corps of Lieut.-general Kamenkoi	18	8	..	4	..	39,000	The nine Cossack Regiments may be estimated at 30 Squadrons.
Corps of Lieut.-general Markow	24	8	..	7	..		
Corps of Lieut.-general Sacken	12	24	..	2	..		
Corps of Cavalry of Major-general Count Lambert	..	36	..	..	..		
Artillery, Pontoniers, and Pioneers of Ponibar	..	..	..	..	3		
Irregular Cavalry	..	..	9	..	..	4,000	
Total	54	76	9	13	3	43,000	

The Generals of Division in this Army were,

LIEUT.-GENERALS KAMENKOI and PRINCE TCHERBATOFF.
„   „   MARKOW and NASIMOFF.
„   „   SACKEN, SOROKIN, and LASSKIN.

DIVISIONS OF THE RESERVE.

Description of Corps.	Battalions.	Squadrons.	Total number in each Corps.	Names of Generals of the Reserve.
7th Corps of Infantry	87	..	18,000	Major-general Hammeon.
3rd Corps of Cavalry	..	54	17,000	Major-general Williamenof.
Total	87	54	35,000	Major-general Zapolskoi.
				Major-general Prince Repnin (Cavalry).

This reserve was distributed at Riga, Dunamonde, Mittau, Dunaburg, Welix to Newel on the right of the Duna, Borisow, Bobruisk, Mozyr, Kiew, and the left of the Boug near Ovipel, as follows, viz.:—

Riga and Dunamonde	5,000
Mittau	3,400
Dunaburg	7,000
Right of the Duna	3,200
Borisow	500
Bobruisk	5,200
Mozyr	6,300
Kiew	2,500
Left of the Boug	1,600
Total	34,800

	First Army.	Second Army.	Third Army.	Reserve Army.	Total.
Grand Totals	129,050	48,000	43,000	34,300	254,350

Exclusively of these armies, the Moldavian army, that had been employed against the Turks, was composed of seventy-two battalions, eighty squadrons, seventeen companies of artillery, and fourteen regiments of Cossacks, that presented a total of above fifty thousand regulars.

This army was commanded by Admiral Tchichagow; but it is not yet the time to particularize the force with which he arrived on the Styr, to unite with the third army and assume the direction of both.

All the enemy's corps had not yet reached the Niemen, but Napoleon determined to effect the passage without further delay, and, dressing himself to appear like a Polish light horseman, proceeded with General Haxo to inspect the banks of the river.

The point having been selected at an angle formed by the river between Kowno and Ponemoni, General Eblé was directed to throw three bridges across, distant from each other about three hundred yards; whilst General Morand, with three companies, crossed in boats to protect the construction. In eleven hours the bridges were ready, "the war javelin was hurled," and the French troops, on the 24th of June, commenced the invasion of Russia, in presence of a few Cossacks, whom the French cavalry repulsed and drove out of Kowno, where Napoleon the same evening established his head-quarters, and ordered a bridge to be thrown over the Wilia.

Alexander, during the same night, whilst at a ball given by General Beningsen in his château of Zaerelt, a mile and a half from Wilna, received the intelligence of this passage, and on the next morning published the following address to his army, which was despatched to S. Petersburg with the letter that announced to his subjects his resolve "not to sheathe the sword till the invaders were driven out of his empire."

It is due to Alexander to put his address on record, for never did a sovereign more faithfully and fully maintain his engagements in the hour of adversity as well as of prosperity.

Proclamation to the Army.

"Wilna, the 25th of June, 1812.

"We had long observed on the part of the Emperor of the French the most hostile proceedings towards Russia, but we had always hoped to avert them by conciliatory and pacific measures. At length, experiencing a continued renewal of direct and evident aggression, notwithstanding our earnest desire to maintain tranquillity, we were compelled to complete and assemble our armies. But even then we flattered ourselves that a reconciliation might be effected while we remained on the frontiers of our empire and, without violating one principle of peace, were prepared only to act in our own defence: all these conciliatory and pacific measures could not preserve the tranquillity which we desired. The Emperor of the French, by suddenly attacking our army at Kowno, has been the first to declare war. As nothing, therefore, could inspire him with those friendly sentiments which possessed our bosoms, we have no choice but to oppose our forces to those of the enemy, invoking the aid of the Almighty, the witness and the defender of the truth. It is unnecessary for me to recall to the minds of the generals, the officers, or the soldiers, their duty and their bravery. The blood of the valiant Sclavonians flows in their veins. Warriors! you defend your religion, your country, and your liberty! I am with you. God is against the aggressor."

Letter to Count Soltikoff, Commander-in-Chief at S. Petersburg.

"Count Nicholas Iwanowicz,

"The French troops have passed the frontier of our empire. The strict observance of the alliance has been repaid by the most perfidious aggression. To preserve the peace I have exhausted all the means compatible with the dignity of my crown, and the interests of my people. All my efforts have been without success. The Emperor Napoleon has resolutely decided in his mind to ruin Russia. The most moderate proposals have remained without any answer. An obstinate invasion has developed in an evident manner the falseness of the pacific protestations again recently renewed. It only remains then for me to take arms and to employ all the means that Providence has placed in my power to repel force by force.

"I have full confidence in the zeal of my people, and in the bravery of my troops: being menaced in their homes, they will defend them with the firmness and intrepidity which characterize them.

"Providence will bless our just cause: the defence

of the nation, the preservation of independence and of the national honour, has forced us to draw the sword. *I will not sheathe it again whilst a single enemy remains in arms on the territory of my empire.*

"My best wishes are with you.

(Signed) "ALEXANDER.

"Wilna, June 25th, 1812."

Napoleon having made his dispositions, advanced on the 26th of June with the cavalry of Nansouty, Montbrun, and Grouchy, under the orders of Murat; and also with the corps of Davoust, Oudinot, and Ney, composing altogether a force of about two hundred and fifty thousand men; and he strained every nerve to reach Wilna, distant seventy-five miles, that he might bring the Russian army to battle forthwith, and before it could have time to concentrate.

Barclay de Tolly had meditated an offensive movement into the duchy of Warsaw with the Cossacks under Platow, to be supported by the second army, that he might delay the enemy's movement on Wilna: but on receiving accurate information of his strength, he represented to Alexander the absolute necessity for the immediate evacuation of Wilna, and a retreat by Swentziany on the entrenched camp of Drissa.

It was an announcement of great mortification to Alexander, who saw himself thus compelled to disappoint all those expectations which had been raised by the preparations for resistance so long witnessed by his troops; expectations which had been further authorized by the language, so recently addressed to them, in his own proclamation.

It was a painful decision to give up to desolation so much country—to create so much discontent in the armies—to cause such high courage, and ardent patriotism eager for the combat, to droop—to incur so much hazard as a retrograde movement under such circumstances rendered inevitable; but the safety of the armies, the preservation of the empire, did not permit a different course to be pursued, and Alexander had no alternative but to yield to the dictates of a stern necessity.

Orders were sent to all the detached corps of the first army to fall back immediately on Swentziany, which lay on the road to Drissa, and was about equi-distant from the right and left wings.

On the night of the 27th, after destroying all the magazines and material which could not be removed, the city was evacuated and the troops withdrew to Nemenczin.

Napoleon had been in hopes, by his rapidity of movement, to have cut off some Russian corps of observation, if he could not anticipate the retreat of the main army; and at all events to have prevented the destruction of the magazines and the bridges over the Wilia; but although he entered Wilna on the 28th, he found himself baffled in every expectation by the celerity and order with which the evacuation had been conducted.

As soon as the bridge was re-established, a division of cavalry was ordered to pursue the Russian column on the route of Swentziany, and Murat with the remainder of the reserve pushed forward in the direction of Nemenczin to overtake Barclay's rear-guard.

The same day that Wilna was occupied, the corps under Oudinot fell in with and engaged the rearguard of Wittgenstein, who was retiring on Wilkomir, which town was evacuated after the magazines had been fired: but no impression was made on the Russian troops; they maintained a steady course, and afforded time for the passage of the Lauta without any confusion.

Wittgenstein, on leaving Wilkomir, retired on Maliatz in the direction of Swentziany and Widzy: this town lay on the road to Braslaw and Dunaburg; but the enemy did not continue the pursuit for more than two miles beyond Wilkomir.

The King of Westphalia, with three corps, the 5th, 7th, and 8th, (Poniatowski's, Regnier's, and Vandamme's), and the corps of cavalry under Latour Maubourg, passed the Niemen on the 30th before Grodno, and was ordered to take the route of Bielitza on Novogrodok, to intercept Bagrathion's communication with Barclay de Tolly.

On the 29th the Viceroy had begun passing his army composed of the 4th and 6th corps (his own and S. Cyr's) and the 3rd of cavalry, across the Niemen at Pilony, between Plensig and Kowno, and on the 4th of July took up his position at Novoi Troki to cover the right of the army at Wilna, where he himself arrived on the 5th of July.

Prince Schwarzenberg had been directed to pass the Boug at Drogiczin, move on Prujany, and endeavour to intercept the communication between Bagrathion and the third army under Tormanssow.

Macdonald, with the 11th corps, had passed the Niemen at Tilsit on the 24th of June, and on the

30th had reached Rossieny, whence he proposed to cut off Wittgenstein from Mittau and Courland.

The following was therefore the position of the confederate armies at this first epoch:—

The 10th corps on the extreme left, Rossieny.
2nd corps, Wilkomir.
3rd corps, between Suderwa and Swirwintz.
Reserve cavalry near Nemenczin.
Imperial Guard, Wilna.
1st corps, on the road of Ochmiani.
4th corps, Novoi Troki.
5th, 7th, and 8th corps, near Grodno.
Austrians, Drogiczin on the Boug.

The Russian army had retired—
The 1st corps, from Wilkomir to Maliatz.
The 2nd corps, from Izerioidty on Gedroitze.

The 3rd and 4th remained in front of Swentziany, which was occupied by the 5th; and the rear guard, commanded by Major-general Korf, was posted between Swentziany and Nemealgin.

The 6th corps, Doctorow's, was on march from Lida to gain Wilkomir.

The second army, under Bagrathion, was at Wolkowich, with orders to march on Wilna.

The Cossacks, under Platow, whose advance had been driven out of Grodno by Poniatowski, had taken the direction of Lida; and the third army, under Tormanssow, was in cantonments between Novgorod, Molynsk, and Dubna.

Although so short a time had elapsed since the passage of the Niemen, and such few marches had been made, notwithstanding that scarcely any resistance had been opposed to their movements, the confederate army was already stricken with a calamity which seemed to be a prelude to its future catastrophe.

Five days' incessant deluge of rain, which had begun on the 29th, accompanied with an icy chill, had caused an epidemy amongst the horses (unable, from the state of the roads, to procure any other food than the green rye growing in the fields), which destroyed several thousand; occasioning the abandonment of a hundred pieces of cannon and five thousand ammunition waggons, and so disorganizing the columns by depriving the troops of the regular commissariat supplies, that numbers fell sick; and no less than thirty thousand stragglers were estimated to be wandering on the road from the different points of passage, committing every deplorable excess on the peasantry.

The march through Prussia, a friendly country, had been a disastrous infliction on the population, from the want of due administrative arrangements; but devastation now became atrociously savage, and terror general.

Napoleon applied all his energy to repair these evils—ordered provisions round from Dantzic up the Niemen, established on the Wilia large magazines which he covered with works, and made a citadel of the Jagellon palace at Wilna to receive and guard his stores.

Kowno was also entrenched, and defended by sixty pieces of cannon; nothing was neglected that might secure this his new basis of operations against incursionary enterprise.

At the same time Napoleon constituted a strong administrative government at Wilna, composed of

Polish nobles, for the direction of all military services in the country as well as of its municipal affairs; but he would not, as was required by the Poles, proclaim the re-establishment of the Kingdom of Poland; and on the 19th of July, when the deputation of Warsaw was presented to him at Wilna, and earnestly urged that concession, informing him that the Diet of Warsaw had, on the 28th of June, voted the re-establishment of the kingdom, he replied in the following measured terms, which caused disappointment and dismay in all:—" I have listened attentively to your representations. As a Pole I should have thought and voted as you have done; I would have voted like you in the assembly of Warsaw. Love of one's country is the first duty of civilized man. In my situation, I have many interests to conciliate, and many duties to fulfil. If I had reigned during the first, the second, or the third division of Poland, I should have armed my people to defend her. As soon as victory had put me in a state to re-establish your ancient laws in your capital and a part of your provinces, I did it without looking to prolong the war, which would have continued to shed the blood of my subjects.

" I love your nation—during sixteen years I have seen your soldiers at my side in the fields of Italy and in those of Spain.

" I rejoice at what you have done; I authorize the efforts that you wish to make; I will do all that depends upon me to second your resolutions.

" If your efforts are unanimous, you may then hope to compel your enemies to recognise your independence; but in countries so distant and so extensive, it is entirely in the unanimous efforts of the population which inhabits them that you can hope for success.

"I held the same language to you from my first entry into Poland.

"I ought to add, that I have guaranteed to the Emperor of Austria the integrity of his dominions, and that I cannot sanction any manœuvre or any movement, that tends to trouble the quiet possession of what remains to him of the provinces of Poland.

"Act so that Lithuania, Samogitia, Witepsk, Polotzk, Mohilew, Wolhynia, Ukraine, and Podolia, may be animated with the same spirit that I saw in Great Poland; and Providence will crown your good cause with success. I will recompense this devotion of your countries that makes you so interesting, and which acquires for you all the esteem and protection that I can give you under existing circumstances."

Napoleon indeed could not prudently take any more decisive step at that moment. He had pledged himself to the Emperor of Austria and the King of Prussia, "not to incorporate Gallicia and Posen into the duchy of Warsaw, unless a suitable and satisfactory indemnity should be provided;" and it was impossible to establish a kingdom of Poland without violating indirectly, if not directly, those engagements.

The importance of the alliance of Austria and the vassalage of Prussia was too great at this crisis for him to risk their defection even for the purpose of gaining the national support of Poland.

It appears also that Napoleon was not well pleased with the complaints made by Poniatowski of the want of pay and due commissariat supplies; for in a letter

to Berthier, dated Wilna, July the 9th, he writes—
"Answer the Prince that you have submitted to the Emperor his letter—that his Majesty is much dissatisfied to find that he is talking of pay and *provisions* when his whole object should be to pursue the enemy.

"That his Majesty is the more surprised when he thinks that the Imperial Guards, who had come by forced marches from Paris to Wilna, are not only without *half rations*, but *bread* altogether, and that, being fed *totally* on meat, they do not make any complaint.

"The Emperor has seen with regret that the Poles are *such bad soldiers and have such a bad spirit* (mauvais esprit) as to put forward such privations, and he trusts he shall hear no more of it."

In another letter, dated the 11th of July, he confirms the loss of horses on the march, and notifies his intention to replace some of them from the contributions he was about to levy; for he directs Berthier to write to Macdonald—"That he, Macdonald, had been in error when he said that the Emperor wanted to purchase three thousand horses in Samogitia. Tell him they must be got by *requisition*, and their price shall be deducted from the general contribution to be imposed on the country."

Another letter of the same date shows that notwithstanding the suddenness of this irruption, and the velocity with which he had swept forward, few prisoners had been made, for he directs that, "when 1,200 *shall have been* collected, they shall be formed into companies of 100 each, and marched to Dantzic. That during the march they shall be confined nightly in churches, and all attempting to escape—'Shot!'"

Whilst Napoleon continued at Wilna, General Balaschieff, Minister of Russian Police, arrived there on some pretext connected with the exchange of prisoners, and with instructions " to procure a suspension of arms, if Napoleon would withdraw his army behind the Niemen;" but as it was evident that this negotiation was only intended to gain time for the reunion of the Russian corps and armies, the proposal led to no result, except an increase of irritation on the part of Alexander at some slanderous expressions used by Napoleon relative to the Emperor Paul's death. This, the subsequent seizure at Wilna, of one of Maret's the Duke of Bassano's fourgons, full of publications in which the most offensive insinuations were introduced on that subject, aggravated to an intense degree of excitement.*

Barclay, who had retired upon Swentziany, where he was joined by the 2nd corps (Bagawouth's), continued on the 1st of July his retrograde movement upon Drissa; Doctorow, and the 6th corps, for whose safety great anxiety prevailed, having previously arrived at Kobylniki, which station was within two days' march, and in direct communication that could not be intercepted, with the main army.

This corps had been posted at Lida, sixty miles from Wilna and seventy from Wolkowich, Bagrathion's head-quarters, when the enemy passed the

---

* This publication, entitled 'Le Progrès de la Puissance Russe,' had been printed at Paris, and several hundred copies distributed in Poland. One of the copies, sent by Sir R. Wilson to Lord Grey, is now extant in the library at Howick. When the Emperor Alexander spoke with Sir R. Wilson on the work, he said he " never would forgive that infamous attempt to shake the allegiance of his subjects."

Niemen, and on Barclay's quitting Wilna, had been directed to fall back on Olchany.

On the 27th of June Doctorow began his retreat on the route of Ochmiani and Solly, and reunited his whole corps on the 30th at Danouchewo; but his flanking parties having found the enemy in Ochmiani, who were reported by some prisoners taken to be the advance of Davoust's army moving on Minsk, Doctorow feared to be preceded by his columns at Mikhalichki, and therefore resolved to continue a forced march on Swir:* and notwithstanding the heavy rain and almost impassable roads he effected it the same day, although Swir was still above thirty miles distant, and the succeeding day reached Kobylniki; thus, by his energetic activity (only with the sacrifice of some baggage) baffling the enemy, and preserving his corps exposed to a flank attack through the whole route.

The detachment under the orders of General Dorokoff was not so successful in its attempt to reunite with the main army, but was conducted through its trials with equal energy and skill.

This detachment, consisting of a regiment of hussars and two of chasseurs, had been stationed at Orany, as the advanced guard of the 4th corps (Schouwaloff's), when the enemy crossed the Niemen. Unfortunately, the order which had been despatched for the retreat did not reach Dorokoff, who, finding himself nearly surrounded, determined on the 27th to retire on Olkiniki.

During this march an order was received from

---

* Nansouty was moving on Swir with the division Morand, a light division, and a division of cuirassiers, sent expressly by Napoleon to cut him off, if he should escape Davoust.

Barclay for the detachment to move by Roudniki on Mikhalichki; but as Roudniki was already occupied by the enemy, he was obliged to make a circuit by Bolchia Solekniki, where he halted to be joined by two companies of chasseurs, who had been posted at Martsikantsy.

On the 30th a detachment from Davoust's corps fell in with and attacked him; but repulsing it with vigour, he gained Demenischi without further molestation.

On the 1st of July he reached Olchany, and there ascertaining that some of Davoust's advances had already entered Ochmiani, and would anticipate his arrival at Zachkewiczi, he relinquished the attempt to unite with the first army, and turned upon Koidanow and Wologin, to join and attach himself to the second army under Bagrathion.

The Russian army under Barclay reached Drissa on the 9th of July, without much interruption. Near Danelowiczi the rear guard had been attacked by the advance of Montbrun; but Korf, who commanded, retired behind the Dissna and succeeded in cutting the bridge, notwithstanding that Montbrun brought to bear on him thirty pieces of flying artillery during the operation.

Wittgenstein reached the Duna, or Dwina, where three bridges were prepared for the passage, and on the 13th of July entered Dunaburg.

Oudinot had so far feebly pressed his retreat, and the advanced guard of Murat did not pass Opsa.

The first army had thus completed its movement, and gained a resting position, without any disaster to its arms, notwithstanding that its alignment had been pierced, and its communications obstructed by an overwhelming superiority of force.

Generals, officers, and soldiers, had all done their duty with exemplary exertion and judgment.

It was suggested that Barclay, when he found his army collected at Swentziany, might have assumed the offensive, as Napoleon's force was separated by the detachments made to prevent that reunion; but Murat would doubtless have retired to gain time for Davoust and the Viceroy to manœuvre in rear of the Russian left, and when its retreat became necessary the difficulty would have been great, and an union with the second army rendered impracticable.

Had Napoleon been able to direct the Russian operations, he could not have traced a plan more suitable to his interests than such an advance would have afforded.

The only error committed by Barclay, so far, was in having pushed the whole army into such forward positions, when it was evidently not his intention nor in his power to defend the Niemen line of frontier. It was perilling the safety of the army, and incurring a certain waste of force; for although the retreat to the Dwina was accomplished without any military reverse, owing to the extraordinary marching and laborious energy of the Russian soldiery, still such marches could not be made with impunity and without a serious prejudice to the general organization and effective strength of the main body: this should have been preserved, as long as possible, from all avoidable reduction and impairment of its numerical and moral force.

The improvident expenditure of men, from movement of masses with an immense material as if they were a handful of light troops, has always been an error in the Russian military direction, and frequent occasions will be presented for recurrence to, and confirmation of, this remark.

Prince Bagrathion.—Second Army.

Bagrathion had been directed so soon as he received positive intelligence of the war having commenced, to sustain Platow in an attempt to create a diversion in the duchy of Warsaw, which might delay the movements of the enemy in Lithuania; but that project had been disconcerted by the advance of the King of Westphalia on Grodno.

Barclay on retiring from Wilna, had therefore ordered Platow to march by Lida and Smorgoni on Swentziany, and Bagrathion to secure his own communications with Minsk and Borisow.

On the 28th Bagrathion retired from Wolkowich on Zelwa. His intention was to march from Zelwa direct on Minsk, but General Benkendorff brought him an order at Zelwa revoking the former order, and directing him "to cross the Szczaya, and effect a junction with the first army in the camp of Drissa."

As the subsequent movements of the Prince were of great interest, and afforded various opportunities for the display of those resources and that activity which always characterized his career, it will be necessary to trace them with minute detail.

On the 1st of July his army marched on Slonim.

On the 2nd to Dworjetz, twenty-five miles.

On the 3rd to Novogrodok, twenty-one miles.

On the 4th his cavalry and detachments reunited with him on the Niemen, in front of Nikolaiew, twenty-four miles from Novogrodok.

Here a bridge was with great difficulty constructed, as the rains had swollen the river, and the materials for forming one were very insufficient.

The baggage was directed on another bridge, thrown across at Kolodnia.

On the afternoon of the 4th a part of the army began to file, and the remainder was prepared to follow on the ensuing morning; but during the night Platow sent information "that having reached Lida on the 1st of July, and being about to march on Smorgoni, he found that the enemy had already occupied Olchany in force; that bending to his right, he had reached Swir the next day, with design to move on Wicknow to join Dorokoff, whence his patrols brought him advice that Wicknow was already in possession of Davoust's corps, which some prisoners taken stated to be 60,000 strong"—a statement subsequently proved to be inaccurate, as Davoust had left three divisions behind under Murat.

Bagrathion, fearing to be attacked whilst entangled in the woods and marshes that intersect the road from Nikolaiew to Wologin, making of it almost one continuous defile, and aware that in case of repulse he could only repass the Niemen over the imperfectly constructed bridges of Nikolaiew and Kolodnia, determined to relinquish the movement on Wologin, and to gain Minsk by forced marches through Koreliczi, Novoi Swerzenn, and Koidanow.

Pursuant to this decision, he repassed his troops over the Niemen, and the whole army forthwith proceeded to Koreliczi.

Platow was ordered to defend Wologin, in concert with Dorokoff, until the 8th of July, and then to retire by Kamen, Khotowo, and Stolbtsy, on Novoi Swerzenn; but Dorokoff, on the 4th of July, had been obliged to retire on Kamen; and on the 5th Davoust had reached Bobrowiczi, close to Wologin, whilst his advance had already gained Perchai and Rachty.*

Platow, therefore, had no alternative but to follow the movement of Bagrathion, who, on the 6th of July, reached Mir.

Bagrathion, on receiving this information, again changed his direction; and, abandoning the hope of reaching Minsk before Davoust, determined to gain Bobruisk by the route of Neswige and Sloutsk.

On the 8th part of his corps reached Neswige, whilst he moved with the remainder on Novoi Swerzenn and Nieswris, distant thirty-eight miles, in the neighbourhood of which place he was joined by Dorokoff, who had successfully evaded all his pursuers. Bagrathion had again intended to push on to Minsk from Novoi Swerzenn; but a Russian officer returning from thence with the report "that he left the French close upon the town, which was in such confusion and consternation that he could not execute his orders to burn, in case of the enemy's near approach, the magazines and stores," Bagrathion struck back into the Neswige road, and made another angle of thirty-eight miles from Mir, instead of keeping a direct line of twenty-one miles.

* Or Rakow.

Since the second army quitted Slonim, a circuitous march of a hundred and fifty miles had been executed, instead of a straight march of seventy four which was the direct distance between Slonim and Neswige.

The army rested for three days at Neswige, to refresh the soldiers harassed by nine successive severe marches, and to allow time for the artillery and baggage to file on Sloutsk.

Had Bagrathion pushed on from Novogrodok upon Minsk, he possibly might have preceded the main body of Davoust's army, which did not arrive there until the 8th; but he had received an exaggerated account of Davoust's force; and, even if the truth had been ascertained, he could not prudently have hazarded a doubtful race, where he would have been exposed to obstructions occasioning detention, which would have permitted the arrival of the King of Westphalia pursuing from Grodno, whence he had marched with three corps on the 30th of June.

Had the King overtaken Bagrathion before he could make himself master of Minsk,[*] Bagrathion would have been placed between two fires, which would have insured his destruction.

It must also be borne in mind, to account for want or inaccuracy of intelligence, that although the Russians were moving in their own territory, the Lithuanians were not originally disposed to aid them; their sympathies were in favour of the invaders, until their merciless treatment by them as if they had been enemies converted them into the most rancorous foes.

---

[*] The failure in the occupation of Minsk must in fact be ascribed to the order brought by General Benkendorff, which diverted "Bagrathion's march on Drissa;" this deviation lost three or four days.

On the 8th Platow had been attacked at Mir by a Polish division of cavalry under General Rozineski, who commanded the advance of the King of Westphalia's army marching on Novogrodok.

Two attempts to make an impression on the Cossacks were brilliantly repulsed, and three hundred prisoners were taken, who were very well treated, notwithstanding that they were marched into the interior under a Kalmouck escort.

On the next day, the 9th, the same general, at the head of six regiments, renewed the attack, to revenge the affront of the preceding combat; but in the mean time General Vasiltchikoff had been detached by Bagrathion with three regiments of cavalry and one of infantry to support Platow, and the Polish General was again foiled with much greater loss.

To assist a clear understanding of the complicated movements of the several armies, and of the intentionally detached and incidentally separated corps, it is necessary to recur to the transactions which had been passing on the Dwina, and to regulate the whole relation by conformity of dates, so as not to anticipate too much in the narrative of partial occurrences.

Barclay had reached the entrenched camp of Drissa on the 9th of July, and on the 11th the whole army had been reunited. Four corps were stationed on the left bank with two divisions of cavalry; a fifth corps, the first, was posted at Balin, on the right bank, opposite Lepel, and was reinforced by the reserve detachment of Prince Repnin, which had occupied Dorina.

The 6th corps, Doctorow's, took a position also on

the right bank, near Proudniki, and on the left of the camp.

On the 9th Alexander addressed the following proclamation to his army:—

"Russian Warriors,

"You have at last obtained the result which you proposed when the enemy dared to invade the boundaries of our empire. You were on the frontiers to observe him.

"Until the reunion of the army, it was necessary by a momentary and indispensable retreat to restrain your ardour for the combat, that you might check the rash march of the enemy. All the corps of the first army are now united on the position preselected.

"A new occasion offers to manifest your tried valour, and to enable you to gather the recompense of the labours you have endured.

"May this day, distinguished by the victory of Pultawa, serve for your example; may the remembrance of your glorious ancestors animate you to equally glorious exploits. In following their steps you will overthrow the projects of the enemy directed against your honour, your country, and your families.

"God, Who sees the justice of your cause, will give you His blessing.

(Signed) "Alexander."

The camp of Drissa had been in process of construction for a whole previous year. The situation was well chosen to cover Livonia and the road to S. Petersburg through Sebije, about forty miles from and beyond Drissa, but not to defend the central provinces of the empire.

The site of the camp was traced on the left bank of the Dwina, in an angle formed by a bend of the river between Drissa and Bredgiowo. The exterior curve of the camp was about seven thousand eight hundred yards in extent, and the chord five thousand two hundred. The camp was defended by a triple line of redoubts, open at the gorge, sustained by batteries not closed and various other connecting works. A chain of ten redoubts resting on the right and left flanks on the river covered the front; but a marshy wood in advance of the left favoured an enemy's lodgment.

Eighty-one squadrons and ninety-four battalions garrisoned the camp; a hundred and thirty pieces of cannon were posted to command the approaches, and two hundred and twenty-two were kept in reserve.

The works of the camp were strongly built and well finished, but the arrangement was in various respects defective. The chief and usual Russian error was, dependence on only *one* bridge for communication with or retreat to the right bank. This single bridge was covered by a tête du pont; but in case of any part of the camp being forced, the confusion to gain this tête du pont would have been fearful and irreparable.

The Russians have had cause to ascribe many of their most remarkable successes in the Turkish wars to the neglect of due precaution for the passage of the rivers under hostile fire and pressure; but the habit at this period was as inveterately Russian as Turkish;

and during the campaigns that had preceded and those which followed this invasion, the Russian armies, from its existence and continuance, were frequently exposed to the greatest difficulties and dangers.

Barclay soon found that the camp of Drissa was moreover untenable from the dispositions making by Napoleon, who was collecting a force at Glubokoie, a hundred and twenty miles north-east from Wilna,* forty-five from Drissa, and sixty from Polotzk; whence he menaced Witepsk, which was at least thirty miles nearer Glubokoie than Drissa, and thus jeopardized the whole line of Barclay's communication along the Dnieper.

Barclay now also ascertained that the junction with the second army on the Drissa side of Witepsk was impracticable. He therefore felt that he had no time to lose in withdrawing from Drissa and filing by his left on Polotzk, in order to reach Witepsk, that he might anticipate the operation of Napoleon; and, having confided to Wittgenstein the defence of the road to S. Petersburg and of the country between Riga and Polotzk, he made the necessary arrangements for total evacuation of the camp on the 18th of July.

The disappointment, the mortification, the excited feelings of the Emperor and army at this decision, which did not admit of opposition or delay, but

---

* The Russians measure their distances by wersts. A werst is about three quarters of an English mile:—

	Wersts.	Miles.
From Dunaburg to Drouia	64	48
,, Drouia to Drissa	37	27¾
,, Drissa to Polotzk	85	61¼
,, Polotzk to Witepsk	130	97
Total	316	234

which should have been foreseen and provided against by due preparations in order to prevent prejudicial impressions, may be better conceived than described. The proclamation of the 9th was a painful record that could not be obliterated.

On the 17th, Alexander, deeply affected, left his army for Polotzk and Moscow, but before he quitted, he signed the ukase for a fresh levy of troops through the empire, in the proportion of five out of every hundred males.

An incident fortunately occurred to favour the Russian retreat.

Oudinot, after following Wittgenstein to Drouia, had moved on Dunaburg, distant fifty-four miles, and reaching it on the 13th had immediately attempted to carry by assault the tête du pont defended by General Oulaneff and fifteen hundred men of the reserve.

Oudinot was repulsed, but partially renewed the attack on the following day. Had he persevered, the Russian General would have retired, and given him up possession of the work; it being no longer of importance to maintain it, as the army was abandoning all operations on the left bank of the river; but Oudinot had also received an order to fall back and unite with Murat at Opsa, which order he obeyed in the night of the 15th and 16th.

Wittgenstein, hearing that the enemy had left only some picquets of cavalry at Drouia, directed General Bouteneff to throw a bridge across the river in the night of the 14th and 15th.

Having constructed his bridge he passed in the night of the 15th, with the advanced guard, and pushing forward on the road to Czernowo, surprised two regiments of Sebastiani's division, and destroying many withdrew again across the river with General S. Geniez and two hundred prisoners.

Napoleon had left Wilna on the 16th, and on the 18th had established his head-quarters at Glubokoie, where his Guards had already arrived.

When leaving Wilna he had been apprized of the check of Sebastiani, and apprehending that Barclay might be assuming a general offensive, he despatched orders to stop all his troops on march towards Witepsk by Uszacez and Kamen. Being assured of the evacuation of Drissa on the 17th and 18th, he ordered the columns to proceed; but it was too late to impede Barclay's movement, and bring the Russian army to battle, or even to harass its march. When Montbrun passed the Dwina at Dissna on the 20th with Murat's advanced guard, the whole Russian force had already reached Polotzk.

Alexander, before he quitted Polotzk for Moscow on the 18th, despatched the Grand Duke Constantine to S. Petersburg to animate the zeal of that city, and also employed him as the bearer of the two following proclamations to the Russian nation and the city of Moscow:—

First Proclamation.

" To the Nation.

" The enemy has passed the frontiers, and carried his arms into the interior of Russia. Since perfidy cannot destroy an empire which has existed with a dignity always increasing for so many generations, he has determined to attack it by violence, and to assault the empire of the Czars with the forces of the continent of Europe.

"With treason in the heart and loyalty on the lips, he flatters the ears of the credulous and enchains their arms; and if the captive perceives fetters under the flowers, the spirit of domination discovers itself, and he calls forth war to assure the work of treason! But Russia has penetrated his views. The path of loyalty is open to her: she has invoked the protection of God; she opposes to the plots of her enemy an army strong in courage, and eager to drive from her territory this race of locusts who consume the earth, and whom the earth will reject, finding them too heavy a burden to sustain.

"We call out sufficient armies to annihilate the enemy. Our soldiers who are under arms are like lions who dart on their prey; but we do not disguise from our faithful subjects that the intrepid courage of our warriors actually under arms needs to be supported by an interior line of troops. The means ought to be proportioned to the object; and the object placed before you is to overthrow the tyrant who wishes to overthrow all the earth.

"We have called on our ancient city of Moscow, the first capital of our empire, to make final efforts, and she is accustomed to make them, by sending her sons to the succour of the empire. After her, we call on all our subjects of Europe and Asia to unite themselves for the cause of humanity! We call on all our civil and religious communities to co-operate with us by a general rising against the universal tyrant.

"Wherever in this empire he turns his steps he will be assured of finding our native subjects laughing at his frauds, scorning his flattery and his falsehoods, trampling on his gold with the indignation of offended virtue, and paralyzing, by the feeling of true honour, his legions of slaves. In every noble Russian he will find a Pojarskoi, in every ecclesiastic a Palistyn, in every peasant a Minin.

"Nobles! you have been in all ages the defenders of our country! Holy Synod! and you members of our Church! you have in all circumstances by your intercession called down upon our empire the Divine protection! Russian people! intrepid posterity of Sclavonians! it is not the first time that you have plucked out the teeth from the head of the lion, who sprung on you as upon a prey, and met his own destruction! Unite yourselves! carry the cross in your hearts and the sword in your hands, and human force never can prevail against you.

"I have delegated the organization of the new levies to the nobles of every province; and I have charged with the care of assembling the brave patriots who will present themselves of their own accord for the defence of the country the gentlemen amongst whom the officers will be chosen. The number of those who will be assembled ought to be sent to Moscow, where they will be made acquainted with the commander-in-chief.

"Given at our camp of Polotzk, the 18th of July, 1812.

(Signed) "ALEXANDER."

Second Proclamation.

" To our ancient City and Capital of Moscow.

"The enemy, with a perfidy without parallel, and with forces equal to his immeasurable ambition, has passed the frontiers of Russia. His design is to ruin our country. The Russian armies burn with desire to throw themselves upon his battalions and to punish by their destruction this perfidious invasion; but our paternal regard for our faithful subjects will not permit us to allow so desperate a sacrifice. We cannot suffer that our brave soldiers should immolate themselves thus upon the altar of this Moloch! We are ready to contend with him in the open field, man against man in equal combat, he for his ambition, we for our country.

"Fully informed of the bad intentions of our enemy and of the great means he has prepared for the execution of his projects, we do not hesitate to declare to our people the danger of the empire; and to call on them to destroy, by their patriotic efforts, the advantages that the aggressor hopes to draw from our present inferiority in number.

"Necessity commands the gathering of new forces in the interior, to support those which are in the presence of the enemy, determined to perish or to form a barrier between him and the liberty of our country. To assemble these new armies, we address ourselves to the ancient capital of our ancestors—to the city of Moscow! She was always the sovereign seat of all the Russias, and the first in every moment of public danger to send forth from her bosom her courageous children to defend the honour of the empire. As the blood flows invariably towards the heart of heroes to recall valour to their energetic souls, the children of our country also from the surrounding provinces spring towards her, seeking in her breast the lessons of courage, with which they ought to defend their children on the maternal bosom and save the tombs of their fathers from a sacrilegious violation!

"The existence of your name in the list of nations is threatened—the enemy announces the destruction of Russia!

"The safety of our holy Church and the throne of the Czars, the independence of the ancient Muscovite empire, all loudly proclaim that the object of this appeal will be received by our faithful subjects as a sacred law.

"We will not delay to appear in the midst of our faithful people of Moscow, and from this centre we will visit the other portions of our empire to advise upon and direct the armaments.

"May the hearts of our nobles and of the other orders of the state, propagate the spirit of this holy war that is blessed by God, and fight under the banners of this holy Church! may the filial zeal extend from Moscow to the extremities of our dominions! The nation then, assembled round its monarch, may defy the thousand legions of the perfidious aggressor; then the evils which he has prepared for you will recoil on his own head; and Europe, delivered from slavery, will hail the name of Russia.

"Camp of Polotzk, the 18th of July, 1812.

   (Signed)   "ALEXANDER."

On the 23rd of July Alexander reached Moscow, and found the patriotism, loyalty, and resolution of all classes excited to the highest degree of enthusiasm.

Barclay had established his head-quarters at Polotzk on the 18th, but finding that the enemy were drawing more and more on his left, he commenced his march on the 20th, and on the 23rd assembled his whole force at Witepsk. The 3rd, 4th, and 5th corps, with the 1st division of cavalry, crossed the Dwina, and took post on the right bank of the rivulet Louczatsa, on the road of Bechenkowiczi, to observe Napoleon's movements from Kamen.

The confederate army had continued its pursuit. On the 23rd Napoleon reached Kamen, and the Viceroy, hearing that Bechenkowiczi was occupied by some Russian cavalry, moved on that place; but the Russians withdrew across the Dwina before his arrival.

The Bavarian light cavalry, without waiting for the bridge being constructed, which the Viceroy had ordered, passed the Dwina at a ford; and Napoleon accompanying, advanced a couple of leagues to reconnoitre in the direction of Kowalochino, where Doctorow was posted: he found to his regret that the Russian main army had already passed, traversing in six days a distance of upwards of a hundred and sixty miles.

Napoleon on his return established his head-quarters at Bechenkowiczi.

Barclay, perceiving that one of the principal objects of the enemy was to prevent the junction of Bagrathion's army with his own, had on the 18th sent an order in the Emperor's name to Bagrathion, enjoining him " to force at all hazards his way to Orsza,* where

* Or Orcha.

he purposed to reunite with him by the route of Babinowiczi;" at the same time he despatched Major-general Touchkoff, with two regiments of chasseurs and a regiment of Cossacks, with six pieces of horse artillery, " to clear the country towards Babinowiczi—distant from Witepsk thirty-six miles, and from Orsza fourteen—which was infested with the enemy's parties; and also to open a communication with the Count Orloff Denisoff in the environs of Sienno."

On the 25th General Osterman, with a brigade of dragoons, the hussars of the Guard and Soumy, with a company of horse artillery, had been marched on Ostrowno, upon the left bank of the Dwina, that time might be gained for the arrival of Doctorow, who was retiring from Kourslofchino, or Kowkowitchino, to Witepsk, from which it was distant thirty miles.

Osterman's advanced guard, composed of two squadrons of hussars and the company of horse artillery, imprudently pursued some advanced parties of the enemy, which, rallying on their reserves, resumed the offensive and drove back the hussars, taking six of the guns.

Osterman immediately moved forward the hussars of Soumy, and supported them with his infantry; but when within a mile and a half of Ostrowno he found himself at once opposed to the whole advanced guard of Murat under Nansouty, in which advanced guard there were ten thousand cavalry and a numerous artillery.

The action commenced by a heavy fire of artillery, and was followed by various charges of cavalry on each other's squadrons and on the infantry. The hussars of Soumy lost two hundred prisoners in one attack, and the enemy's general, Ornano,[*] was repulsed in another, with great loss, by the fire from the Russian infantry; but the Viceroy eventually supporting Nansouty with the division Delzon's, the force became too preponderating, and Osterman withdrew in unbroken order upon a wood, where he took up a position.

During the night of the 25th and 26th Barclay sent Konownitsyn with his division and the 1st corps of cavalry to relieve Osterman, who posted himself at Dobrieka, whilst Konownitsyn took post in advance at Peczouka.

At ten in the morning Murat ordered the division Delzon's to attack Konownitsyn, strongly posted behind a deep ravine, with his left resting upon a thick forest.

The attack on the right had partially succeeded, but that on the left had been checked: profiting by this check, the Russian reserve was brought to the aid of the right, which animatedly resumed the offensive, and drove back the assailants; but pushing too eagerly beyond the ravine, it was charged by the enemy's cavalry, and obliged to recross in disorder.

The enemy's right being reinforced, the Russians could no longer maintain the wood which, as the enemy proceeded to outflank the left, was gradually abandoned; but every rood of ground that permitted defence was disputed, and so leisurely was the retreat conducted, that the Russians did not reach Kukowiaczi, only two miles distant, till five in the evening: here they were reinforced by the divisions Touchkoff and Strogonoff, when the whole retreated on Dobrieka, and united with Osterman.

[*] A Pole.

Napoleon, who passed the night at Kukowiaczi, about five miles from Dobrieka, which is near eight from Witepsk, had arrived towards the conclusion of the combat, and urged its continuance.

As the Russians until they reached Kukowiaczi could only oppose nine thousand infantry and three thousand horse to twelve thousand infantry and between seven and eight thousand horse actually engaged, it was a combat that did them great credit; but in fact no troops in the world can and do defend ground in retreat better than the Russians. Their artillery is so well horsed, so nimbly and so handily worked, that it bowls over almost all irregularities of surface with an ease, lightness, and velocity that give it great superiority. The vivacity of their cavalry, and the unquailing steadiness of their infantry, make it a pleasure to command them in extremest difficulties; for, like the British soldier, the most unbounded confidence may be reposed, to use a sailor's expression, "in their answer to the helm" in every stress of situation.

Barclay, being assured that Napoleon was advancing with his whole army, and that he could not continue his projected movement on Orsza, to join Bagrathion, without exposing his right flank, nor sweep round by Suraje and Poreczie without entirely separating the two armies, once again made up his mind to hazard a general battle, although he had but eighty thousand men in his position, whilst Napoleon could bear on him with a hundred and eighty thousand, at the lowest calculation of the force with which he was approaching; viz., the Guards, Ney's and the Viceroy's corps, three of

Davoust's divisions, and Nansouty's and Montbrun's cavalry.

The Russian army extended along the right bank of the river Lausetza, running parallel to the road of Babinowiczi, with its right resting on the Dwina.

Osterman and Konownitsyn were recalled into the line, and relieved by Pahlen, whose force was composed of eight battalions, all the light regular cavalry of the army, and two regiments of Cossacks.

Every preparation was made for the battle that was now believed by all to be inevitable; but during the night an aide-de-camp of Bagrathion's arrived at the Russian head-quarters, who brought the intelligence "that Bagrathion had not been able to force his way through Mohilew on Orsza, and therefore had been obliged to pass the Dnieper and gain the Soje, with the intention of reaching Smolensk." After this information had been received, there was no longer any justifiable motive for maintaining Witepsk, with the assurance of a battle under such disadvantage of numbers. The army was therefore immediately directed on Poreczie to secure Smolensk and the union with Bagrathion.

The march commenced in the evening of the 27th in three columns, Doctorow, who had arrived from Kourslofchino, commanding the right column.

Pahlen had been attacked at dawn on the 27th, but in retreating obstinately disputed the ground, as he knew the importance of delay and felt that it became him to make the greatest efforts, and even sacrifices, to procure it.

His cavalry, supported by his batteries, one of which, a masked one, caused great carnage in the plain of the Dwina, executed several successful charges, and it was not until the division Delzon's had been brought up to support the division Broussier, that Pahlen retired behind the Lausetza. The enemy admitted that during the action, when a regiment of cavalry was withdrawn to make way for the advance of the division Delzon's, a panic seized part of the troops and was communicated to the followers of the army, who fled several leagues under a cry of "Sauve qui peut!"

In these three combats each party lost between three and four thousand men.

On the side of the Russians General Akouleff was killed, and on the enemy's General Roupel, but it was said through a mistake of one of his own sentries.

In the evening the enemy advanced along the left bank of the Dwina, whilst Montbrun moved on the right bank, and approached Witepsk; but such were the activity, diligence, and method with which the Russian army and rear guard under Pahlen had withdrawn from the town and environs, after destroying the magazines, that not the slightest vestige or remnant of the retired force was perceptible on the ensuing morning, the 28th. One of the enemy's historians, General Vaudoncourt, writes, "not a patrol, not a picquet, not a vidette was to be seen on a plain which had been covered the preceding night by a hundred thousand men: not even a peasant was to be found—all had vanished."

Napoleon, on the 28th, entered Witepsk with his Guards, a deputation having come out of the city with the keys; but notwithstanding this submission, and the presence of Napoleon, to whom in person the keys were delivered, and who had some time previously prohibited pillage "under pain of death," the greater part of the city was sacked as if it had been a storm prize.

The confederate army, indeed, (and it cannot be too often repeated for due impression of its consequences,) from the moment of its entrance into the Russian territory, notwithstanding order on order, and some exemplary punishments, had been incorrigibly guilty of every excess. It had not only seized with violence all that its wants demanded, but destroyed in mere wantonness what did not tempt its cupidity. No Vandal ferocity was ever more destructive.

Those crimes, however, were not committed with impunity. Want, sickness, and an enraged peasantry inflicted terrible reprisals, and caused a daily fearful reduction of numbers, which successive reinforcements could not adequately meet and replace.

Napoleon, under the incertitude of the Russian line of retreat, directed Ney to pursue on the road to Babinowiczi, and the Viceroy to follow and support.

Murat was despatched on the road to Suraje and Poreczie with the cavalry of the reserve, and after some hours' forced march fell in with Pahlen's rear guard.

Napoleon, on receiving this information, left Witepsk with his Guards, and ordered the Viceroy to fall back and join Murat; but, finding that the Russians were decidedly moving on Smolensk, he returned to Witepsk, and determined to rest his army for some days, a repose of which it stood in the greatest need.

The Viceroy was instructed to take post at Suraje, and Ney at Liosna, on the road to Smolensk.

Murat occupied Janowiczi.

Barclay had continued his movement on Poreczie, where the columns of his left and centre united: thence Doctorow was detached to Smolensk, garrisoned by Winzingerode with fourteen reserve battalions and eight squadrons: from this force, however, he had detached several battalions and some cavalry on the road of Orsza, to watch the movements of Davoust's detachments advanced from Mohilew towards Doubrowna.

Second Army.

Bagrathion, on the 8th of July, had, as has been stated, reunited all his force at Neswige, with the intention of reposing three days, whilst his artillery and baggage filed on Sloutsk.

Davoust had on the same day, the 8th, entered Minsk, where he found considerable magazines, stores, and supplies, with some cannon but the greater part not mounted.

On the 10th of July Bagrathion recommenced his march, and on the 13th reached Sloutsk, viâ Temkolowiczi and Romanow.

Platow followed, and, on the 14th, was attacked at Romanow by Latour Maubourg, at the head of a Polish regiment of chasseurs.

The Cossacks, however, repelled the assailants with great loss, and drove them back upon their reserves. Latour Maubourg endeavouring to repass a bridge with another regiment, was exposed to a severe fire of artillery, which rendered his attempt to renew the combat costly and abortive.

Several hundred prisoners remained in the hands of the Cossacks.

Bagrathion being informed that the enemy's parties sallying from Minsk had already been seen at Swislocq on the Beresina, only thirty miles above Bobruisk whilst Sloutsk was distant eighty, ordered Raeffskoi to march immediately on Bobruisk, and, if opposed, "to force a passage without regard to numbers," whilst he himself, with the 8th corps and the cuirassiers, followed to support. Platow continued to form the rear guard, on which it was expected that the King of Westphalia would press.

On the 14th Raeffskoi began his march, and Bagrathion on the 15th: on the 18th he reached Bobruisk, where he had been preceded by Raeffskoi, whose progress had not been resisted.

Platow had only been followed by the enemy to Oureczie.

Napoleon, displeased with the little vigour shown by the King of Westphalia in the pursuit of Bagrathion, and in his co-operation with Davoust, placed him under that Marshal's orders, which so offended the King that he withdrew from the army altogether, and, by this abrupt step, delayed the execution of the orders sent by Davoust on receiving the command, which circumstance greatly favoured Bagrathion's movement on Bobruisk.

The corps of Junot and Poniatowski with the cavalry of Latour Maubourg, hitherto serving under the King's command, eventually joined in the operations of Davoust, but too late to obtain the advantages that might have been derived from their presence at Mohilew, as the relation of succeeding events will show.

The Saxon corps under Regnier, which had also belonged to the King's army, was directed to put itself under the orders of Schwarzenberg, and therefore retrograded on Slonim, where it arrived on the 19th. Davoust, leaving a regiment of the division Desaix to garrison Minsk, marched on the 13th, and entered Igumen on the 15th. A detachment of his cavalry the same day fell in with a convoy of artillery train belonging to Bagrathion's army at Chelni, near Swislocq. Having burnt the carriages, the commander carried off several hundred horses, and about one hundred and fifty artillerymen. Major-general Grouchy, with a corps of cavalry, reached Borisow on the 15th, and occupied its tête du pont, which had been evacuated by a detachment of four hundred horse, who retired on Mohilew, leaving some magazines uninjured. On the 18th Grouchy reached Kockhanowo, and from thence joined Napoleon's army by Sienno and Babinowiczi: one of his parties, on entering Lepel, captured some magazines and two companies of miners. The division Chastel, which had been under Grouchy's orders, remained attached to Davoust's command. Colbert, who with his brigade had made a similar sweep, after taking possession of some magazines at Orsza which had not been destroyed (as the officer charged with that order had been taken) reunited his detachment with the main army.

Davoust, continuing his march on Borisow, crossed the Beresina, and on the 20th entered Mohilew.

Bagrathion, who had crossed the Beresina under the protection of the ramparts of Bobruisk, and who had hoped to anticipate the arrival of Davoust at Mohilew, commenced on the 17th the march of his advanced guard, formed by the Cossacks under Platow, and the detachment of Dorokoff supported by Raeffskoi. The following day Bagrathion himself moved on with the eighth corps, and composed his rear guard of the division of grenadiers under Woronzow, a regiment of chasseurs, and one of dragoons. On quitting Bobruisk, Bagrathion reinforced his army with six battalions of the reserve that had been stationed there, leaving in it a garrison of five thousand and a few Cossacks, and directing the remainder of the reserve at Mozyr "to maintain the communications with Generals Tormanssow and Kiow."

Bagrathion's army, thus reinforced, consisted of thirty-five thousand infantry, ten thousand cavalry, and six thousand Cossacks, with a considerable artillery.

On the 21st Platow reached Workalabowo, and Raeffskoi Staroi Bykhow. Bagrathion arrived there the next day, and receiving an order from Barclay to send Platow with his Cossacks to join the main army, he directed him "to proceed by the road of Czaury and Mstislaw," and at the same time he ordered a bridge to be constructed at Novo Bykhow, that he might secure a passage for himself in that direction, if it should become indispensable.

On the 22nd Raeffskoi reached Dachkowka. On the same day Davoust, expecting to be attacked at Mohilew, had sent forward a regiment of chasseurs to reconnoitre the road on which he presumed that Bagrathion might be approaching. About eleven miles from Mohilew, near Novo Selki, this regiment fell in with a corps of Cossacks, under Colonel Syssoref, which Raeffskoi had also pushed on to ascertain the enemy's positions, and which on its advance had met the three Russian battalions of reserve retiring from Mohilew upon Davoust's entrance. The Cossacks, without pausing, charged; one squadron of the enemy was instantly taken, the remainder fled leaving many men; and Davoust and General Haxo, who were riding after the regiment, were themselves all but made prisoners.

The pursuers were only stopped by some cannon-shot fired from a post within three miles of Mohilew, where a regiment of infantry was stationed.

Davoust, after the withdrawal of the Cossacks, advanced his force from Mohilew, which force, as the enemy said, amounted only to twelve thousand men; the two corps of Junot and Poniatowski, with Claparède's division of cavalry, not having then joined; but the disposition of troops will prove that it far exceeded that number in infantry alone.

Having reached Saltanowka, about eight miles from Mohilew, Davoust barricaded the bridge thrown over a broad and deep ravine that traversed the road, extending its left to the Dnieper, and right to the hamlet of Fatowa—a total length of about two miles.

An inn near the bridge on the high road was loop-holed. The bridge of the mill was cut, and the buildings also loop-holed. Strong batteries were moreover established at both posts.

Three battalions occupied Saltanowka, one battalion Fatowa, with three in reserve; four battalions were stationed between Fatowa and Selets, to guard an intervening wood; and two battalions in front of a ravine that covered the last village; the rest of the force was posted between Selets and Mohilew—in all twenty battalions, besides the cavalry of the division of cuirassiers Valence, of the light cavalry of Chastel, and a regiment of chasseurs of the brigade Bordesoult. Thus protected, it was a position of great strength, and twelve thousand men were fully adequate to its defence against any numbers endeavouring to force it by a front attack; but the Russians say that Davoust had twenty-eight thousand, whilst Raeffskoi did not bring into the field twenty thousand, so that he could not attempt to turn the position by the right, which was certainly the most practicable approach on which to manœuvre.

Raeffskoi, at eight in the morning of the 23rd, arrived at Saltanowka from Dachkowka, and immediately commenced an attack on its bridge. The Russians, exposed to an enfilading battery, suffered severely, and all the efforts of their persevering courage could not make any impression at this point.

An attack at the same time on the mill and hamlet of Fatowa was more successful; both were carried, and some of the Russians even passed the ravine, but could not maintain their lodgment after the arrival of two of the enemy's battalions in reserve.

The enemy, elated with this success, in their turn endeavoured to cross the ravine and regain the mill and buildings. Notwithstanding the fire of twelve guns whch played on them from a commanding height, they effected a passage; but then the two battalions executing this enterprise were charged, overthrown, and obliged to fly back across the ravine, swept down by showers of grape; nor could the enemy during the combat afterwards dispossess the Russians of their conquest.

Raeffskoi and General Vasiltchikoff again renewed their efforts to pass the defile of the bridge at Saltanowka, and dismounting, led their men on to the attack; but Davoust had brought up all his reserves, and the weight of their fire, added to the natural obstruction of the ground, rendered their attempts and brilliant example unavailing. The impediments were insurmountable.

The Russians, obliged to continue on the borders of the ravine to prevent the enemy's descent, being quite exposed, experienced great loss. The action continued *en tirailleur* with an incessant cannonade until near four in the afternoon, when Bagrathion, who had arrived, ordered a retreat, that the enemy might not, on receiving reinforcements hourly expected in Mohilew, embarrass his movement at a later and more inconvenient period.

Raeffskoi gradually withdrew, nor was he, after quitting the wood near Novo Selki, molested in his retreat.

At six the troops under Bagrathion, which had marched the same day from Staroi Bykhow, united with the corps of Raeffskoi at Dachkowka.

The loss of both antagonists had been heavy, nearly four thousand killed, wounded, and prisoners on each side.

This combat has been the subject of much controversy.

Bagrathion proposed to execute his orders; but as the event proved, it was not a judicious proceeding, after information had been obtained by the retiring troops from Mohilew of Davoust's having reached that city. His passage was then too irresistibly barred.

Had he moved on with his whole force, and turned by its right the position of Saltanowka, he might have gained the rear and Mohilew by Selets, Staroi Bouiniczi, and Tichewka; but with the assurance that Davoust was about to be strengthened by such great addition of force as reached him immediately after the affair, it would have been an unjustifiable risk to have hazarded such a flank movement.

The Russians were certainly foiled in their operation, but they had displayed a fortitude which impressed great respect on their enemy, and contributed much to maintain the national as well as military spirit.

On the 24th the army regained Staroi Bykhow; on the 25th Novo Bykhow, where, on the 26th, it passed the Dnieper, and moved to Propoisk, upon the Soje. On the 27th it arrived at Cherikow; on the 28th at Kriczew, and on the 29th at Mstislaw, whence it opened for the first time an assured line of communication with the first army.

Davoust had not pursued Bagrathion, or endeavoured to precede his arrival at Mstislaw, which might easily have been done, for Mstislaw is only distant a little more than fifty miles from Mohilew, and Bagrathion had to make a détour of nearly a hundred and twenty-five miles.

Davoust continued till the 28th at Mohilew, to collect all his force. He then remounted the Dnieper by its right bank; and passing through Syklow and

Orsza repassed the Dnieper at Doubrowna, where he established his head-quarters.

Poniatowski with his corps occupied Mohilew on the same day on which Davoust quitted it, and Junot took post at Orsza.

First Army.

Barclay, on the 30th, had broken up his camp at Poreczie, and, covered by a strong rear guard under Pahlen, moved on Kholim: thence he pursued his march on Smolensk, where the first army had arrived on the 1st of August, and took up a position on the right bank of the Dnieper.

Platow, who had effected his junction without incident with the first army, fell back on Chelametz; and Pahlen, who had not been interrupted in his movements since quitting Poreczie, took post at Kholim.

Whilst such had been the marches and countermarches, conversions and combats of the main armies acting on the centre, the operations and transactions which had occurred in the extreme wings of the right and left had been no less active, varied, sanguinary, and important.

Schwarzenberg, with his thirty thousand Austrians, had passed the Boug, on the 1st of July, at Drogiczin, and moved on Slonim, taking possession with an advanced detachment of some valuable magazines in Pinsk.

Tormanssow, who had originally but two divisions of infantry under his command, had been reinforced by two more under Markow, belonging to Bagrathion, whose army they had been unable to reach on its retreat.

Tormanssow had also a considerable cavalry force of regulars, Cossacks, and Kalmoucks, with a very large supply of artillery. Altogether his troops might amount to forty thousand; but amongst them were many new levies.

On the 17th of July Tormanssow determined to undertake an offensive movement from Lutsk (his head-quarters) in the direction of Wolkowich, to menace the enemy's communications with and in the duchy of Warsaw.

Regnier, who, with the Saxons, had been ordered back by Napoleon to join Schwarzenberg when Napoleon placed the army of the King of Westphalia under Davoust's orders, reached Slonim on the 19th of July, and there received directions to march on Kobrin to oppose Tormanssow's movement.

Schwarzenberg, who was to have advanced on Minsk by Napoleon's orders, finding that Tormanssow had collected his forces in such strength, suspended his movement; and although Napoleon approved of this suspension under the stated circumstances, still, unwilling to credit what he disliked, he expressed great doubts of the accuracy of the information, and noted his belief in one of his letters to Berthier, in which he observed "that Tormanssow nevertheless would be found not to have more than eight or nine thousand bad troops."

On the 25th of July a brigade of Regnier's corps, commanded by Klingil, entered Kobrin, where it was surrounded by Tormanssow; and after a brave resistance of nine hours, in which it lost two thousand men killed and wounded, was obliged to surrender: two thousand three hundred men laid down their arms, with four stand of colours, and eight pieces of cannon.

Regnier endeavoured, by a forced march, to support Klingil; but finding, when in the neighbourhood, that he had arrived too late, he fell back on Slonim, where he united with Schwarzenberg.

Tormanssow marched with a portion of his force on Prujany, and detached some light troops in rear of the Austrians towards Bialystock and Warsaw, where the consternation was so great, and whence the panic so widely spread, that Loison, who commanded at Königsberg, marched thence on Rastenberg with ten thousand men to reinforce Schwarzenberg and Regnier.

Tormanssow, embarrassed for provisions and jealous of his magazines in Wolhynia, on finding that Schwarzenberg and Regnier were advancing upon him, retired and took post at Gorodeczna, half-way between Kobrin and Prujany.

Schwarzenberg and Regnier pressed forwards, eager to avenge the affront at Kobrin; but all the enterprises against the detached Russian corps were baffled by the vigilance and judicious dispositions of their commanders.

Unfortunately, Tormanssow, not having been joined by his reserve consisting of thirteen thousand men, could only place eighteen thousand in position, whilst the confederate force was composed of thirteen thousand Saxons and twenty-five thousand Austrians. But the position was a strong one. A marsh lay in front and swept round it, affording security to the rear of the right, and skirting the left for about three miles to the source of the rivulet by which the marsh was formed, and where a thick wood, nearly as long and a mile and a half deep, continued to bend round within two miles of the Kobrin road, the only line of retreat for the Russians and which lay through Tewele.

The position may therefore be described as a great half-moon battery, with the marsh as its glacis and partial wet-ditch. Over this marsh ran three dykes: the first formed the great road from Prujany to Kobrin; the second, the route of Poddoubno, was not practicable for artillery; the third made a route from Cherikow to Kobrin and Brest Litowski.

Tormanssow had only proposed to defend the first route, as being the one most likely to be assailed. The enemy, perceiving this disposition, changed their plan of attack, and moved in force along the third route, whilst at daybreak of the morning of the 12th of August they directed also an attempt to surprise and seize a passage by the second causeway. A Saxon detachment had already passed the marsh, when it was attacked by Kamenskoi and driven back.

Twenty-four pieces of cannon playing vigorously upon the opposite ground, at Bolkoia Poddoube, kept the enemy in check at that point.

The main attack, directed by Regnier in person, and which was conducted along the third route to turn the left of the position, was more successful.

The advanced guard, chiefly composed of cavalry, passed the marsh without any interruption, and, gaining the source of the marsh stream, entered, and deployed from the wood into the plain behind the Russian left.

The supporting columns followed.

Tormanssow had not expected this movement. He had been led to suppose that the ground would not permit it; but he applied great energy to correct the oversight; and, feeling no longer any uneasiness for his right, where he left only one regiment of infantry and one of dragoons, he withdrew the remainder of the force to the point attacked, and formed with it a new line of defence opposite the Saxons, who kept extending to their right in order that they might gain the Kobrin road at Zawjurie, and thus encircling the position, close the Russians within it and force a surrender.

During the time these movements were making the artillery on both sides was fiercely engaged.

Two regiments of Saxon cavalry—the Hohenzollern and Polentz—in an attempt to pass the left of Lambert's division, were charged by the hussars of Pavlograd and of Alexander, and were cut to pieces. Some few fugitives flying upon the road of Brest Litowski fell into the hands of a detached party commanded by Colonel Rosen, and were made prisoners.

Regnier, baffled in his hope of making a lodgment in the rear of the position, ordered an attack on the Russian centre near Poddoube, and covered it with a heavy fire from the Austrian batteries which had been established at that point; but the attack failed, although made with great intrepidity.

The 2nd regiment of Saxon light infantry preserved

itself and acquired much credit by forming a square, and beating off a vigorous charge of cavalry.

Towards evening Regnier renewed his attack at this same point; and a battalion of the Austrian regiment of the brave Colloredo, wading up to its knees, and laboriously struggling through the presumed impracticable part of the marsh near Poddoube, gained the heights crowned by the Russians, and opening a fire on their flank, enabled Regnier to establish himself on the crest; but only for a short period, as before nightfall the high ground was recovered; but the enemy remained immovable on the southern side of the marsh.

Another attempt of the Saxons to turn the Russian left was also foiled, and the Russian regiment left to guard the first dyke—the dyke of Gorodeczna—successfully resisted several attempts made by the Austrians to advance.

This combat cost the confederates between four and five thousand killed and wounded, and the Russian loss was nearly equal.

Tormanssow had no alternative but to retire; for Regnier during the night might draw considerable reinforcements from the Austrian corps at Gorodeczna, as he had yet engaged but eighteen battalions and forty-eight squadrons out of the thirty-nine battalions and sixty-six squadrons of which the united army was composed.

On the 13th of August Regnier advanced to make another effort against the Russian left; but he found in the position only a rear guard under Lambert, which fell back quietly through Tewele. The enemy entered Kobrin the same day, and the Russians retired behind the Mouk Nawelsa.

Schwarzenberg, in his despatch giving an account of this combat, wrote:—"Another hour's light would have ensured the destruction or the surrender of the Russians." On which Napoleon is said to have observed—"Or another Austrian brigade sent before dark to Regnier."

Tormanssow, in not watching better his left, and guarding the wood at the source of the marshy rivulet, certainly compromised the safety of his corps; but happily for Russian chiefs, the valour of their soldiery will always repair the faults they commit, if reparable by fortitude and invincible stedfastness.

On the 15th of August the Russian rear guard was attacked without any serious impression being made on it near Novo Selki, and the next day at Divin. On the 17th it reached Samary without any molestation.

Tormanssow had arrived at Ratno on the 17th, and having reinforced himself with the detachments of Tchaplitz and Prince Khewarskoi, mustered a force of twenty-eight thousand men; but as he learned that the army of the Danube under Tchichagow was about to join him, in consequence of the peace with Turkey being ratified through the mediation of the English at Constantinople, he determined to retrograde behind the Styr, where, on the 29th, the whole army was established, with Lutsk as its head-quarters.

Schwarzenberg, whose march had been impeded by the swollen state of the rivers, and who also now heard of the approach of the Danube army, stopped his pursuit at the Styr.

These operations had been advantageous to the Russian central forces, as they had prevented the execution of Napoleon's order for the junction of the Austrians with Davoust, and thus crippled the movements which might then have been rendered disastrous to Bagrathion. They had also kept the troops in the duchy of Warsaw and neighbourhood on an uneasy defensive, and favoured political transactions in progress by the means and energy displayed in resistance to the invader.

WITTGENSTEIN.—ESSEN.—EXTREME RIGHT WING OF THE RUSSIANS.

When Barclay retired from Drissa, Wittgenstein was left at Pokemtsy with about twenty-five thousand men, exclusive of the garrison of Riga, to check the corps of Macdonald and Oudinot, which it was supposed were manœuvring to gain the line of communication with S. Petersburg through Pskow.

Macdonald, who had quitted Rossieny on the 4th of July, had advanced towards Riga, and with the Prussian corps occupied Mittau, Brausk, and Jacobstadt.

The governor of Riga, Essen, had posted his advance at Eckau, whence it was dislodged after a sharp combat, in which the loss on each side amounted to about five or six hundred men.

On the 10th of July Essen had burnt the suburbs of Riga, as the enemy had taken possession of the island of Daklenholm.

Wittgenstein, hearing that Oudinot with the second corps was preparing to march by Rejitza and Lioutzin on Sebije, which lay in his rear, whilst Macdonald, by crossing the Duna at Jacobstadt, contemplated a junction at that point so as to cut him off from Pskow, determined to march direct on Sebije, and disconcert the plan of combination.

Finding, however, that Oudinot had already reached Kliastitsy, he summoned a council of war, where it was agreed "that the safety of S. Petersburg required the attack or defeat of Oudinot wherever he might be reached."

The advanced parties of Oudinot and Wittgenstein first met on the 30th of July at Jakabowo, about a mile from Kliastitsy, and a skirmish commenced, which afforded time for the arrival of both the advancing corps, when the action was continued with increased spirit.

The Russians having a considerable advantage in artillery—as the enemy's front, contracted by a wood on the right and a village on the left, only permitted the employment of twelve pieces, whilst the Russians could bring to bear forty pieces on it—the enemy fell back behind Jakabowo.

At three in the afternoon the Russians recommenced the action, with a regiment of chasseurs, on the château of Jakabowo; the chasseurs had penetrated into the inner court, but were there repulsed.

Oudinot hoping to profit by that check, advanced on the Russian centre with the mass of his force, but was driven back by the batteries, and notwithstanding reinforcement, was unable to make any progress.

Wittgenstein in his turn moved forward, and the enemy, overpowered by the impetuosity of his attack, abandoned Kliastitsy and withdrew behind the Nitcha.

At eight on the ensuing morning, the 31st. the Russians threw a bridge over the river, when Oudinot, finding himself turned on his right, set fire to his own bridge, and abandoning Kliastitsy, in which he had left the preceding evening a feeble rear guard, withdrew on Polotzk; but the enemy's bridge was only partially consumed, for the Russian grenadiers, rushing through the flames, gained the opposite side, and succeeded in extinguishing them, so as to permit the passage and an almost uninterrupted pursuit.

Oudinot during the night crossed the Dryssa, leaving a brigade to watch the fords, and took post at Oboiarzina.

Wittgenstein's whole force had not exceeded twenty-eight thousand men; Oudinot's amounted to about twenty thousand.

The enemy lost much of their baggage, and a thousand prisoners; the numbers of killed and wounded were also considerable.

The most important issue, however, of the success was that the enemy's plan of lodging himself on the road to Pskow was baffled; that result in all its bearings was of vast advantage to the general interests.

General Koulnieff, who with a strong advanced guard had pushed on to the Dryssa, under orders "not to cross that river until the main body, distant fifteen miles, had approached," being over zealous, deviated from his orders, and crossed at a ford near Dernowiczi in the night between the 31st of July and the 1st of August; and urged forward by a first partial success, plunged suddenly upon the whole corps of Oudinot, awaiting his advance in the position of Oboiarzina.

Thus compromised, and embarrassed in a close defile into which his reserve had also heedlessly thrown itself, arrested in front by an artillery ranged in form of an amphitheatre, that poured its fire into and ploughed the whole pass, Koulnieff in vain endeavoured to bring forward some guns and force a débouchement. Every effort was ineffectual: his column was obliged to recede in confusion, and regain the Dryssa in a "pêle mêle" disorder, abandoning a thousand dead, fifteen hundred prisoners, twelve guns, tumbrils, &c.

Koulnieff did everything that a brave officer could do to repair his fault and mitigate the misfortune gallantly exposing himself to restore order, and under the heaviest fire he was rallying the hussars of Grodno, when he fell, struck dead by a cannon ball, and thus honourably paid the penalty of his impatient zeal.

Verdier, who had been sent in pursuit with his division, prevented the Russians from rallying at Siwokhina, as was proposed, and pushed them back on Sokolitza, where they were joined by a succour despatched by Wittgenstein on receiving notice of the disaster and distress of his advanced guard; Wittgenstein himself also pressed forward with his whole corps to Golowrszczina, where he immediately took up a favourable position, with his right resting on a wood, and his left on the Nitcha.

Verdier, unmindful of Koulnieff's fate and the lesson it should have taught, persisted in his scrambling advance, and suddenly also found himself in the presence of Wittgenstein's whole force, whose first line was formed by sixteen battalions, with four battalions in front of the flanks, and nine battalions in the second line, the whole in columns.

The cavalry under Prince Repnin was stationed in rear of the centre, with some squadrons advanced on the left of the first line to watch the plain on the left of Golowrszczina. Above sixty pieces of cannon swept the approaches to the position.

Verdier's audacity did not forsake him in this emergency, and he judiciously attempted to extricate himself by a bold offensive demonstration, but the troops which he threw forward were crushed at once by the Russian artillery fire.

Wittgenstein, seeing the impression made, ordered an immediate attack with his whole force on the enemy's wings. Their left gave way on the first onset. Some battalions, favoured by a wood on the right, into which they had thrown themselves, offered a short resistance, but all in the wood were finally cut to pieces, or laid down their arms.

Wittgenstein himself, who led this attack, was wounded in the head, but he had the wound dressed in the field, and would not withdraw.

The enemy, overwhelmed and menaced in rear of both flanks, fled beyond the Dryssa, crossing the river at Siwokhina. During the night the Russian light troops passed the Dryssa, and pushed on to Borartchina.

Oudinot on the 2nd of August collected his shattered force at Beloie; the same night he retired on Polotzk. The Russian picquets took post at Beloie, and the main body at Siwokhina.

The enemy lost in these three days' combats at least eight thousand killed, wounded, and prisoners; the Russians five thousand.

Alexander, on receiving the official accounts, immediately conferred on Wittgenstein the Cross of S. George of the second class, with a pension for himself, and for his Countess in case of her survivorship.

Such had been the vicissitudes of fortune in one

and the same day; but not of a capricious fortune, for the penalties inflicted were due and just consequences of inconsiderate ardour: as Verdier had been the most to blame, from contempt of recent example and its admonition, so was his reverse the most severe.

The French general Ricard, at the head of some Prussians, had entered Dunaburg on the 1st of August, and burnt or otherwise destroyed all the material left there, including, as the French say, forty heavy guns.

On the other hand, the town of Schlock, on the Aa, was retaken by a small flotilla of English and Russian armed boats which advanced to the city of Mittau, whence it took away several boats and caused general alarm in the enemy's cantonments.

The English portion of the flotilla was commanded by Captain Stewart, R.N., who led the expedition in British naval style, to the admiration of foes as well as friends.

Alexander.—Moscow.

Whilst the Russian military were making these heroic efforts, and shedding so copiously their blood in a conflict where the predominating superiority of force against them had been regarded as irresistible, even by most of the sincerest well-wishers to Russia and the European cause for which she was contending, Alexander himself was calling into action all the emulous energies of the nation, and electrifying it by his speeches, addresses, and personal exertions.

The nation responded to his appeal with an enthusiastic adoption of his views—religion and loyalty raised their patriotism to the highest point of exaltation—one spirit pervaded all classes—one cry of "victory or death" resounded through the empire.

There was no exaggeration of professions. The feelings excited and expressed were pure and holy emanations of virtue, duty, and loyalty—qualities that characterise and constitute genuine love of country, and on which, as exhibited by the Russian people, time and events have stamped the immortal seal of truth.

Money, material, equipments, and supplies of all kinds, horses, conveyances, and personal service were voted by acclamation, and contributed with voluntary zeal.

On the 23rd of July the Emperor arrived in Moscow.

On the 27th, after divine service, he repaired to the hall of the Noblesse, and then to the hall of the Merchants, "to thank them for their aid, and to avow without any concealment the increasing dangers of the country."

His reception was accompanied by so many affectionate proofs of attachment and fidelity, that he could hardly control his emotions; and the largesses of all kinds were so considerable, that he felt obliged to limit the excess, in a proclamation published on the 30th of the same month.

Alexander then proceeded to S. Petersburg, where the same cordial welcome greeted his arrival, and where he forthwith issued all the orders suitable to the crisis.

From S. Petersburg Alexander repaired to Abo with the English ambassador Lord Cathcart, to ratify the treaty of offensive and defensive alliance with the King of Sweden.

UNITED RUSSIAN ARMIES OF BARCLAY AND BAGRATHION—FIRST AND SECOND ARMIES.

The armies of Barclay and Bagrathion had united at Smolensk on the 3rd of August, and composed a force of a hundred and twenty thousand men.

On the 6th a council of war was held, in which it was resolved to break into the enemy's quarters at Roudnia, Babinowiczi, and Orsza, with the hope of falling upon the separated corps, or compelling a hasty retrograde movement of concentration at some marches' distance under great disadvantage, by which the Russian commanders might profit.

On the 7th the army, divided into three columns, commenced its movement. Touchkoff commanded the right, Doctorow the centre, and Bagrathion the left column.

Neveroffskoi was detached with eight thousand men to occupy Krasnoi, and guard, until he was united with Bagrathion, the line of the Dnieper on its left bank from thence to Smolensk.

On the 8th the army, which had taken post in advance of Prika Wydra and Katana, instead of continuing the march on Roudnia by Inkowo, inclined to its right, and gained the road from Witepsk to Smolensk at Stabna, as Barclay had taken an alarm at the possible attempt of the enemy to turn his right by that route through Poreczie, where they had unexpectedly appeared.

Thus on the very second day Barclay resumed the defensive.

The advanced guard under Platow not being

informed in time of this change of direction, continued its forward movement, and at Molewo Boletto fell in with an advance of Murat's, consisting of six thousand horse, with a regiment of light infantry commanded by Sebastiani.

An action commenced, in which Platow made about five hundred prisoners.

On the 9th Barclay moved to Metchiaki, and was replaced at Prika Wydra by Bagrathion.

Platow fell back on Gawriaki, and the next day marched to Kholim, and Pahlen to Leutcha.

Bagrathion finding that the original plan of offensive operations was abandoned, and dissatisfied at these vacillations, determined to return to Smolensk, assigning officially as his reasons, "that his troops were suffering greatly from the bad water at Prika Wydra, and that his division at Krasnoi by the enemy's advance from Orsza on Rasassna was too much exposed."

Barclay ascertaining that the enemy had quitted Poreczie, and being no longer uneasy for his right, announced his intention to execute the original design of his movement from Smolensk.

On the 14th he occupied Leutcha and Chelametz, and on the 15th Kasplia and Wolokowaia.

Bagrathion, who had been recalled from Smolensk almost as soon as he had reached it, moved on Nadwa.

Platow re-established himself at Inkowo.

Napoleon, who had discovered from the affair at Molewo Boletto the intentions of Barclay, and who had finally made up his mind to move on Moscow instead of S. Petersburg, which some of his generals had advised, felt that his army was committed by the great dispersion of the cantonments, and that not a moment should be lost for reunion and operation.

With remarkable energy and activity he brought his left from Suraje to Janowiczi on the 9th of August. On the 13th he reached Weleckowiczi; on the 14th, Liosna. Grouchy with the cavalry from Nikoulino marched to Rasassna, where General Eblé the same day threw three bridges over the Dnieper, and a fourth at Khomino, whilst the Viceroy entered Lubawiczi.

Davoust, who moved along the left bank of the Dnieper, united his army at Doubrowna; and Ney with his corps and the cavalry of Nansouty and Montbrun, breaking up from Mohilew arrived at Romanow on the road to Krasnoi, whilst Poniatowski and Junot marched from Orsza in the same direction.

The whole of these forces amounted to two hundred and fifty thousand combatants, including thirty-five thousand cavalry; and the combinations for their reassemblage, the accuracy of the dispositions, and celerity of the execution (Junot's corps alone not arriving till after the occupation of Smolensk through some mistake of an order) entitled Napoleon and all the chiefs to much credit. It was a memorable military lesson.

Exclusively of this operating force, Macdonald, Oudinot, and S. Cyr, who had been detached to reinforce Oudinot after Verdier's disaster at Golowrszczina, remained with their corps in front of Riga and of Dunaburg, and at Polotzk, to watch Wittgenstein and Essen, who were expecting reinforcements from Finland.

Garrisons were also established at Kowno, Wilna, Minsk, Slonim, Borisow, Mohilew, Orsza, Witepsk, and various other stations.

Schwarzenberg and Regnier continued in Wolhynia; Dombrowski observed the Russians at Bobruisk; and Mozyr and Augereau, with nearly sixty thousand men as a disposable reserve, occupied the country between the Rhine and the Vistula.

Napoleon had himself reached Rasassna on the 14th. Grouchy the same day had driven two regiments of Cossacks out of Liady; and Ney with his advanced division had surprised and attacked Neveroffskoi at Krasnoi, carrying the town defended by one of his battalions, which was supported by the remainder in a position behind the town.

Neveroffskoi, pressed in his rear by an enemy formidably superior in numbers, and environed by at least eighteen thousand cavalry which had collected during the combat headed by Murat, formed his columns into hollow squares that gave shelter to the dragoons of Kharkow attached to the division. He continued to make good his retreat through an open country: fortunately the high road along which he marched was planted with trees on both sides, like the chaussées of France, and these formed his defence against the charges of the enemy.

When towards dark he had gained Korytnia, fifteen miles from Smolensk and as many from Krasnoi, the enemy desisted from their attack. This gallant corps, composed chiefly of new levies, lost five guns and fifteen hundred men, but acquired for its commander and itself much honour.

The next morning Neveroffskoi retired unmolested on Smolensk, meeting about half way the corps of Racffskoi, which Bagrathion had sent to his succour.

Bagrathion had himself proposed to cross the

Dnieper at Katana to assist Neveroffskoi; but, on learning that his retreat was assured, he withdrew the three bridges which he had constructed, and hastened to Smolensk.

Barclay, on receiving this intelligence, abandoned all his offensive projects, if ever any were seriously entertained, and moved with the utmost rapidity to regain Smolensk.

On the 15th of August Murat and Ney reached Loubnia, nine miles from Smolensk. On the 16th Ney presented himself before Smolensk, when a severe fusillade commenced at the outskirts of the city into which Bagrathion had entered, and close to which the same evening Barclay again took up his position upon the right bank of the Dnieper, after eight days' fruitless marching and countermarching.* These vain efforts were most injurious to the morale as well as the efficiency of Barclay's army, which was reduced to the extent of at least six thousand† men by fatigue, sickness, and marauding, the inevitable consequence of such inconsiderate and rapid movements without any preparation for the regular issue of supplies to man or horse.

Barclay, from the commencement of the campaign, never seriously proposed to hazard a general battle; but he had not firmness, power, or weight enough to avow his object, even to the Emperor. He felt himself obliged to coquette with the opinions of others possessing almost equal authority from personal influence, and thus he appeared to be always wavering and wandering in paths of uncertainty, without any fixity of system by which to regulate his operations, and shape their course.

* See App. No. 8. † Some of the generals affirmed ten thousand.

He might have been right in a plan for weakening the enemy by removing him from his resources, and entangling him in a hostile country, knowing the destructive elements on which he might rely for aid; but he should have spared more his own troops, by less hurried and harassing movements, and by giving to the mass a true direction from the outset, in conformity with his secret views: this he might have done without making his intentions manifest to the enemy.

Every regular soldier was of too great value to be improvidently imperilled.

Barclay, having constructed bridges over the Dnieper, opposite Smolensk, ordered Bagrathion to recross the river, and take post at Kolodnia, about six miles from Smolensk, on the road to Moscow, but to leave four regiments of Cossacks, under Karpow, to watch the Chien Ostrog ford. He then replaced Bagrathion's corps in Smolensk with thirty thousand men drawn from his own army, who were distributed in the suburbs, advanced works, and covered ways, and behind the loopholed battlements of the walls.

Smolensk is distant five hundred and thirteen miles from S. Petersburg, and about two hundred and eighty from Moscow. A brick wall, with loopholed battlements, about thirty feet high and eighteen feet thick at the base, surrounds it, and forms a semicircle of about three miles and a half. Thirty towers, irregularly placed and built, some being round, some square, with roofs made of wood, butt out from the wall. The walls of these towers, which are hollow, are not more than half the thickness of the curtain walls.

In front of the walls are a deep dry ditch and a covered way and glacis, but the covered way had no regular communications with the town until they were made by the Russians at the moment of the attack. There were three gates: one by the side of the river led over a bridge covered by an old tête du pont to the S. Petersburg suburb, and which was called from its size "La basse Ville." This suburb was populous and wealthy, but the houses were made of wood.

Two other gates, Malakhofskia and Nikolskia, opened on the country; a half-moon work of earth covered the Malakhofskia or Krasnoi gate, which was flanked on the left by an old bastion, also of earth, and on the right by an earthwork polygon of five bastions, not palisaded, easily scaleable, and open in the rear.

The towers could not receive artillery, and the Russians had no heavy guns to plant in any part of the works.

There were five suburbs close up to the glacis, one on each flank, which descended to the river's edge, whilst three in the centre of the southern front connected together favoured an enemy's approach.*

The city was full of churches, with painted domes to the belfries, of which generally one was in the centre, surrounded by four small ones. Many of the houses were of wood and separated by gardens; in these houses, when afterwards fired, most of the wounded miserably perished. Altogether it was one of the least regularly defensible places that could be

---

* The three central suburbs, making in fact but one, were called Mistilaul, Roslaul, Nikolakoi.

imagined, and when the enemy entered, its weakness caused them much mortification and surprise.

On the 17th, about eight in the morning, Doctorow, who commanded in the city, finding that the enemy had crept during the night into the suburbs Mistilaul and Roslaul, and Nikolskoi on the southern front, whence they annoyed his troops by a sharpshooting fire, ordered a sortie, and quickly cleared them.

Napoleon, expecting to be attacked, drew out his army, arraying seventy thousand men in his first line, and displaying thirty thousand cavalry; but, finding that the Russians only defended the suburbs, against which a galling attack had been maintained all day, he determined, about two in the afternoon, to carry Smolensk by storm.

Ney directed his corps against the bastion called the citadel, and the suburb of Krasnoi. Davoust directed Gudin to carry the Mistilaul, and Morand the Roslaul and Nikolskoi suburbs. Friant connected Morand with Poniatowski, who was charged with the assault on the Raczenka suburb and the eastern quarter of the city. Murat at the same time charged and drove in the Russian cavalry stationed on that flank; their retreat enabled Poniatowski to establish sixty pieces of cannon on the height above Raczenka, whence he enfiladed the Russian bridges till a Russian battery was established on the opposite side of the river, and on equal heights, by the English General Sir Robert Wilson, which raked his line of battery, and compelled its removal from the position: by this withdrawal the bridges were preserved.* The battle now raged with mutual fury and carnage through the

* See the English General's despatch that follows.

whole semicircle, and continued for two hours before the Russians withdrew from the suburbs; but even then they left troops in the covered ways. Once, indeed, the suburb of Nikolskoi was re-occupied by a sally with the division of Konownitsyn, but again relinquished.

As soon as the suburbs were in possession of the enemy, a hundred and fifty pieces of cannon, many of them twelve, and some eighteen-pounders, played incessantly upon the wall of the curtain to batter a breach; and about five o'clock a daring assault was made on the gate Malakhofskia, which for a moment was gained; but Konownitsyn and the gallant Prince Eugène of Wurtemberg, always most conspicuous in every danger and who had just been sent by Barclay to reinforce the garrison, charged forward and recovered possession.

The enemy's grape and shells continued to pour into and sweep the covered ways, compelling their abandonment, and setting on fire the roofs of the towers and many of the houses in the city; but neither projectiles nor flames could dislodge the Russians from the ramparts.

At seven o'clock the enemy renewed the assaults, but in vain. They were even driven out of the suburb of Krasnoi by a reinforcement which Barclay had despatched across the river to strengthen that quarter.

At nine the cannonade ceased, and the Russians again occupied the covered ways, to give alarm in case of any attempts to approach and undermine the walls.

The incidents of the night will be found in the despatch of the English General, and therefore it will suffice here to state that the city was voluntarily evacuated before morning.

The French having entered found themselves in possession of only burning ruins. Napoleon must have regretted that he had not avoided the bloody sacrifice of twelve thousand of his bravest troops—and none ever behaved better—by a movement direct from Witepsk, on the right bank of the Dnieper, which would have alarmed Barclay for his communications with Moscow, and necessitated his retreat from Smolensk. Barclay, as has been stated, had directed Bagrathion " to take the high road to Moscow along the right bank of the Dnieper, as far as Kolodnia, six miles from Smolensk, and there post himself behind the Kolodnia river; but to leave four regiments of Cossacks, under Karpow, opposite Chien Ostrog, three miles from Smolensk, where there was a ford over the Dnieper, which they were vigilantly to watch."

The Russian army, on abandoning Smolensk, bivouacked on some heights about two miles beyond, in the direction of Poreczie, and awaited there during the whole day the enemy's expected attack : this, however, was confined to some feeble attempts made to effect a lodgment in the suburb of S. Petersburg. For this purpose various detachments crossed at different fords; but Korf, attacking them with his rear guard, easily drove them out and back over the Dnieper, taking amongst his prisoners some Spaniards and Portuguese who had been the first to pass, and maintaining the suburb till daybreak on the following morning.

At seven in the evening of the 18th, the left column

of the Russian army under Doctorow commenced its sweeping march by Zykolino, Priklowa, Marchoulki, Soutchowo, and Prouditche.

The column under Barclay began its march two hours later, and then moved by Krathotkino, Poloniewo, Gorbounowo, Jonkowo, Jabino, Kochawiewo, and Loubino, on Bredechino, which was distant from Smolensk by the high road only fifteen miles.

Korf with the rear guard followed this column. Platow, extending his curve in the direction of Poreczie, was instructed to reunite with the whole army at Slobonewa, where the Vop falls into the Dnieper at the distance of about thirty miles from Smolensk in a direct line.

Bagrathion's orders were to "quit the Kolodnia, and move on Dorogobouche, but still not to withdraw the four regiments of Cossacks appointed to watch the ford at Chien Ostrog."

By this disposition Doctorow had to make a circuit of fifty long miles before he reached the Moscow road and Slobonewa, the point of rendezvous.

Barclay had to make a march of fifteen miles by map measurement, but nearer twenty * by actual distance of ground, before he could gain the Moscow high road at Loubino, where he still would be distant more than twenty from Slobonewa. Loubino being scarcely nine miles from Smolensk by the direct road, the enemy sallying from thence had not merely the advantage of six miles less distance, but a good road, whereas the route by Krathotkino and Jabino was a cross route, intersected by deep ravines running

---

* The cross roads not being measured, there was difficulty in making accurate calculation; but in general they are much longer than computed.

through a marshy country, and where a piece of cannon had never been seen to pass in the memory of man.

Barclay, however, apprehending the mischief that might occur, despatched Major-general Touchkoff with three regiments of Cossacks, a regiment of hussars, and two of chasseurs, with a battery of light artillery, to support the Cossacks ordered to be kept by Bagrathion, under Karpow, at Chien Ostrog ford.

Barclay, at the eleventh hour, had made these dispositions to conceal his movement from the enemy, for the direct road of his retreat ran along the Dnieper, and therefore would have been exposed to the enemy's observation and fire; but it was one of the most critical movements ever hazarded, and which required for its successful execution [*] not only all the good fortune and valour of the Russians, but the errors committed by their adversaries.

Ney having constructed two bridges passed the Dnieper on the 19th, at dawn of day; Murat with the cavalry followed.

Junot had orders to pass the Dnieper at Proudichewo, nearly opposite Waloutina Gora, about four miles from Smolensk, to march on Latichino, and thus cut off all the Russian detachments between that place and Smolensk.

Ney moved direct on Gorbounowo, instead of following Barclay's column in its bend by Krathotkino, and thus gained two hours on its march.

At Gorbounowo he fell in with the rear of Baga-

[*] The subsequent movement of the Allied Armies, retiring from Dresden through the defiles of Bohemia, covered and saved by Osterman at Culm, may in some respects be compared; but there necessity governed the movement.

wouth's corps, and made himself, by a brisk attack, master of the village. In this post he would have intercepted Korf, who with the rear guard of the army, was not further in advance of the defile between Krathotkino and Gorbounowo than Poloniewo. Barclay, who had preceded, being informed of this danger, ordered Prince Eugène of Wurtemberg "to return and retake Gorbounowo," which he succeeded in effecting after two hours' combat, and thus opened a passage for Korf, who opportunely arrived, to pass without impediment.

The enemy say "that Ney withdrew of his own accord, not knowing that Korf was behind, and that Napoleon, who had joined him, on hearing that he was seriously engaged, approved, and directed his march by a more direct road on Waloutina Gora, to cut in upon, if he could not gain the head of the retiring column, and co-operate with Junot."

Touchkoff, after twelve hours' march, had halted to repose his troops between the villages of Toporowtchino and Latechino, on the lower or Dnieper road; but going forward himself to reconnoitre, he perceived a column of the enemy (Ney's corps) in full march on the high Moscow road from Smolensk, and another body (Junot's) forming a bridge over the Dnieper at Proudichewo. Touchkoff made the best dispositions that time and means would permit, throwing his infantry into the small woods which lay on the right and left of the road; he established his battery on some heights that commanded it, and sent the Cossacks towards Lapina to watch the corps making its preparations to cross the Dnieper.

In this position he covered Loubino, where the

cross road by which Barclay's column was advancing joined the high Moscow road.

On the preservation of this position, therefore, depended Barclay's safety. Some of his advanced parties had already passed Loubino, and continued their march on Bredechino; but several regiments, as they cleared the cross road, were successively stopped by Lieutenant-general Touchkoff, and sent to the assistance of his brother.

Ney, unable to force the Russians, sent for more troops.

Napoleon ordered Gudin's division of Davoust's corps that was following Ney to join him, and imagining that the whole Russian army had taken post at Loubino, recalled General Morand who was penetrating what the enemy called a virgin wood, as never having been pierced before by troops with cannon or by wheel carriages, to turn the enemy's right, "lest he should be compromised by a superiority of force when he debouched upon it;" but such was the density of this virgin wood, that Morand's artillery had to move forward one mile and a half before it could find space to turn.

At three in the afternoon Touchkoff, who had most valiantly defended his ground, found himself obliged to retire and form behind the Stragan, where he was reinforced by eight eighteen-pounders, two regiments of cavalry, three of infantry, and a battalion which had cleared the cross road.

This was "the last ditch" for the protection of Loubino, and though its defences were not in many respects favourable, it was indispensable "to set the die upon that cast."

Ney renewed his attack with increased animation on finding that his reinforcements were approaching; and Murat, who had also advanced, endeavoured to overthrow the cavalry on the Russian left.

The Russian artillery, supported by the grenadiers, bravely and successfully covered the cavalry; and though the Cossacks were driven back on a regiment of hussars which they threw also into disorder, Orloff Denisoff, with the gallant regiments of Madiapol and the Elizabethgrad hussars, checked the enemy and re-established the position.

More beautiful conduct in the field was never seen than that displayed by these two victorious regiments. The courage, the steadiness, the skill of the manœuvres were most admirable, and could not be surpassed.

Junot, who had crossed the Dnieper with his corps, unaccountably remained passive; and when urged to advance in rear of the Russian left by Murat and Gourgaud speaking in the Emperor's name, he positively, as they said, "refused;" under the declaration "that his orders were limited to the passage of the river, and that a marsh in his front would prevent the deployment of his force." He, however, at last consented to throw forward a battalion as skirmishers.

About five in the afternoon Gudin, having reached the line of action, was ordered with his own regiments to force the wood of Boubliewo in the valley on the left of the road, and also the batteries on the heights. The divisions Lédru and Marchand were designated to support.

The Russians in the valley, unable to resist such great superiority, had given way. The centre was shaking and its rear flying, when Barclay arrived and, placing himself at the head of the rallying fugitives, charged forward, electrifying all by his personal example, and giving an impulse that snatched victory from the enemy and attached it firmly and finally for the remainder of the combat, to the Russian standards.

Konownitsyn cleared the valley, but Ney continued the action until near nine o'clock, when it ceased, after an endeavour previously made under favour of the obscurity to pass the Stragan and surprise the Russian right. A charge with the bayonet of the Ekaterinoslav grenadiers baffled the attempt: unfortunately however, Touchkoff, who had led on too eagerly to the charge, was made prisoner.

This affair cost the enemy six thousand men killed, wounded, and prisoners; amongst the slain was the lamented General Gudin, who, like Moreau * at Dresden, was struck by a cannon ball, and had both his legs smashed to shreds.

The enemy had thirty-five thousand infantry engaged, and the Russians, who, when first attacked, had but two thousand five hundred, never brought up more than sixteen thousand, of which they lost five thousand. The cavalry experienced also some inconsiderable loss.

The column of Barclay, entangled in the cross road, could not altogether extricate itself till near midnight.

Had the enemy gained the hill over Loubino, the débouche would have been closed, for from the hill not only the egress of the defile was commanded, but a single bridge, with loose rafter planks, intersected the main road a few yards beyond, and within grape

---

* Moreau was struck at the side of, and whilst he was talking to, the English General, Sir Robert Wilson.

shot,—on which Duke Alexander of Wurtemberg, and other generals, indeed Barclay himself, stood many hours during the night crying "Tishe—Tishe"—"Gently—Gently"—to the drivers of the artillery and carriages of all sorts, of which there were ten thousand, under the apprehension that a quick pace might break up the platform.

The inaction of Junot had been most providential for the Russians.

Well might Napoleon say "he had lost the marshal's staff,"—he could with truth have added, "Moscow also, without another battle."

The French historians affirm that Napoleon himself was not on this occasion so stirring, decided, and judicious as usual; but genius, and aspirations which create and feed the excitement of the hero as well as of the poet, must occasionally "slumber," for they animate but a human frame, subject to lassitude, internal derangement, and decay.

By many it was thought that Napoleon during the whole of this campaign, even at Borodino, was less vigorous than heretofore; if so, perhaps he was then beginning to feel the weakening influence of his mortal malady.

On the 20th Barclay's column continued its retreat in Slobonewa, where it effected its reunion with Doctorow's column, that had not been molested on its march.

On the 20th and 21st the whole army repassed the Duieper; excepting Platow, who with a strong rear guard of regular cavalry as well as Cossacks, remained on the right bank, whilst Rosen with six regiments of chasseurs and some flying artillery took post on the left bank to afford him support.

The same day Bagrathion reached Dorogobouche and established his communication with Moscow, and with Barclay who took up his position at Ouswiatic on the Ougra. Platow, being attacked, retired across the fords of the river, which the enemy also attempted to pass in pursuit, but were prevented by Rosen.

On the 22nd Barclay marched to Andreiewka, and announcing again his resolve to fight a general battle, ordered up Milaradowitch to Wiazma with the new battalions which he had been forming at Kalouga, Mojaisk, and Woloklamsk.

The enemy having thrown three bridges across the Dnieper, advanced on Mikailouka, where Rosen was posted.

Platow with his Cossacks drew them on under the fire of some infantry in ambuscade, and of several masked batteries, by which they were severely galled.

Murat, not having any infantry with him, applied to Davoust for a detachment; but Davoust declined to send any without the Emperor's direct orders, as he saw that no essential object was to be gained by a combat gratuitously engaged in, and which the army was not ready to sustain. The useless action, however, continued till night, without any particular incident.

On the 23rd Bagrathion returned from Dorogobouche, and formed on the left of Barclay.

The advanced guard fell back on Ouswiatic.

Bagrathion, not approving the position selected by Barclay for battle, as the enemy might cut off the communication with Dorogobouche and throw the armies into the concave formed by the Ougra and Dnieper, recommended a retrograde movement on

Wiazma; and in the night of the 23rd and 24th Barclay moved on Dorogobouche, and Bagrathion on Bregino, whilst the corps of Bagawouth took post on the right of the Dnieper.

Reference has been made to the despatch of the English General relative to the transactions at Smolensk and Loubino; and that despatch never having been published, it is now inserted, not so much for the details which it communicates as because it is expressive and confirmative of the impressions made at the moment on the Russian army, as well as on himself who was commissioned to ascertain and report the truth to his Government.

It is in these respects a document of more value for history than any later narrative furnished by compilation.

Written amidst the hurry and confusion of the events and movements which it describes, it could only pretend to give a hasty sketch of the most prominent circumstances demanding attention; but it possesses the merit of being a faithful representation of facts, transmitted under the guarantee of official responsibility and military accuracy.

Brigadier general Sir Robert Wilson had been sent from England with Mr. Liston (the British ambassador to the Ottoman Porte in succession to Sir Stratford Canning) to assist in the conduct of the negotiations for peace between Turkey and Russia. Arriving at Constantinople subsequently to the signature of the preliminaries, he was despatched by the ambassador to the Emperor of Russia, but was directed in the first instance to proceed to the Grand Vizir at

Shumla, and then to Admiral Tchichagow commanding the Russian Danube army, whose head-quarters were established at Bucharest.

The object of his instructions with reference to the two last missions was "to prevent the threatened renewal of hostilities, which the increasing influence of the French in the Turkish councils was instigating; and which renewal Admiral Tchichagow was believed to be disposed to promote, that he might force his way to Dalmatia and invade Italy."

Sir Robert Wilson, who quitted Constantinople the day but one before the arrival of Andreossi,—who it was known, through the French diplomacy there, intended to protest against his departure,—proceeded to Shumla, where he obtained from the Grand Vizir the most solemn and satisfactory assurances "that he would forbear from all hostile operations," and the most unequivocal pledges of his sincerity.

His negotiation with Admiral Tchichagow was equally successful; for the Admiral assented to "the immediate evacuation of Servia, for which the treaty did not stipulate, and the march of his disposable force, thirty-six thousand men in the highest possible effective order, to act in rear and on the line of the enemy's Polish communications." These transactions Mr. Liston acknowledged in the outset as being very auxiliary to his influence at the Ottoman Porte; for he wrote in his first reply, "I feel very sensibly the able manner in which you have conducted the important negotiations committed to your charge, and the beneficial advantages which have already resulted here," &c., &c.

DESPATCH TO EARL CATHCART, BRITISH AMBASSADOR TO THE EMPEROR OF RUSSIA, &c. &c.*

"MY LORD, "Andreiewka, August the 22nd, 1812.

"I have the honour to transmit to your Lordship a detail of a series of operations which have occurred since the date of my letter that communicated to your Lordship my arrival at Smolensk, in the expectation of finding His Imperial Majesty at the head-quarters of the first Russian army.

"I must, however, for your Lordship's information, commence my statement by noticing the previous movements of General Barclay de Tolly from Smolensk, and the subsequent march of the second army under Prince Bagrathion in the direction of Roudnia, with the intention of attacking the enemy in the neighbourhood of that place, Babinowiczi, and Orsza.

"A division under General Neveroffskoi had been left at Smolensk, and was ordered to proceed on the left bank of the Dnieper, as far as Krasnoi, to reunite with Prince Bagrathion after his passage of that river.

"The enemy, by his superiority of cavalry, was enabled to mask his movements, and suddenly collecting his forces, marched upon Smolensk.

"On the 14th of August the advanced guard, under the command of Marshal Ney supported by Marshals Murat and Davoust, unexpectedly attacked the division of General Neveroffskoi near Krasnoi, entered the village, which it occupied with a battalion before the

* The paragraphs within brackets were intended to be confidential communications for Lord Cathcart and the British Government.

division could be formed, and made several hundred men prisoners, with seven pieces of cannon; the remainder of the division, posted outside the village, recovering from the first disorder, rallied, and by an exertion of steady valour equal to the exigency, critical as it was, secured its retreat to Korytnia, within eight wersts (six English miles) of Smolensk, notwithstanding the vast superiority and incessant attacks of the enemy.

"The total loss of the division on this occasion amounted to fifteen hundred men.

"The next morning, the 15th, General Neveroffskoi received some succours from Prince Bagrathion, but was obliged in the evening to approach Smolensk. The movement was effected without any disorder, and with small loss, although the number of the assailants exceeded all proportion, and the ground admitted of their movements with an extended front.

"During the night General Raeffskoi arrived with more troops, and took the command of Smolensk, which the enemy attempted, about eight o'clock in the morning of the 16th, to carry by assault at the north-west angle; but the attempt was repulsed, and the loss of the enemy was considerable in his retreat up a hill affording no cover.

"In the course of the morning Prince Bagrathion took up a position on the right bank of the Dnieper to support the town; and in the afternoon General Barclay arrived with his army, when he ordered two pontoon bridges to be thrown across the river, in addition to the one already established there.

"As Smolensk will be in the history of this war a feature of importance, I deviate from the narrative to acquaint your Lordship that it is built on the side of a hill rising immediately above the Dnieper, to which it forms a tête du pont; that it is about a mile square, surrounded by an old brick wall eighteen feet thick at the base, flanked by thirty towers, some square, some round, jutting from and flanking, but not of equal solidity with, the wall.

"It resembles in its enceinte the towns of Spain, but with the additional advantage of its three gates being covered by redoubts raised above a deep dry ditch with a covered way beyond, and a glacis, but on which five suburbs prejudicially encroach.

"The exterior semicircle of the whole may be about seven wersts, with both flanks resting on the Dnieper.

"Smolensk is, nevertheless, not so defensible within as a Spanish town, since the streets are very wide and laid out at right angles; many of the houses are moreover built of wood, and the lofty conical roofs of the towers of the wall are of the same material.

"A cannonade and partial musketry employed the enemy on the 16th.

"During the night Prince Bagrathion marched with his army to take a position on the high Moscow road, and watch one of the fords of the Dnieper about seven wersts distant from Smolensk, as the enemy indicated an intention of crossing the river in that neighbourhood.

"On the 17th the enemy commenced, soon after daybreak, a sharp musketry fire against the post stationed in front of the western face of the town, on the Krasnoi road: this was sustained by the Russian chasseurs with a personal gallantry that amounted to a fault; for by an unnecessary exposure of themselves many were killed and wounded unprofitably.

"During this partial action the French army, expecting to be attacked, had been drawn out in order of battle, presenting a very great force of cavalry and, it was thought, of at least seventy thousand infantry in their first line.

"Napoleon, finding that the Russian army continued within the walls, commenced a violent assault, about mid-day, on the southern suburbs of the town: the attack was executed and maintained with such vigour that the enemy, after encountering for two hours as resolute a resistance, obtained possession of the three central suburbs; but he was repulsed in numerous attempts to make a more forward lodgment. Finding that every effort, notwithstanding high encouragement* to those efforts, was unavailing, towards the afternoon he wheeled his right flank forward to the eastern face of the town, and opened on that side a very heavy fire from above sixty pieces of cannon under the direction of Prince Poniatowski. But a Russian battery † which was established immediately on the right bank of the Dnieper, and on a corresponding elevation, although very inferior in number of guns and weight of metal, obliged the enemy's guns which it enfiladed, to withdraw from the position whence they commanded the pontoon bridges and the original wooden bridge of the town, dismounted several of them, and occasioned six different explosions of powder waggons.

"But the enemy's bombardment with above a hundred and fifty pieces of cannon, although failing to make any impression on the walls and works, suc-

* "Promise to let the town be sacked."
† "The site of the battery was selected by myself."

ceeded in firing the town in several different places, and in enveloping the northern suburb in a volume of flames that extended above half a mile; a spectacle that no person present can ever forget, and a calamity (for it was a holy city) which every Russian resolved to avenge.

"A cannonade and musketry fire continued until sunset, when the enemy fell back into their original position, with a loss of not less than ten thousand men.

"The Russians had been favoured by the shelter of ramparts and battlements, but their loss amounted to six thousand men, exclusive of many officers, amongst whom were two generals.

"The retention or evacuation of Smolensk was a question of measures, that excited the deepest interest in the Russian army; every commander, officer, and soldier was desirous of forming its garrison, and resisting the future attacks of the enemy, who, notwithstanding his severe check, would, it was hoped, from a characteristic irritation of temper, persevere in an attempt to storm the town, and thus fruitlessly expend his bravest men.

"But General Barclay conceived that the enemy might make a movement towards his left, which would oblige him to evacuate Smolensk in the day time, an operation that he thought would be attended with great inconvenience; and, moreover, he did not choose to engage in a defence that would require a daily expenditure of his own men, and thus perhaps enfeeble his army too much for the execution of his other plans.

"General Barclay therefore resolved to withdraw

from Smolensk; and at night the evacuation was completed and the bridges burnt; and the whole army took up its ground in columns of attack opposite to the town. The advanced guard crowned the heights that rose above the Dnieper.

"[General Barclay had sent me about eleven at night back into the town to inquire into its state: Prince Eugène of Wirtemberg, General Doctorow, and all the generals of the different stations, assured me 'that they would hold out for ten days more, if supplied with provisions, for not the slightest impression had been made on the defences.' After I had made this report to General Barclay, and urged the detrimental moral effects which they had stated would be made on the country by the evacuation of 'the venerated city of Smolensk,' he observed—'There is nothing to fear on that account; I have provided against it: the Holy Virgin' (a picture) 'is safe, and we have her in our camp; she is the only object that gives importance to the city in the eyes of the Russians; she shall be carried in a car of triumph with the army, and a battalion constantly appointed to escort and mount guard over her.']

"The enemy soon after daybreak entered the city, and commenced a tiraillade across the river.

"Towards eight o'clock a Spanish and Portuguese brigade crossed the river about mid-deep under the walls of the town, and entered the suburb on the right bank; but they were attacked, and many of them killed, wounded, or made prisoners.

"[When General Barclay heard from some of the prisoners that the town was full of artillery and powder waggons, he ordered some shells to be thrown into it;

but the artillerymen executed the order with great reluctance, as, notwithstanding the removal of their Saint, they did not feel sure that the bombardment would not be considered a religious offence.]

"General Barclay wished to induce the enemy to attempt the passage with his whole force, and therefore about mid-day withdrew his army some distance from the river; but the enemy seemed still rather to expect than to propose an attack.

"In the evening a heavy cannonade was opened by the enemy against the Russian guns in position and the troops stationed on the heights of the left, whence the enemy's guns had on the preceding day been driven from their ground. Some tirailleurs were also thrown across the Dnieper; and the suburb of S. Petersburg catching fire, in about an hour several hundred houses, extending above a mile, were blazing, in addition to the other fires not yet extinguished.

"At night the General deemed it expedient to retire; for although the enemy had refused battle so offered to him, he might, without a battle, gain the Moscow road.

"The direct route on Dorogobouche from General Barclay's position ran parallel with the Dnieper for five wersts, but was commanded by the enemy's guns and musketry: the General therefore judged it necessary to march by a cross road.

"The march of so considerable an army with more than five hundred pieces of cannon, even in two columns, must in any case have been attended under existing circumstances with great embarrassment; but unfortunately in this instance there were two very steep hills on the route of General Barclay's column, and the Russian ammunition waggons on two wheels had not proper aid in carriage-tackle or harness, there being no breechings or other apparatus for their safe descent.

"[I had been sent forward by General Barclay to ascertain why the column was halted, and I found that the first four ammunition waggons, with two pieces of cannon, twelve-pounders, had overpowered the horses in the descent of the nearest hill, and that they lay at the bottom, with wheels or limbers broken, and all the horses killed or maimed; every succeeding gun and ammunition waggon had therefore to be held back by the soldiers fixing ropes on them, and that could not be done till daylight; and moreover, as too frequently occurs in night marches, most of the drivers fell asleep.]

"'The enemy, finding that the Russian army had withdrawn from the plain of the Dnieper, passed the river with a large force, and furiously attacked part of the rear guard, threatening to cut off a portion under General Korf. It was found necessary to make the division of Prince Eugène return and recover the village which the enemy had occupied.

"Whilst this effort was directed against the Russians slowly advancing in the cross road, another column of the enemy moved along the main road upon the left bank of the Dnieper, and another upon the right, where it crossed the Dnieper about seven wersts from Smolensk, threatening to establish itself beyond the point where the cross road united with the main road, and which point of junction both columns, it was to be presumed, hoped to reach before the Russians; but happily, General Touchkoff had been detached with a small corps in that direction, to cover the débouchement on the cross road, as soon as it was known that Prince Bagrathion with his army had withdrawn as directed on Dorogobouche.

"The enemy's attack on General Touchkoff commenced, about three o'clock in the afternoon, with great vigour, and before General Barclay's column had gained the main road mutual charges were given and repelled; but the superiority of the enemy's numbers increasing every moment, they must have prevailed if some of the infantry first débouching from the cross road had not opportunely arrived to check their advance.

"It was about sunset when the enemy on the main road upon the left bank, flattering themselves that their right was gaining ground, made a desperate effort to force the hill, on which several Russian guns were placed, and which commanded the whole position and also in reverse the outlet of the cross road, beyond which a boggy rivulet ran intersecting the route; over this only one bridge with loose planks afforded passage for the artillery and infantry until night, when two others were thrown across by Duke Alexander of Wirtemberg. For an instant the Russian guns and troops supporting, overwhelmed with shells, shot, and musketry, flew back to seek shelter behind the crest of the hill; but General Barclay, who had been superintending the action with his rear guard, admonished by the cannonade at Loubino and Waloutina Gora of the new danger to his advanced guard, opportunely arrived at this moment, and seeing the extent of the danger to his column, galloped forward, sword in hand, at the head of his staff (including myself, with two Russian officers attached to me as aides-de-camp), orderlies, and rallying fugitives, and crying out, 'Victory or death! we must preserve this post or perish!' by his energy and example reanimating all, recovered possession of the height, and thus, under God's favour, the army was preserved!

"The loss on each side was not much more than six thousand men. The Russians had suffered most by the attack on their rear guard. The French had in the other attacks been the most exposed.

"The Russian army, after a short repose, was again put in motion, and marched thirty wersts to repass the Dnieper, about forty wersts in front of Dorogobouche.

"The enemy, discomfited in their design of intercepting the march of the Russian columns, remained the next day almost inactive, and thus confirmed the Russian pretensions to the honour of rendering abortive with thirty thousand men, the most that were engaged from first to last during the whole day, the attempt which the French army, with the exception of one corps that had remained unaccountably inoperative on the banks of the Dnieper, had been moved forward to execute.

"The next night the Russian army continued its march.

"Yesterday morning, the 21st, the General determined to remain in his position, and accept battle; but as he subsequently issued an order for the army to march on Dorogobouche, I left the head-quarters that night to proceed to S. Petersburg.

"It is yet doubtful whether the enemy will advance upon Moscow immediately. It is rather conjectured that he will desist from that undertaking until he has converted Smolensk into a place of arms, secured possession of the rich governments of Tchernigow and Kiew, revolutionised Podolia and Wolhynia, and endeavoured to prevent the union of the Moldavian army under Admiral Tchichagow with the army of General Tormanssow.

"On the other hand, the Russian army, although very powerful, requires some time for the arrival of its reinforcements to permit an offensive movement having for its object to dislodge the enemy from Smolensk and the line of the Dnieper; but the battalions of recruits which are on march are reported to be in very fine order, and some of them have had a year's discipline.

"Having been a participator in the events which I have partially traced for your Lordship's information, I can with authority assure your Lordship that, notwithstanding the painful marches which the Russian army has incessantly made, notwithstanding its harassing retreats and severe services, its original high condition is but little impaired, and that its confidence has augmented by the incidents in every field of combat. An impatience for a decisive battle is perhaps expressed in a tone that infringes on strict discipline; but the sight of a much loved country in desolation adds to the feeling of mortification which each individual experiences, under the buoyant belief 'that it has been an unnecessary sacrifice of reputation and property.'

"Against the undeniable numerical superiority of the enemy, it is urged [by the advocates, and they are the whole army, for a change of system] 'that the enemy does not present a national force, nor one of that same experienced description against which they had to contend before the Spanish war. They insist upon the reduced condition of the enemy's cavalry, and the comparatively increased vigour of their own; the indisputably greater efficiency of their artillery, although weaker in point of numerical amount; and finally, the devotion of every man in the army, as if the fate of the country depended on his single efforts.'

(Signed) "R. T. WILSON,
"Brigadier-General.

"Despatched from Dorogobouche, 22nd of Aug., 1812."

When Sir Robert Wilson reached the Russian army he found the Generals in open dissension with the Commander-in-chief, General Barclay, for having already suffered the enemy to overrun so many provinces, and for not making any serious disposition to defend the line of the Dnieper. Some wished that General Beningsen should have the command, others Prince Bagrathion; and General Beningsen, fearing that he might be forced into the command by a military election when it was known that Smolensk was to be evacuated, left the army and withdrew several marches to the rear, that the Emperor's orders for the appointment of a new chief might arrive during his absence. Before his departure for S. Petersburg, however, it had been resolved to send to the Emperor not only the request of the army "for a new chief," but a declaration in the name of the army, "that if any order came from S. Petersburg to suspend hostilities, and treat the invaders as friends (which was apprehended to be the true motive of the retrograde movements, in deference to the policy of Count Romanzow), such an order would be regarded as one which did not express His Imperial Majesty's real sentiments and wishes, but had been extracted from His Majesty under false representations or external control; and that the army would continue to maintain his pledge and pursue the contest till the invader was driven beyond the frontier." Since the execution of such a commission might expose a Russian officer to future punishment, and the conveyance of such a communication by a subject to the Sovereign was calculated to pain and give offence, when no offence was proposed, it was communicated by a body of generals to Sir Robert Wilson, "that under the circumstances of his known attachment to the Emperor, and His Imperial Majesty's equally well known feelings towards him, no person was considered so properly qualified as himself to put the Emperor in possession of the sentiments of the army; that his motives in accepting the mission could not be suspected; and that the channel was one which would best avoid trespass on personal respect, and prevent irritation from personal feelings being humiliated."

Sir Robert Wilson, after that deliberation which such a grave proposition required, agreed to be the bearer of the message, as far as the question of war and peace was concerned; but agreed solely that he might mitigate the unavoidable distress which the Emperor must experience during the execution of such a commission.

The dismissal of Count Romanzow was not made a *sine quâ non*; but Sir Robert Wilson was directed to state "that his removal from the ministry could alone inspire full confidence in the Imperial councils."

Sir Robert Wilson on his way deviated a few miles to inform Count Panin of the evacuation of Smolensk, the continued retreat of the army, and the probable arrival of the enemy in a few hours at his residence. The Count had not the slightest suspicion of the danger, but immediately ordered off all his papers and valuable effects to Moscow, where they were shortly afterwards burnt in the conflagration of the city! Prudence itself was here in fault, for the French officer who commanded the detachment had the most positive orders from Napoleon "to respect the Count's person, house, and property."

Sir Robert Wilson reached S. Petersburg on the 24th of August.* The Emperor was then at Abo, where he had gone with the English ambassador, Lord Cathcart, to meet the King of Sweden, and where those negotiations were concluded " which rendered disposable the Russian army of Finland and secured the co-operation of a Swedish force, assuring Norway to Sweden under the guarantee of England, with one million sterling as subsidy ; which moreover held out to the King the prospect of ascending the throne of France, Alexander having declared in his presence " that he should consider it vacant in case of Napoleon's overthrow," and having replied to the King's question, " To whom then would it be given ?" with a pointed emphasis and accompanying inclination of head,—" Au plus digne."

The information brought by Sir Robert Wilson as to the patriotic spirit, the brave conduct, and effective

* The Russian calendar causes frequent discrepancies in dates.

condition of the army produced a very beneficial effect; and Lord Cathcart, adverting to that arrival, wrote, "Your arrival and conduct in the capital at this very critical moment has rendered important service:" the fact being that so much alarm had then prevailed at S. Petersburg, that all the archives and treasure of the state and palaces were packed up for removal.

Of course the special communication with which Sir Robert Wilson was charged had been confided only to those whose interests and affections were identified with the interest and welfare of the Emperor, and whose co-operation for the attainment of the object had been thought indispensable.

The Emperor arrived on the 3rd of September at S. Petersburg, and Sir Robert Wilson was immediately honoured by a command to dine with him, as he had previously done several times with the Empresses. His reception was of a nature to give encouragement, and to strengthen him in the execution of a purpose to which his word was committed, and on the success of which so many serious interests depended.

When the dinner was over, the Emperor withdrew with Sir Robert Wilson to his cabinet, where the conference commenced by Sir Robert Wilson glancing over the subject of his mission from Mr. Liston, the state of Turkey, the condition and movements of Admiral Tchichagow's army, and the details of the battle of Smolensk. The Emperor, having satisfied himself on all these points, directed the conversation to the dissensions existing among the Generals, observing that " he had heard that the Hetman Platow had even said to General Barclay, on the evacuation of Smolensk, 'You see I wear but a cloak; I will never put on again a Russian uniform, since it has become a disgrace.'" These expressions having been used in Sir Robert Wilson's presence, he could not pretend ignorance of them. The Emperor then asked "whether Sir Robert Wilson thought that Marshal Kutusow (who had been appointed Commander-in-chief) would be able to restore subordination?"

Sir Robert Wilson observed "that Marshal Kutusow, whom he had met going to the army, was fully aware of the temper in which he would find the army; that he had thought it his duty to communicate to the Marshal the facts with which he was acquainted, and that the Marshal had conjured him to conceal nothing from His Imperial Majesty; that he, Sir Robert Wilson, had undertaken a charge which his affection and gratitude towards His Majesty had made a duty under all circumstances; that in incurring the chance of displeasure, he was devoting himself to the Emperor's service, and for the protection of his dignity;" and then, entering at once into the matter (carefully avoiding the designation of individuals who might be regarded as leaders), he concluded "by earnestly imploring His Majesty to bear in mind the perilous state of the empire, which might justify patriotic alarm, and which alarm, from the gravity of its cause, extenuated a trespass on authority instigated by the purest motives, and intended for the permanent preservation of that authority itself; that the chiefs were animated by the most affectionate attachment to the Emperor and his family; and if they were but assured that His Majesty would no longer give his confidence to advisers whose policy they mistrusted, they would testify their allegiance by exertions and sacrifices which would add splendour to the crown, and security to the throne under every adversity."

During this exposition the Emperor's colour occasionally visited and left his cheek. When Sir Robert Wilson had terminated his appeal, there was a minute or two of pause, and His Majesty drew towards the window, as if desirous of recovering an unembarrassed air before he replied. After a few struggles, however, he came up to Sir Robert Wilson, took him by the hand, and kissed him on the forehead and cheek, according to the Russian custom. "You are the only person," then said His Majesty, "from whom I could or would have heard such a communication. In the former war you proved your attachment towards me by your services, and you entitled yourself to my most intimate confidence; but you must be aware that you have placed me in a very distressing position.—Moi! souverain de la Russie!—to hear such things from any one! But the army is mistaken in Romanzow: he really has not advised submission to the Emperor Napoleon; and I have a great respect for him, since he is almost the only one who never asked me in his life for anything on his own account, whereas every one else in my service has always been seeking honours, wealth, or some private object for himself and connections. I am unwilling to sacrifice him without cause; but come again to-morrow—I must collect my thoughts before I despatch you with an answer. I know the generals and officers about them well; they mean, I am satisfied, to do their duty, and I have no fears of their having any unavowed designs against my authority. But I am to be pitied, for I have few about me who have any sound education or fixed principles: my grandmother's court vitiated the whole education of the empire, confining it to the acquisition of the French language, French frivolities and vices, particularly gaming. I have little, therefore, on which I can rely firmly; only impulses; I must not give way to them, if possible; but I will think on all you have said." His Majesty then embraced Sir Robert Wilson again, and appointed the next day for his further attendance.

Sir Robert Wilson obeyed His Majesty's commands, who renewed the subject almost immediately by saying "Well! *Monsieur l'ambassadeur des rebelles*—I have reflected seriously during the whole night upon the conversation of yesterday, and I have not done you injustice. You shall carry back to the army pledges of my determination to continue the war against Napoleon whilst a Frenchman is in arms on this side the frontier. I will not desert my engagements, come what may. I will abide the worst. I am ready to remove my family into the interior, and undergo every sacrifice; but I must not give way on the point of choosing my own ministers: *that* concession might induce other demands, still more inconvenient and indecorous for me to grant. Count Romanzow shall not be the means of any disunion or difference—everything will be done that can remove uneasiness on that head; but done so that I shall not appear to give way to menace, or have to reproach myself for injustice. This is a case where much depends on the *manner of doing it*. Give me a little time—all will be satisfactorily arranged."

The Emperor then entered upon the subject of Mr. Liston's mission relative to the treaty of Bucharest, the proposed object of which mission was "to induce the Emperor to secure the amity of Turkey by restoring the acquisitions in Asia obtained by that treaty; a proposition to which the Russian generals had added their concurrence, as they attached no military importance to the new boundary line, either for defensive or offensive operations."

Sir Robert Wilson, however, told the Emperor "that the Turks attached the greatest value to the recovery of the ancient limits, and that the Grand Vizir had offered him purses to the amount of 50,000*l*., exclusive of great rewards from the Sultan, if he succeeded in his negotiation."—"And what reply did you make?" asked the Emperor.—"A laugh, and a hope that the Grand Vizir did not found his proposition upon any purchased experience of English envoyés"—"on which," said Sir Robert Wilson, "the Grand Vizir gave an Allah il Allah, and joining in the tone of mirth, he told me that the moment he saw a smile on my countenance he was convinced that he could not drive a bargain; for all the diplomatic jobbers he ever had to do with pretended great wrath till he had soothed it by offering at least double the sum." The Emperor in great good humour remarked that "he knew, to his cost, how the Turks spoiled the market by their extravagant prices;" for, he added, "we generally employ the same contractors and agents."

When Sir Robert Wilson assured the Emperor that "the military reform proposed by Selim would be executed by Mahmoud, the reigning Sultan," he seemed much struck by that intelligence, and it became the subject of frequent discussion at that epoch, and afterwards when the Emperor joined the army.

During the stay of Sir Robert Wilson at S. Petersburg, His Imperial Majesty continued to heap distinctions on him, as if anxious to make more manifest through him his sentiments and feelings towards the parties whom he had represented; and when the Emperor sanctioned his return, His Majesty, with the greatest solemnity, " declared upon his honour, and directed him to repeat in the most formal manner the declaration, that His Majesty would not enter into or permit any negotiation with Napoleon as long as an armed Frenchman remained in the territories of Russia." His Imperial Majesty said, " he would sooner let his beard grow to his waist, and eat potatoes in Siberia." At the same time he *specially authorized Sir Robert Wilson* (who was to reside with the Russian army as British Commissioner) *to interpose, and intervene with all the power and influence he could exert, to protect the interests of the Imperial Crown in conformity with that pledge, whenever he saw any disposition or design to contravene or prejudice them.*"

Each of the Empresses, who at that time took an active part in the transactions that were passing to sustain the Emperor in his resolution against subscribing to a peace, severally communicated to Sir Robert Wilson " her positive confidence in the Emperor's firm adherence to his word;" and they directed him " to give this their personal assurance to those influential chiefs of the army who had the honour of their confidence."

On the subject of Turkey, the Emperor acceded to the principle of the cession solicited, provided that Turkey maintained peace inviolably, but said " he would conclude that negotiation with Lord Cathcart." Sir Robert Wilson despatched that information to Mr. Liston, and Lord Cathcart undertook to bring the transaction under the Emperor's notice at a suitable moment, but thought it not delicate to press him further at the instant: nevertheless, in consequence of waiting for a more decorous opportunity, the object was never accomplished, for after the retreat of the French, the Emperor waived all attention to the application—a proceeding of which Turkey had much reason to complain, as Russia owed her a great debt of gratitude for the rejection of Andreossi's propositions. Had she listened to them, the Moldavian army never could have left the Danube, and the fortune of the war in Russia might have been most disastrously influenced by that result alone. This debt was, however, partly discharged when the Emperor sent the Russian corps to the aid of the Sultan at Unkiar Skelessi (after our reiterated refusal to take any measures to stop Ibrahim's march), and preserved by so doing the Sultan's life as well as his throne.

Confederate Army.

Napoleon, after the affair which the Russians call Loubino, and the French Waloutina Gora, returned to Smolensk, much chagrined at the result of that day, and the escape from his grasp of the Russian army. He hesitated whether to proceed at once to Moscow, or delay that great undertaking until another year, according to his original intention conveyed to the Poles and deputies at Wilna, whom he had questioned on the subject of distance. "You tell me," he said, "that it is but six weeks' march to Moscow, but I shall take two years."

There were serious objections to his progress as well as to his pause.

His inability to satisfy the demands of the Poles and set up their kingdom was becoming more and more embarrassing, for the Poles, oppressed by the devastating violence of friends and foes, were growing impatient, and reluctantly contributed to the heavy charges made to support a war of which they began to find that they were to be only the victims.

Napoleon foresaw that concession to their pretensions of independence must accompany a prolonged occupation of the country; for not only might their succours be withheld, but resistance might be opposed to requisite exactions under any other administrative system.

Many of his generals, agreeing with that view, nevertheless urged the necessity of a winter's repose, and founded their reasoning on the advanced period of the season, and various other considerations which presented themselves with irresistible force. But Napoleon could not listen to the counsels of a prudence which, not unnaturally, influenced the judgment of others. The structure of his empire contained too many discordant materials to be consolidated by procrastination. It was indispensable to coerce and maintain adhesion by continuous action and audacity of enterprise. As has been before observed, he ruled solely by the impressions entertained of his superiority of talent, the lofty tendencies of his destiny, and the irresistible power that he wielded.

Napoleon had been alarmed for the safety of

Witepsk, to which place he sent a strong detachment, but was enabled to recall it when he found that the Russians were not advancing from Suraje; the uneasiness also which he had felt at Wittgenstein's threatened movements was opportunely in this moment of hesitation removed by a despatch from S. Cyr, "who announced the total failure of the Russian general's attack on Polotzk, after several sanguinary combats."

Army of Wittgenstein.

Wittgenstein, imagining that Macdonald had dispersed his corps into cantonments so wide as to expose them to a successful irruption, made his dispositions with that view, and in the first instance prepared to cut off General Ricard, who, with a brigade, occupied Dunaburg. Suffering still from his wound, Wittgenstein gave the active command to General Dawray, who began this movement on the 4th of August.

It so happened that Oudinot, about the same time, finding that he was to be supported by S. Cyr, determined on assuming the offensive, and marched on Wolkyntsy, where he arrived on the 9th of August; but as soon as Wittgenstein and Dawray heard that Oudinot had left Polotzk, they relinquished the intention of surprising Dunaburg, and proceeded with their whole force to meet S. Cyr.

The enemy's detachments were first fallen in with in front of Swolna; they were immediately attacked, driven and pursued across the river, the château of Swolna was stormed, and, before nightfall, fifteen hundred of the enemy were killed, wounded, and taken. The Russians lost about half as many killed and wounded; none were made prisoners.

General Hamen, who had been stationed to watch Dunaburg, joined the army on the 13th, and formed its reserve.

Wittgenstein, having resumed the command, advanced on Wolkyntsy, which the enemy had evacuated the preceding day.

On the 15th a Russian detachment occupied Dissna, and the enemy were driven from all their outposts into Polotzk, where S. Cyr had already arrived with his corps.

The two corps united amounted to forty thousand combatants, notwithstanding that both, and particularly S. Cyr's, had suffered much by sickness.

Wittgenstein in this expedition had but twenty thousand men under his immediate command.

Polotzk is situated on the Dwina.

In front of Polotzk, on the north-west or Baltic side, is a plain girded by a wood.

The river Pelota, running from the north by east, intersects the plain for a mile and a half, and covers the town in its course to the Dwina.

The farm of Pressmenitza stands near the wood in the centre of the plain, and the convent of Spass, with a few adjoining houses, is situated on the right bank of the Pelota, about half a mile from the farm. This convent was strongly occupied by S. Cyr's advance, and supported by his own corps, which was covered by the Pelota.

Oudinot established his corps between the Dwina and Pelota, on the plain, with the right thrown forward toward Spass.

Wittgenstein directed his chief attack on the 17th against Spass and S. Cyr, hoping to force S. Cyr's left, and penetrate the right of Oudinot, so as to cut off the communication between the two corps.

The attack was protected by the fire of a powerful artillery.

Oudinot, on seeing S. Cyr pressed, endeavoured to make a diversion by an advance against the Russian centre, but was foiled in two attempts, and, being wounded in the shoulder, was obliged to quit the field and give up the command to S. Cyr.

Spass, after a desperate resistance, was carried, and Wrede who had crossed the Pelota to support it, after firing the buildings close to the convent, retired again behind the Pelota, which the Russians were unable to cross.

During the day the enemy had made a demonstration against the Russian right, but it had been feebly supported. Night put an end to the conflict, which had continued fourteen hours, each party losing nearly three thousand men.

Wittgenstein, reinforced by his reserve from Repno, watched for a favourable opportunity to recommence his attack; this he calculated would be afforded during the evacuation of Polotzk, on which event he confidently relied, as being the certain consequence of the operations of the preceding day, and of the demonstrations he had made by ordering a bridge to be thrown over the Dwina, as if he were about to cross and invest Polotzk on that side.

S. Cyr, to encourage this delusion, directed his baggage, under a strong cavalry escort, to file behind the Dwina along a road in view of the Russians, and to return into Polotzk by another road hidden from their observation ; a stratagem the more likely to succeed as it was studiously reported that S. Cyr had actually recommended the evacuation to Oudinot before he himself obtained the command in chief.

S. Cyr, finding that Wittgenstein did not attack, and that his troops did not even keep under arms, opened all his guns on the Russian lines at five in the afternoon of the 18th, and simultaneously sallied from Spass in three columns.

The Russians were taken quite unawares, but, as is admitted and admired in all the enemy's records, fell into their ranks without any disorder, and formed steadily in their position.

Shattered, however, by the artillery, which raked its columns, their left, notwithstanding an obstinately protracted resistance, was obliged to recede and fall back into the wood behind the farm.

The Russian centre, assaulted with equal impetuosity, was unsettling, and abandoning the farm that was on the point of being carried by Legrand's division, when Hamen, seeing the necessity of a desperate effort to save the army about to be cut off from Repno, the only route of retreat, charged forward at the head of nine battalions, and recovered the lost ground. · Three squadrons of the Chevalier guards, darting on the enemy at the same onset, overthrew with much loss several columns attempting to turn Hamen's left; various other movements of the enemy were also successfully baffled.

S. Cyr, seeking to recover the advantages thus wrested from him, ordered a mass of cavalry, aided by the concentrated fire of fifteen pieces of artillery, to pierce the Russian centre. The Russian cavalry met it at speed, overwhelmed it and all that opposed them on their way, pursuing the fugitives to the suburbs of Polotzk and taking the fifteen guns (of which, however, they could only bring away two for want of means of removal) before the Bavarian reserves arrived, who opening their fire from the houses of the suburbs, compelled a prompt retreat.

The Russian right, which covered the road of Dissna, had successfully maintained its ground, and in every part of the field the Russians remained masters of their original posts.

A detachment of Grodno hussars, and a battalion of the Pawlask regiment of grenadiers, gained great credit during the affair; for being cut off near the Pelota, where they had been watching two fords on the left of the Russian line, instead of surrendering as was expected, they forced their way through the enemy's alignment, and even making some prisoners in their progress, gained triumphantly the Russian position.

S. Cyr finding that he could make no impression on the immovable tenacity of the Russians, gradually relaxed his fire, which ceased towards night.

The Russians withdrew between Repno and Pressmenitza, and continued till the 22nd their retrograde movement, when they reached Siwokhina and Tokolitchie Tchitar on the right bank of the Drissa, and posted a small rear guard under Wlastoff at Beloie, on the left bank: here it continued unmolested until the 22nd, when the enemy, who had quietly and unexpectedly remained in Polotzk, made an attack, under Wrede, on the post of Beloie, and for a moment obtained possession of a farm, which turned the Russian right, but they were quickly driven back on Garuzelewo, with the loss of two hundred prisoners, and five hundred killed and wounded. Wittgenstein then commenced throwing up works to defend the position of Siwokhina, and also fortified Sebije, where he proposed to establish his magazines, artillery-park, and depôts. S. Cyr also occupied his troops in making defences at Polotzk.

The last day's action at Polotzk had cost the Russians three thousand men, seven guns, and three generals wounded.*

The enemy lost as many, including five hundred prisoners; and they had four generals wounded, of whom two died.†

Wittgenstein never had warrant with his inferiority of force to undertake the dislodgment of two of the enemy's corps entrenched in Polotzk—he should have been satisfied with the discomfiture of Oudinot's offensive enterprise; but lured on by the dispositions and stratagem of S. Cyr, he was involved in a snare from which he was extricated by the zeal, nerve, and discipline of his officers and soldiers.

Some have thought that Wittgenstein should have made his chief attack on Polotzk, but he had not force enough, even after the capture of the Spass Convent, to keep S. Cyr's corps in check behind the Pelota; and had he advanced on the town, his rear would have been uncovered, and all his communications lost.

S. Cyr seems to have missed an opportunity of turning the Russian right (whilst the centre and left

---

* Berg, Hamen, and Kosaczkoffskoi.
† Generals Verdier, Deroy, Siebien, and Raglowich. Deroy and Siebien died a day or two afterwards.

were wholly engaged) by a reserve which he might have drawn from the Pelota; but he conducted his manœuvres, in all other respects, with skill and well-considered assurance of his enemy's impetuosity and erroneous calculations of his intentions: his success was, however, confined to a victorious defence of his position, for he was too crippled by his adversary to reap any other advantage.

The intelligence of this amount of success, nevertheless, was most satisfactory to Napoleon. Sending S. Cyr a marshal's staff as a proof of his approbation, he resolved forthwith to discuss no longer the question of his own advance to Moscow but to move on Ueviat, where he understood that Barclay proposed to give him battle.

Quitting Smolensk on the 23rd, he despatched an order, on his way, dated the 25th, "for Victor to march from the Niemen with his corps, and making Smolensk his head-quarters, to take under his charge the governments of Mohilew and Witepsk." He also directed Augereau to "replace Victor with the corps of new levies which he had been forming;" adding that "Macdonald was about to besiege Riga; that Wittgenstein could not again make head against Oudinot and S. Cyr; and that Dombrowski with his division was in strength enough to maintain the communications from Minsk to Orsza and Smolensk, without any interruption from General Ertel at Bobruisk, whose garrison was weak, and whom Schwarzenberg would keep in check."

Imperial Russian Army.

On the 26th the Russian army retired in three columns on Louchki, Semlewo, and Afanasiewo.

The enemy attacked the rear guard behind the Osma, but could not force it, and Rosen kept his ground till the evening, when he retired behind the Kostra.

On the 27th the army of Barclay united near Wiazma, and Bagrathion took post at Skoblewo.

Murat attacked the rear guard at Rybki—the action was sharp, but without any result.

On the 28th the two armies retired on Federowskoie.

The rear guard was more hotly pressed, but it was not compromised, in its retreat on Wiazma.

On the 29th the united armies took post at Tsarewo Zalomich.

The rear guard commanded by Konownitsyn (for Platow, heart-sick at the evacuation of Smolensk and interminable retreats, had withdrawn on the plea of physical indisposition), approached within twelve miles of the army, after firing the magazines at Wiazma: the conflagration consumed half the town before the enemy could enter, which they did early on the same morning.

Barclay, on hearing that Napoleon headed his army again, expressed his determination to accept battle in the plain of Tsarewo Zalomich, and ordered forward from Gjatsk, Milaradowitch the gallant and emulous rival of Bagrathion, who had arrived there conducting sixteen thousand infantry of the new levy and twelve hundred horse; but in the evening of the 29th Barclay's oscillations and responsibility terminated by the

K

arrival of Marshal Prince Kutusow, who superseded him in the command.

A change of chief had become indispensable. Barclay no longer could command any confidence in his judgment or firmness of purpose. He had seemed to be governed by the chapter of accidents, and to have wasted his force by continual movements without explicable or defined object.

The spirit of the army was affected by a sense of mortification, and all ranks loudly and boldly complained; discontent was general, and discipline relaxing.

The nobles, the merchants, and the population at large, were indignant at seeing city after city, government after government abandoned, till the enemy's guns were almost heard at Moscow, and S. Petersburg doubted of its own safety.

The removal of a general who had not been able to make a more favourable application of the sacrifices which they had so nobly made, and the blood so lavishly shed, had become an universal demand.

The difficulties of Barclay, as already stated, were immensely beyond his capacity to regulate satisfactorily or to overcome: he sought to palliate them, and in the endeavour he but aggravated their evils till they were too formidable for further trust in his direction.

He was a brave soldier and a good officer, but not a captain with a master mind equal to the need.

Marshal Prince Kutusow was born noble, and was still more nobly allied by marriage. In his youth he was regarded as a very gallant officer, and had served with distinction. Wounded several times, on one occasion he lost an eye, but the expression of his countenance was still engagingly intellectual.

At the battle of Austerlitz he commanded the Russian corps; but as he disapproved the fatal flank movement that occasioned the loss of the battle almost before it was commenced, his reputation did not suffer by that event.

In the year 1811 he had obtained great successes over the Turks, and in the following year, by the aid of English and Swedish influence, concluded the peace which contributed so much to the safety of the Russian empire.

He had passed some of his time at Paris, and preserved a predilection for the French; he distrusted and yet was not personally disinclined to Napoleon.

A bon vivant—polished, courteous, shrewd as a Greek, naturally intelligent as an Asiatic and well instructed as an European—he was more disposed to trust to diplomacy for his success than to martial prowess, for which by his age and the state of his constitution he was no longer qualified.

When he joined the army he was seventy-four years old, and though hale, so very corpulent and unwieldy that he was obliged to move about, even when in the field, in a little four-wheeled carriage with a head, called a droska.

Such was the successor of Barclay, whom, as Alexander told the English General Sir Robert Wilson, "the nobility of Russia had selected to vindicate the arms of Russia, and defend their remaining possessions."

Bound to the stake by the circumstances of his appointment, he could not decline the battle which he had heard vociferously demanded wherever he had passed; but not approving for the arena of combat of the plain selected by Barclay, he withdrew the army on the 30th to Jackowo, where Milaradowitch's reinforcement was distributed amongst the regiments of the army, as it was not found to be in a fit state to form an independent corps.

On the 2nd of September the army again fell back on the convent of Kolotskoi, and on the 3rd entered the position of Borodino.

Napoleon had latterly pressed on with great activity, and on the 1st of September reached Gjatsk.

The march of the enemy from Smolensk had been accompanied with the most barbarous destruction and disorder of every kind. Even the towns which they were occupying were set on fire with recklessly mad ferocity, and disregard of their own interests.

Gjatsk and Dorogobouche suffered this fate, and Junot himself nearly perished in the flames. Nothing was respected; a demon spirit raged, and revelled with exterminating fury, preparing a day of vengeance no less savage and calamitous.

The movements of the confederate army were also more and more encumbered by increasing baggage and ambulance of every kind, so that Napoleon at last issued an order, which was never executed, " that all carriages found contravening the regulations for their march and parking should be burnt."

" Take care," he wrote to Berthier, " take care, dear cousin, that the first baggage I may have to consume be not that of the head quarter staff."

On the 2nd of September another order was issued directing the generals and chiefs of regiments to " collect all the soldiers that were lingering behind, to inspect arms, and adopt every measure to render their force as efficient as possible, for they were on the eve of a decisive battle."

The official returns in conformity with this order gave one hundred and three thousand infantry under arms, and thirty-one thousand cavalry. Total in round numbers, including artillery, staff corps, &c., *one hundred and forty thousand fighting men.*

The infantry was reported in good order, but the cavalry was generally in bad condition from fatigue, and from want of good water and proper food. Murat one day complaining to Nansouty that "the cavalry had not vigorously executed a charge," Nansouty is said to have replied, " The horses have no patriotism: the soldiers fight without bread, but the horses insist on oats."

When Napoleon commenced hostilities, the same corps which now mustered only one hundred and forty thousand men, exceeded two hundred and eighty thousand : deducting thirty-five thousand employed on detachments, the deficiency amounted to a hundred and five thousand, and this loss had been sustained before some of the divisions had even been engaged.

On the 4th of September Napoleon marched on Gridnewa, where Konownitsyn was stationed with a rear guard of twenty battalions and ninety-five squadrons.

A severe action was prolonged till night, during which the hussars of Isoum and the Cossacks surrounded and sabred five whole squadrons of the enemy; but Konownitsyn seeing that his right flank was being turned, retired leisurely, and entered the position of Borodino.

The position of Borodino, which the enemy call "of Mojaisk,"* rested its right flank on a wood, distant about five hundred yards from the Moskwa.

The rivulet of Kolocza, fordable everywhere, but running through a deep ravine, covered the front of the right, and part of the centre as far as the village of Borodino.

The left extended from the heights above Borodino beyond the village of Semenowskoie.

The ground was here more open, but deep ravines and brushwood intersected it, and rendered approach difficult for compact bodies.

Field works were constructed in front of the wood, on the right of the position.

On the heights in front of Gorki—which may be considered the right centre of the whole position—two strong redoubts were established, commanding Borodino, the Kolocza, and the high road from Smolensk to Moscow called the new road, which ran through

---

* The post route from Smolensk to Mojaisk makes the distance 284 wersts, or 211 miles.

Smolensk to	Bredechino	..	23
	Pneva	..	17
	Mikailouka	..	24
	Dorogobouche	..	23
	Jackowo	..	28
	Semlewo	..	28
	Wiazma	..	26
	Tepelouka	..	29
	Gjatsk	..	30
	Gridnewa	..	29
	Mojaisk	..	27
	Total	..	284

From Mojaisk to Moscow is a post distance of 99 wersts, or 75 miles.

Mojaisk to	Chelkowka	..	24
	Koubinskoie	..	22
	Pekrouchekowo		26
	Moscow	..	27
	Total	..	99

Borodino, Gorki, and the centre of the army to Mojaisk. The advanced battery was constructed within four hundred yards of the battery nearest Gorki, and was capable of holding twelve hundred men.

The left of the position being the weakest, a bastioned battery with curtain prolongations was established on the heights that overlooked all the plain that lay in its front; this battery served as a point of contact between the centre and left.

The village of Semenowskoie, which lay in front of the left, had been destroyed to prevent an enemy's lodgment in it; and a considerable redoubt had been projected in advance, but it was no more than traced.

In front of this ruined village ran a deep ravine, beyond which three flèches or redans were constructed, destined to support the advanced chasseurs; and again in advance, on a hill situated between two small woods, about eighteen hundred yards in front of the village of Chewardino, was another field work intended to delay the progress of an enemy moving on Semenowskoie.

The three villages in front of Chewardino, called Aleksinki, Fomkino, and Doronino, were occupied by light troops.

The old road from Smolensk to Moscow ran immediately on the left of the Russian position through Jelnia, and then, taking a direction through Oulitsa, swept round behind the whole through Psarewo to Mojaisk, where it united with the new road.

Thus the field of battle ranged from the Moskwa to the old road of Smolensk at Oulitsa, a distance of about eight thousand yards; but the principal ground of contest was confined to the space between Borodino and Oulitsa, i.e. about five thousand yards.

The whole surface was broken, billowy, and uneven.

The Russian army consisted of ninety thousand effective regulars, ten thousand militia of Moscow and of Smolensk, which had joined a day or two previously, and seven thousand Cossacks.

Bagrathion commanded the left, Beningsen the centre, Barclay the right.

On the 5th of September Murat appeared in front of the position by the road of Golowino, and immediately deployed his cavalry and the division Campans, by which it was supported.

The Viceroy took the direction of Borodino, and Poniatowski moved through Jelnia along the old Smolensk road.

At two o'clock in the afternoon, Napoleon, who had come forward to reconnoitre, ordered an attack to be made on the Russian light troops in the villages of Aleksinki, Fomkino, and Doronino, and on the redoubt of Chewardino.

At four o'clock the enemy passed the Kolocza, dislodging the Russians from the three before-named villages, and establishing themselves behind an elevation in front of the redoubt which was armed with twelve field pieces, and from which elevation they kept up a galling fire on the Russian cannoneers.

As soon as Campans had planted his guns on an eminence that favoured the operation, he opened his fire on the redoubt.

Murat then attempted to charge between the redoubt and a wood on the left, but was driven back.

Prince Gorchakow, who was entrusted with the defence of this redoubt, had supported it with two regiments of infantry, supported again on their right by two regiments of dragoons and four pieces of flying artillery, and on the left by a division of cuirassiers and eight pieces of flying artillery; two regiments of dragoons had also been employed in covering the chasseurs on their retreat from the villages.

After a heavy cannonade on the redoubt, which had silenced several of its guns, the enemy made a rush at the redoubt and carried it. The Russians rallying recovered it—again lost it—again retook it—and a third time, having been driven out, forced a re-entrance, but were at length obliged to give up the conflict, and leave the enemy for a time in possession.

At eight o'clock Bagrathion, finding Gorchakow too much pressed, reinforced him with a division of grenadiers, and going forward himself to examine the enemy's strength and dispositions, ordered the grenadier division to proceed and storm the redoubt that had been abandoned.

Two columns of the enemy bore down on the advancing division to attack it in flank, but the cuirassiers of Little Russia and Gloutchkow threw them into confusion, and pushing on carried the enemy's battery in front of Doronino, bringing away five pieces of cannon out of eight; whilst the dragoons of Kharkow and Tchernigow attacked two columns advancing from Fomkino on Doronino, and carried off their two guns.

Under favour of this successful diversion, the grenadiers possessed themselves of the redoubt, and retained it till an order came from the Marshal at ten o'clock at night "to withdraw from it, as it was out of the main defensive line of the position, was turned by Poniatowski, who had advanced to Jelnia, and by checking, as it had done, the enemy's approach, had fully accomplished the object of its construction."

The enemy soon afterwards crept forward, and found the redoubt unoccupied, except by five guns—of which the artillerymen and horses had been killed—and one thousand of their own slain and wounded comrades, who were strewed in and around.

Napoleon's head-quarters were that night established at Waloniewa, near Fomkino, but on the other side of the Kolocza. The day of the 6th was passed in mutual preparations for the engagement that was probably to decide not only the fate of Russia and of its invader, but of Europe.

Napoleon, doubtful whether the Russians had remained in their position, mounted his horse before day-dawn. Finding that they had not moved, he reconnoitred them in detail, and having made his dispositions, published to his army the following proclamation :—

"Soldiers—the moment for that battle you had so long ardently desired is at hand. The victory now depends on yourselves—it is necessary—it will assure us abundance of good winter quarters, and a speedy return to our own country.

"Behave as at Austerlitz, Friedland, Witepsk, and Smolensk—that the most distant posterity may cite your conduct on this day—that they may say of you, 'He was in the great battle under the walls of Moscow.'"

This address, so unusually low in tone, was adapted, however, to the feelings and condition of the army.

The army required subsistence, repose, and the prospect of an early return to their homes.

Privations, fatigue, and disgust had enfeebled their passion for glory; and yet on the morrow, when arrayed on her field of blood, all forgot their griefs, and emulously strove to win her crown, though cypress were enwreathed with its laurel.

Kutusow, preceded by the holy image rescued from Smolensk, had also passed his army in review, and published a proclamation to his troops, which, after adverting to the cruel ravages committed by the enemy, concluded in these terms:—

"Soldiers, fulfil your duties. Think of the sacrifices of your cities to the flames—of your children who implore your protection. Think of your Emperor, your Lord, who regards you as the source of all his strength; and to-morrow, before the sun sets, you will have traced your faith and your allegiance to your Sovereign and country, in the blood of the aggressor and of his hosts."

The troops responded to the announcement with shouts that evidenced their resolve to discharge undauntedly their duty, and to conquer if victory could be achieved by bravery, or if foiled by superior numbers, to raise by the sacrifice of their lives an imperishable monument to their courage, fidelity, and patriotism.

On the morning of the 7th the sun that was to shine for the last time on so many thousands of the brave rose extraordinarily bright.

Napoleon is said to have hailed the ascending refulgent orb as a twin sun of Austerlitz; and he proceeded to place himself, with full confidence in the auspicious omen, on the hillock near Chewardino, to superintend the movements.

On the eminence beyond this spot he had ordered three batteries, each of twenty-four twelve-pounders, to be constructed during the night; the first to play on the Russian centre, nearly in front of the corps of the Viceroy; the second to bear on the redoubt above the ruins of Semenoffskoie; the third on the three flèches which covered the front of the Russian left, where Bagrathion commanded.

Poniatowski had orders to move from Jelnia along the old road of Smolensk to Mojaisk, to advance out of the wood, and to gain the rear of the left of the Russian position; Davoust to attack in front the Russian left, with the divisions Campans, Desaix, and Friant; Ney, with his own corps and Junot's, to attack the right of the left and left centre, extending from Chewardino to Aleksinki; and the Viceroy with his army and the cavalry of Grouchy, supported by the divisions Gerard and Morand, to keep in check the Russian right centre and right, and thus to form on the left bank of the Kolocza the left wing of the confederate army.

The Imperial Guard, old and new, was posted as a reserve on the right of Fomkino.

Eight corps were thus collected to storm in the first instance the redoubts and works located between the Kolocza and the wood contiguous to the old Smolensk road.

The Russian army during the night had also moved into its order of battle positions.

The village of Borodino, as being advanced beyond the Russian line of defence, was only occupied by the chasseurs of the Guard.

On the extreme right, extending to the Moscow road, and within a thousand yards of the Moskwa, Bagawouth was stationed with his corps en échelon, and a reserve formed of the first corps of cavalry with seven regiments of Cossacks under Platow. On his left stood Osterman, with his left established on the eminence above the Kolocza. Then Doctorow, who was charged with the defence of the great battery above Borodino, and under Gorki. Raeffskoi occupied the ground between this battery and Semenoffskoie. Woronzow and Borosdin supported the flèches in front of Semenoffskoie, and were sustained in the second line by the division of Neveroffskoi.

Prince Charles of Mecklenburg with his grenadiers remained in reserve behind Semenoffskoie; whilst the second division of cuirassiers formed in extended line behind the grenadiers of Prince Charles, to carry aid to the whole left as might be required.

Touchkoff, with the divisions Konownitsyn and Strogonoff, with the ten thousand militia in reserve, were employed to defend Oulitsa, and prevent the enemy from reaching Psarewo, and thus establishing himself in the rear of the army to endanger its communication with Mojaisk.

The Imperial Guards were stationed in reserve behind the centre, and they were supported by the division of Depreradowitch's cuirassiers.

The reserve artillery was parked at Psarewo.

The cavalry formed behind the infantry, guarding the intervals between the lines and columns.

The Cossacks attached to the different corps were distributed on the flanks, and the chasseurs along the ravines and brushwood that lay in front.

Barclay was charged with the superintendence of the right, Beningsen of the centre, and Bagrathion commanded his own army on the left.

The Russians had six hundred and forty guns, the enemy a thousand.

The Kolocza was fordable everywhere, but as the banks were rugged and steep, bridges were thrown across to facilitate communication.

At six in the morning of the 7th of September the enemy suddenly opened fire from their right battery under the direction of General Sorbier, with a thundering peal, which was followed by lightning flashes from all the other batteries.

The Russians, who had also been standing at their guns, returned the fire with equal alacrity and vigour.

Davoust, leaving Friant in reserve, moved the division Desaix along the skirts of the brushwood upon its right, whilst Campans, preceded by thirty pieces of artillery, advanced directly in front under showers of grape and musketry: when he had approached sufficiently near, one of his regiments rushed towards the most advanced flèche.

The impetuous onset was stedfastly repulsed, and General Rapp, who led it, was severely wounded. The next in command was also shortly afterwards obliged to leave the field, being struck by a cannon ball.

Ney, seeing that the division was wavering, advanced to its support with Junot's corps as his reserve. This succour permitted the renewal of the attack and the capture of the flèche; but it was recovered almost as soon as lost by Woronzow at the head of his grenadiers formed in solid squares, and by a charge of the cuirassiers under Dourka, supported by the division Neveroffskoi. The conflict had been most sanguinary, and the enemy were obliged to suspend their further attempts until reinforcements could be obtained; but there was no pause in the cannonade and musketry.

Poniatowski about that time, having forced and cleared the wood in which he had been long detained to the great prejudice of Napoleon's original plan, deployed his force, and drove the Russian light troops out of Oulitsa, notwithstanding that the Russian guns had poured a most destructive fire upon his columns in their advance to that point.

Touchkoff, on retiring, fell back on a height that commanded the plain in front where till mid-day he maintained an unremitting combat.

The Viceroy, after an obstinate opposition, in which his guns had been several times silenced by the Russian batteries, succeeded in occupying Borodino permanently.

Leaving a division of infantry and some light cavalry to watch his rear in the direction of the Moskwa, he crossed the Kolocza with the remainder of his army, and formed in front of the Gorki batteries and the great bastioned battery that covered the Russian right centre.

Ney, who had been compelled to desist from his onslaughts until further strengthened, awaited impatiently the reinforcement for which he had applied to Napoleon, who delayed compliance until he had received reports from other corps, but at length he gave the order for Friant to join.

About nine o'clock Davoust and Ney moved forward.

The Russians also, during this interval reinforced by cavalry sent by Barclay, continued a successful defence for an hour, when exhausted by their efforts and loss, they were obliged to abandon the flèches with the guns standing in them.

Some of the enemy, following up their advantage, passed the ravine of Semenoffskoie, and established themselves in the ruins of the village; but Borosdin, at the head of his grenadiers, charged, repassed the ravine, and regained the flèches.

In this charge Prince Charles of Mecklenburg was wounded.

Nansouty and Latour Maubourg bore down upon the Russians before they had time to re-arm the flèches, and they were again relinquished, when Konownitsyn, coming up with his division, replanted in them its gory standards. In this conflict Major-general Touchkoff was killed, and, on the side of the enemy, General Romanow of Davoust's staff.

Napoleon, seeing that no impression had been made on the Russian left, now ordered the Viceroy to carry the bastioned redoubt in front of his right.

The difficulties which the ground presented to the advance of the divisions Broussier, Gerard, and Morand had been great, but were spiritedly surmounted.

The first lodged itself in a ravine between Borodino and the redoubt, whilst Morand, supported by Gerard, gained the esplanade in front of the work, whence, notwithstanding the showers of grape that poured on his column, he continued the impulse that he had communicated, rushed upon, reached, stormed, and carried the redoubt!

Koutaisow and Yermolow sprang instantly forward with some battalions taken from the corps of Doctorow, and, uniting with the rallying remains of the division Passkewitch which had been driven back from the redoubt, and supported in their movement by Raeffskoi, they charged the victors in front and on both flanks, in hopes of dislodging them and intercepting their retreat.

The attempt merited and obtained success.

Almost all those who were in the redoubt (the 30th of the line) were bayoneted; but General Bonami, who commanded in it, and who was severely wounded, had his life spared.

Plauzanne, who had advanced to cover the flying remnant, was killed; and Gerard's division, which had moved on to support Morand, being charged by Korf with two regiments of cavalry whom Barclay had detached to sustain the assault, was thrown into great disorder.

The Russians had to lament the death of Koutaisow.

The Viceroy, having failed in his coup-de-main, played on the redoubt with all his artillery, and with such effect that the division occupying it was necessarily relieved on account of its destructive loss.

Ney, despairing of carrying the flèches in advance of the Russian left by a front attack, and of afterwards holding them, determined to push Junot's corps between the Russian left and the corps of Touchkoff, which formed the extreme left. Thus he expected to gain his object by turning the flèches, whilst Touchkoff might be simultaneously placed in jeopardy.

L

Prince Galitzin, with his cuirassiers, defended the space on which Junot directed his march; but Prince Eugène of Wurtemberg (who had been detached by Barclay to support the left), on finding that he had more than sufficient force to guard the right under the enemy's now manifested dispositions of battle, opportunely arrived at the menaced point, attacked the head of Junot's column, and baffled its proposed operation.

The arrival of Prince Eugène again disconcerted Napoleon's plan, for he had felt assured that the Russian left would be forced back, or turned, before any succour from their right could arrive to its aid.

The attack of Junot had ceased; but Poniatowski, finding his left sustained by that corps, renewed the offensive, and, under cover of forty pieces of cannon placed in a battery on the right of Oulitsa, moved on to force Touchkoff's position.

The attack, conducted with energy, obtained at first some success; and even the eminence from which the Russian battery had been so long sweeping the plain in front was gained. But Touchkoff, uniting all his troops, met the enemy boldly, repulsed them, and recovered the lost ground; nor could the enemy make any subsequent impression. But the brave Russian general was mortally wounded, and Bagawouth was sent for to succeed to the command.

It was now mid-day, and the enemy had secured no positive advantage, nor made any essential progress.

The loss on both sides had been enormous; but the Russians, being in their own country, could better repair that loss, and save and mitigate the sufferings of their wounded.

Napoleon felt that it was necessary to combine for a concentrated and conclusive effort. Collecting all his disposable force in one mighty mass, planting four hundred pieces of cannon to cover and support the shock, a general movement in advance was ordered to storm the Russian left.

The collection of this mass, and its unequivocal object, determined the march of Milaradowitch and of Osterman in support of Bagrathion; all the disposable cavalry was also assembled to form a reserve to the centre, whilst, with the view of distracting the enemy's attention to his communications in rear of the Viceroy, Ouwarrow with the first corps of cavalry, and Platow with his seven thousand Cossacks, were directed "to move forward from the right of the position, make then a conversion to the left, pass the Kolocza, and alarm the enemy at Borodino and along his rear, as much and as far as circumstances would permit."

During those movements the artillery battle raged with terrible effect, the Russians having opposed three hundred pieces to the enemy's four hundred.

As the enemy's columns approached, successive charges of cavalry and infantry were interchanged under torrents of missiles, that poured as if discharged from a bursting thunder cloud, but neither party quailed under their suffering.

The collision was terrific: all but the reserves were engaged—the confusion became indescribable—every individual seemed to be animated with the fiercest excitements of hatred and revenge—each endeavoured to kill an enemy without regard to his own life.

Victory hung in the balance equally poised, when Bagrathion, S. Priest, Woronzow, and numerous other generals and chiefs, were wounded and obliged to withdraw.

Konownitsyn assumed the command, but even his valour and energy could not repair the sinister effect of these misfortunes.

The Russians, in their several divisions, no longer under the direction of the commander and of the individual chiefs who had so often led them to the combat, relaxed their resistance, and Konownitsyn was obliged to take up a position behind Semenoffskoie, abandoning the flèches, but re-establishing his batteries with great promptitude on the heights above the village, by which he checked the progress of the enemy.

The enemy's cavalry, under Nansouty and Latour Maubourg, made a daring attempt to break through the Russian left; but the two regiments of the Imperial Guards, Ismailowskoi and Lithuania, when surrounded by the enemy's squadrons, formed squares, and though crushed by a murderous artillery fire, beat off the French cuirassiers; and when they were eventually succoured by the Emperor's and Empresses' cuirassiers, by those of Astrachan, Ekaterinoslav, and S. George, they re-advanced, and forced their assailants back across the ravine.

All the enemy's corps had now been engaged except the Imperial Guards; and during this last desperate struggle, when both parties were evidently exhausted and unable to make further decisive exertion, Napoleon had been earnestly urged by some of his generals to reinforce Davoust and Ney with that formidable corps, and accomplish the triumph partially gained; but he inflexibly refused, saying "And if the Russians should give battle again to-morrow, what force should I have left to command the victory?"

At this moment he received the intelligence that the Viceroy was attacked in his rear at Borodino by the Russian cavalry. Alarmed at the possible consequences of such an irruption from the Russian right, if making in force, he suspended all orders until he was more fully acquainted with the real object of the movement.

Ouwarrow and Platow, passing, as directed, the Kolocza, and moving in the direction of Borodino, fell suddenly upon the Viceroy's cavalry, and threw them back with great loss and disorder on the division of infantry Delzon's, left to guard that village. The infantry had but just time to form into squares of regiments, and the Viceroy, who, on hearing of the attack, had hastened to the menaced point with his Italian guards and cavalry, was obliged to throw himself for personal safety into one of the squares.

Ouwarrow and Platow, not having any infantry to support, dispersed when they had accomplished their object by alarming the Viceroy, drawing off his forces, and distracting the attention of Napoleon at the most critical moment of the battle; for the attack on the centre had been delayed, and time gained for the Russian left to re-organize and crown with their batteries the new position, which now presented a front of little more than three thousand yards.

The Viceroy finding that there was no further cause of apprehension in his rear, and being reinforced by the legion of the Vistula from the Imperial Guards, which Napoleon had ordered to his aid on the first notice of the enemy's appearance in his rear at Borodino, recrossed the Kolocza, and prepared to make, as ordered by Napoleon, a decisive assault on the bastioned battery with his whole force.

His artillery redoubled its violence, and the battle again raged with increased animation at all points.

Montbrun having been killed, Caulaincourt had succeeded to the command of his division of cuirassiers.

Murat, seizing the moment when the divisions of Morand, Gerard, and Broussier were beginning to make an impression on the Russian columns, ordered Caulaincourt to charge through their intervals, and then, by a wheel on his left, to enter the great redoubt by its open gorge.

Executing his order with the most exemplary bravery and ability of direction, he ran the gauntlet through the columns, and, sweeping round, gained the gorge; but the cannon from the supporting battery and works, and the fire from the infantry in the redoubt, nearly exterminated all the assailants, the intrepid Caulaincourt being one of the first to fall in this his bed of imperishable honour. The redoubt, though penetrated, was still Russian, when four infantry regiments of the enemy rushing forward again stormed it successfully, putting all its brave defenders to death: every Russian, indeed, refused quarter, and contended hand to hand even in the last agonies.

In vain the Russian artillery from the supporting

redoubt and works round Gorki poured their fire upon the enemy lodged in the captured redoubt and contiguous ground which afforded shelter. In vain the Russians endeavoured, with the shattered means still left them, to regain the whole portion of the position lost, and perhaps isolate within it, if successful, some of the enemy's corps. Ardour the most enthusiastic—courage the most devoted—could not achieve any progress against the tremendous carnage power now bearing on them; but still their heroic daring and endurance extorted from Napoleon language of admiration that will for ever constitute their proudest eulogium.

The enemy's further success was, however, arrested; and an attempt made by Grouchy at the head of the cavalry of Chastel stationed upon the left of the Viceroy, in the hope that the Russian cavalry could not reach the ground in time to repel it, as well as all subsequent attempts to force back the Russian alignments, proved ineffectual.

Napoleon expressed an inclination to continue the combat by an attack on the works and heights of Gorki, that he might break in upon the Russian right; but, as the French say, "his generals unanimously represented that the loss would be too great in achieving that attack, if success were attainable, which was doubtful; for Barclay, foreseeing the impending danger, had moved up already his last reserves to defend the point and strengthen the position between the captured redoubt and Semenoffskoie."

Poniatowski, emulous of the Viceroy's exploit,

moved forward upon the old road of Smolensk; but Bagawouth, who had taken the command of Touchkoff's corps, retired to a hill near the source of the rivulet of Semenoffskoie, where he steadily maintained himself in spite of every succeeding movement to dislodge him.

About three o'clock Napoleon, finding his whole army under fire, except his twenty thousand Guards, and that it was rapidly extenuating, ordered a cessation of active operations, but the cannonade and tirailleur fire continued till nightfall.

At this hour a detachment of the enemy, suddenly débouching from Semenoffskoie, made a momentary lodgment in a wood beyond the village, but the Finland chasseurs, charging with the bayonet, drove them out and back.

When the active battle ceased at three o'clock, the enemy were masters of the bastioned redoubt and the flèches of Semenoffskoie, but these were in fact only the exterior works of the position.

The position occupied behind the ravines of Goretskef and of Semenoffskoie was intact and entire. The army had only retired its centre and left.

To have gained a decisive victory it would have been necessary to pierce this main position, or by reinforcing Poniatowski sufficiently to cause its evacuation, as then the retreat on Mojaisk would have been in peril, and delay of retreat till night would have been too hazardous; but Napoleon found his force, after the resistance he had experienced and might expect to see continued, unequal to either undertaking without endangering its total safety, and impairing too much, even if he succeeded, his own strength for the prosecution of the campaign.

At night the enemy retired to the positions they had occupied before the battle: their advanced posts only were left at Borodino, Oulitsa, and amongst the brushwood that intervened.

Napoleon entertained the opinion that the Russians would not decline battle on the next day: he therefore took every possible precaution against surprise.

Barclay, Beningsen, Yermolow, and Tol were also as actively employed under the same expectations in making their dispositions of the Russian army.

Doctorow's corps appuied its right on the height of Gorki, beyond which, towards the Moskwa, four regiments of chasseurs, with the Cossacks of Platow, were stationed.

Osterman formed on the left of Doctorow's corps, and occupied the interval between that corps and the village of Semenoffskoie.

The right of Bagrathion's army, now under the command of Doctorow, approached its right to Osterman, and linked its left with Bagawouth, who had succeeded Touchkoff.

The cavalry supported, and the Imperial Guards, with the cuirassiers, formed the principal reserve in rear of the centre.

The Russians had lost in the two days' battle forty thousand killed and wounded: the enemy had lost full as many.

On the side of the Russians three generals were killed, seventeen wounded, and eighteen hundred officers killed and wounded.

On the side of the enemy there were eight generals killed, and thirty wounded, with the same proportion of officers as the Russians.

Neither party made prisoners to any amount, and the capture of cannon, the total number being very small, was nearly balanced.

The Russian generals killed were Koutaisow and Touchkoff; wounded, Bakhmitcheff, Gorchakow, Yermolow, Krapowitze, Likaczew, S. Priest, Woronzow, Galitzin, Gouchkoff, Prince Charles of Mecklenburg, Bakmeloff, Kratow, and Bagrathion.

The French generals killed were Montbrun, Plauzanne, Lepel, Marcin, Louabère, Caulaincourt, and Huart. Amongst those most known of the wounded generals were—Grouchy, Nansouty, Latour Maubourg, Rapp, Campans, Morand, Desaix, Laboissaye, and Bonami, who was made prisoner in the bastioned battery.

It certainly was one of the greatest battles of the revolutionary war, and has often been compared to that of Eylau; but the loss at Eylau, with due reference to the relative strength of both armies, was considerably greater. The Russians in that battle, including the ten thousand Prussians who reached the field late in the day, amounted only to seventy-five thousand men, out of which they lost forty thousand, whilst the French had but ninety thousand, out of which they lost at least as many as the Russians. Eylau was a parade battle,—each army being drawn up in an open space, with a front of not more than two miles (until evening, when an attempt was made to turn the Russian left and gain its rear, which was baffled by the Prussians); the whole of the contending forces were moreover not only entirely within view of each other, but scarcely at half cannon shot distance. Borodino was a battle of points, on ground much diversified by eminences and ravines, which gave the army a broken appearance: therefore Eylau, as Beningsen described it, was "une bataille rangée, and Borodino une bataille dérangée." At Eylau the ground was a surface of frozen snow, which greatly aggravated the misery of the wounded, though the night after the battle of Borodino was also cold; and in both cases no supplies for man or beast could be obtained.*

The conclusion of both battles was, however, very similar: each army imagined itself lord of the field, and Kutusow was solicited by many generals, as Beningsen was at Eylau, to form the remnant into columns of attack and engage in a night combat; but the army of Eylau was composed entirely of veterans, trained by numerous combats and unremitting operations to the highest degree of military qualification for all services that required maintenance of the greatest discipline in their execution; whereas the army of Borodino contained a great proportion of new levies, and the militia of Moscow and of Smolensk were the

* At Eylau the Russians, being without bread or water, ate the snow. Beningsen and his staff had but one bowl of small potatoes for food from mid-day of the preceding day till midnight after the battle, when nothing would induce Beningsen to take more than one potato, there being only enough to give one to each individual. This sufficed him till he reached Königsberg the next morning, after a long night's march.

There were about a hundred soldiers having legs and arms cut off in the room where the potatoes were distributed, there being no other tenement on the Russian field of battle.

only corps that had not been actively engaged; but they had displayed great steadiness during the whole day, and especially under Poniatowski's fire, when he had attempted to force back Touchkoff.

A night alerte, with some of the light troops, might have been hazarded perhaps advantageously, but not a general affair that would have exposed the position.

The Russian second army had been much distressed by the loss of so many distinguished officers at the moment of greatest need and effort, but Bagrathion's wound and relinquishment of the command occasioned the pause to that impulse which promised to decide the victory in his favour if the vigour which he was imparting could have been maintained.

Bagrathion was by birth a Georgian, of short stature, with strong dark features, and eyes flashing with Asiatic fire. Gentle, gracious, generous, chivalrously brave, he was beloved by every one, and admired by all who witnessed his exploits. No officer ever excelled him in the direction of an advance or rear guard; nor had any officer's capacity in these commands ever been more severely tested; especially in the retreat from Pultusk to Eylau in the former war—a retreat of seventeen days, and of as many furious combats, in which his skill, unwearying energy, and daring courage were incessantly exemplified. They were indeed so many days of triumph for his fame.

On the evacuation of Moscow, he was borne towards the interior in a litter by relays of grenadiêrs, and to the last was as anxious for all the details of what was passing as if he had been still at the head of his army.

When Sir Robert Wilson told him what the Emperor had declared with regard to the rejection of all treaty with Napoleon "whilst an armed Frenchman should be in Russia," he pressed his hand convulsively, and said "Dear General, you have made me die happy, for then Russia will assuredly not be disgraced."— "Accipio solatium mortis."

Mortification coming on, he breathed his last on the 24th of September at Sima, on the road to Wladimir.

Kutusow, having received the returns and reports from all the different corps, resolved on retiring; but in his despatch to the Emperor dated the 8th, relating the battle, he suppressed the account of his actual march on Mojaisk, for he stated in it—"The batteries passed from the possession of one to the other, and the result has been that the enemy in no one part has gained *an inch of ground.* Remaining at night masters of the field of battle, so soon as I shall have recruited my troops, supplied my artillery, and augmented my forces by reinforcements from Moscow, I shall see what I can undertake against the enemy."

This statement so persuaded the Emperor that a complete victory had been gained "*to save Moscow,*" that he immediately appointed Kutusow Marshal general of his armies, and gave him a donation of a hundred thousand roubles in silver; to the officers appropriate remunerations, and to each soldier five roubles—rewards to which no army ever established more just claims: but the representation of Kutusow was nevertheless not correct, nor candid towards his Sovereign.

On the morning following the battle, before dawn, the Russian army, preceded by its wounded, artillery, equipages, &c., began filing towards Mojaisk and took up a position on the heights beyond. The head-quarters were established at Inkowo.

Platow, who commanded the rear guard, did not quit his ground till near ten o'clock in the forenoon, and halted his cavalry in the plain to the left of Mojaisk, lodging his infantry in the town.

Napoleon, finding that the Russians had actually withdrawn, rode over the field of battle, observing that "It was a magnificent one." He then ordered Murat to pursue, and the army to march in three columns.

The Viceroy, reinforced by the division Pino, which had joined the same morning from Witepsk, moved on Rouza; the main army on Mojaisk; and Poniatowski on Fominskoie, to gain the Kalouga road.

By this order of march the enemy acquired greater freedom of movement, and better chance of supplies; and the Russian rear guards, from fear of being turned on both flanks, could less obstinately defend positions to favour delay.

The enemy's army was in a frightful state of destitution and distress; some of the divisions were even then living on horse flesh; the multitude of wounded embarrassed the road; the desertion of the towns and villages by every inhabitant greatly inconvenienced and exasperated the soldiery; and ninety thousand rounds of gun ammunition having been expended, there was a great want of the reserve park, which was several days' march behind.

To diminish this want, the artillerymen were employed in collecting cannon balls from the field of battle.

Napoleon himself was also suffering from a severe rheum.

Murat having come up with Platow, about four in the afternoon attempted to force his infantry out of Mojaisk. Night put an end to the combat; and he failed to accomplish that object, much to the disappointment of Napoleon, who had designated Mojaisk as his head quarters, and had ordered Murat to proceed two leagues farther, to cover the town.

On the 9th the Russian army retired on Zembino.

Murat the same morning renewed the attack on Platow, who evacuated Mojaisk at ten o'clock, leaving ten thousand wounded unable to proceed farther; their sufferings were greatly aggravated by the arrival of the enemy's wounded, who dispossessed them of their asylums.

Milaradowitch having joined Platow with a strong reinforcement, and taken the command of the rear guard, Murat was in his turn attacked and driven back two or three miles.

On the 10th the Russian army crossed the Nara near Kroutitsa, placing head-quarters at Repetebe.

Milaradowitch halted at Koyaskoi.

Murat, galled by the affront of the preceding day, furiously attacked him in a contracted and strong position. Night closed the combat, in which both parties had lost between two and three thousand men, and towards the conclusion of which Ouwarrow with the cavalry had rendered essential service.

On the 11th the Russians retired on Wiscorna, and the rear guard took post at Koubraskoie.

On the 12th the march continued on Mamonowo, where some field works were thrown up, which had induced a report that Moscow was to be defended.

On the 13th the Russian army took up its last position, within a mile and a half of Moscow, in front of the barriers called Dorogomelow. The village of Fili lay behind the right, that rested on an elbow of the Moskwa. The centre was continued between the villages of Troitskoie and Wolynskoie, and the left to the heights of Worobiewo.

The Moskwa flowed behind the alignment that covered the suburb of Dorogomelow, and intrenchments were already thrown up along its front.

The rear guard took post at Setouna.

The pressure of the enemy's advance had been relaxed after the combat of the 10th; the expenditure of effective force was found too costly, and further useless waste was controlled by Napoleon's express order.

Napoleon did not himself quit Mojaisk till the evening of the 12th. He had remained there to cure himself of his cold, and to direct the necessary measures for the administrative reorganisation.

On the 12th he moved to Tartuka, half way from Mojaisk to Moscow, above fifty miles; but on the morning of the 13th he suddenly stopped the march of all his columns.

Murat had reported "that the Russian rear guard was composed only of cavalry;" and Napoleon apprehended that the army might have withdrawn by its left on the road to Kalouga, and thus might be manœuvring to gain the rear of his line of movement.

On Murat's sending further information " that the

whole Russian army had taken post in front of Moscow," Napoleon renewed his advance; and Murat on the 14th arrived within sight of the capital, whose grand extent crowned with glittering domes suggested the idea of vast treasures and redundant resources within his grasp, and fed hopes of repose and revel as vain as those of the thirsty traveller in the desert when he first beholds the mirage's evanescent flood.

Beningsen, whose services had been of the most essential use in every council and field, whenever he was permitted to render them, had strenuously urged Kutusow at Mojaisk "not to fall back on Moscow, but to move with the main body of his force in the direction of Kalouga, on which line he would be most advantageously posted, in case the enemy persisted in his movement on Moscow, to baffle his operation or render it finally disastrous." He urged that "if Kutusow were in this position, the march on Moscow would at all events be suspended, if not totally prevented; that delay was of essential importance for the arrival of reinforcements and the construction of defences for Moscow itself, which, if time were gained, might, with its garrison reinforced from Kutusow's army, with its own militia and armed population excited to a devotion capable of any effort however desperate, be able to offer a formidable and probably an insuperable resistance; that Moscow could be saved by no other disposition or measures; that the operation exposed the army to no mischances, but assured the safe arrival of its expected reinforcements and supplies; affording at the same time protection to Toula, the greatest establishment in the empire for the manufacture of small arms."

The rejection of this plan, specially adapted for the exigency, and capable of execution without the slightest obstacle, was a fatal decision : a great national misfortune was gratuitously incurred, for events proved that it might have been avoided. Napoleon had not force sufficient to act against the Russian army so located, and to undertake the storm or investment of Moscow, for the defence of which an armament of eighty thousand men, one moiety trained soldiers, could have been arrayed in position, with an abundant artillery, and this armament would have been daily increasing from the contiguous governments.

Kutusow declared to Beningsen and his generals " that he intended to approach Moscow with the object of covering and defending that city, the loss of which he could not hazard;" and he succeeded in impressing Rostopchin, the governor of Moscow, with the firm conviction that his intention was sincere.

Rostopchin had avowed his resolve, " if the city were not to be defended by the Russian army, to convoke all the authorities and inhabitants for the purpose of arranging a general and municipally regulated conflagration, a sacrifice which he was confident would unhesitatingly be made by their patriotism excited by their horror of the invader."

As a further security against the counteraction of his design, he insisted on and obtained a solemn promise from Kutusow "that if any change should occur in his resolution to defend the city, he would give him *three full days' notice.*"

Whilst Kutusow was retiring on Moscow, the uncle

of the Emperor, Duke Alexander of Wurtemberg, submitted to him a written proposal to resume the offensive. Kutusow, however, had made up his own mind to avoid all further general action; but compromised by his demonstrations, professions, and promises, pressed by the clamours from the city as well as those of his officers and soldiers, to fulfil the expectations which he had raised, he determined on assembling a council of war at Fili on the 13th.

Barclay spoke in favour of a retreat on Niznei Nowogorod; Konownitsyn for an offensive movement against the enemy before they could unite their three separated columns; Osterman and Yermolow leaned to that opinion; the Quartermaster-general Tol recommended that a position should be taken in front of Moscow, with its right on Worobiewo, and left on Woronowo, there being still sixty-five thousand old soldiers in the army, which, including six thousand Cossacks, mustered ninety thousand men under arms, and which might be rendered considerably more efficient by the support of the population; Beningsen and Doctorow agreed with the Quartermaster-general as to the defence of Moscow being a military as well as a patriotic duty, but preferred the position of Fili.

Kutusow's opinion, however, prevailed, and it was voted that there was no position in advance of Moscow that afforded sufficient local advantages for the construction of an entrenched camp that would protect the city; that the ground, forming an inclined plain descending towards the city, presented to an enemy after forcing the camp great facility for the destruction of the retiring army; that the greatest part of the wealthy inhabitants having already left Moscow, and the most valuable property having been removed or destroyed, the enemy would only gain a town which, however heretofore venerated, had by consent of the people foregone its claim to such a consideration as would justify the sacrifice of greater interests; that the Russian army in another battle before Moscow might be so shattered as to be rendered incapable of resuming offensive operations in conjunction with the other armies on march or manœuvring to act on the rear and flank communications of the enemy, the success of whose operations, as well as their own safety, depended on the co-operating support of the Russian main army; that the enemy would be obliged to weaken his disposable force by the occupation of Moscow, whereas the Russian army would be daily gaining strength; and finally, that it must always be kept in mind that "the contest was for the Russian empire, and not for the preservation of any particular city or the capital itself." The retreat and evacuation being thereupon ordered, such arrangements were made as the pressure of the time permitted.

On the morning of the 14th, before day-dawn, the troops commenced filing through the city, and were soon accompanied by all the inhabitants and populace who could find any means of conveyance.

A hundred and eighty thousand souls out of two hundred thousand, with sixty-five thousand carriages of every description, exclusive of the artillery and military ambulances, passed the barriers in funeral march; and the colonel of a garrison battalion, who was allowing his music to play as if he were moving out with the "honours of war," was very nearly sacrificed by the indignant multitude.

Many thousand wounded and sick, who were unhappily incapable of removal from the hospitals, were abandoned necessarily to the doom of the city.

The incidents and the whole scene of the evacuation of a great capital may be conceived better than described. The Russians, however, have preserved so much of their nomad habits, that they were much more quickly packed and equipped for their emigration than the inhabitants of any other European city would have been. The army indeed, since the first day's retreat from Smolensk, had been accompanied by a wandering nation. All the towns, villages, and hamlets were abandoned as the columns appeared. The old and infirm, the women and children, were placed with the movable effects, and the "Dii Penates," on their kabitkas or telagas (one and two-horse carts which no peasant is without), and these not being permitted to move on the high road, which was preserved for the artillery and military equipages, formed a variety for themselves of frequently a dozen flanking columns: it was a wonderful spectacle to see the number, the order, the ingenuity and facility with which they wended their way through streams, and over morasses and ravines that had been thought heretofore, even by the inhabitants themselves, to be perfectly impracticable; "not leaving a wheel (as the French bulletins admitted) to mark any disorder, hurry, or trace of their direction."

Whilst Kutusow, with the Russians, was proceeding on the road to Kolomna, Milaradowitch was charged with the conduct of the rear guard.

Murat having reached the barrier of Dorogobouche, made dispositions to force an entrance, although he had pushed forwards with but one division of infantry.

Milaradowitch, seeking to gain some hours for the desertion of the city, sent Murat a flag of truce, stating, that if he were molested, he would defend the streets to the last extremity, and then fire the town.

Murat, unable to employ such a force as might seize possession at once of the whole city, and fearful of endangering a prize of such reputed value and essential importance to the army, consented to suspend hostilities until seven in the evening, and not to interrupt the military march; a convention of immense advantage to the Russians, who actively employed the interval: nevertheless, about two thousand workmen of the garrison battalions, engaged in clearing the arsenal, not being withdrawn in time, were made prisoners.

Milaradowitch had cut the wooden bridge over the Moskwa: Murat was therefore obliged to pass at a ford.

About two in the afternoon he entered the city and proceeded towards the Kremlin, whence suddenly a smart musketry fire was directed on him and his advanced guard. This unexpected attack caused at first much confusion, but it was soon ascertained that it was only the frantic act of some desperate men, who had been left behind accidentally, and who preferred the death they thus ensured, preceded by some hoped-for vengeance, to passive surrender ; but some of the populace as Murat rode forward rushed upon him with maniac fury. In an intercepted letter from him to the Queen of Naples he wrote, "I never was in my whole life in such wild danger; but fortunately having two pieces of artillery with me, which immediately opened their fire with discharges of grape, I was rescued, and the assailants were dispersed: one of the demons, however, sprang upon a colonel of engineers on horseback, tore him to the ground, stabbed him in the back when falling, threw himself upon him to suffocate him, fixed his teeth in his neck, and perseveringly retained his hold until the surrounding French, recovering from their terror, despatched him by beating out his brains with repeated blows." These particulars Murat afterwards at Bologna, in Italy, related, and fully confirmed, to Lord William Bentinck and Sir Robert Wilson when they were dining with him.

Napoleon arrived with his Guards about three o'clock in the afternoon, also by the suburb of Dorogomelow, and was astounded at the solitude which reigned everywhere.

His feelings had been excited to the highest degree of pride and glowing expectation. He had anticipated his reception by a submissive magistracy and humbled people, imploring clemency ; and dreamt that in the palace of the Czars he would have it in his power to promise pardon, protection, and peace to themselves and their sovereign.

He proceeded gloomily to his residence in the suburb, adopting every measure of precaution against surprise, and at the same time against a pillage that might exasperate the inhabitants; but his precautions against pillage were vain, for though he would not allow any of the corps to enter the city, but made them bivouac without, the soldiery after such long privations would not be restrained; and when night favoured their ingress, numbers penetrated, and disorders of every kind rioted, in defiance of threats and punishment.

Towards dark, alarms of fire were spread in various quarters. The bazaar with its ten thousand shops, the Crown magazines of forage, of wine (thirteen millions of quarts), of brandy, of military stores, and gunpowder, burst into a simultaneous blaze.

No engines could be procured—no carts, no conveyance, not even buckets for the carriage of water—all had been destroyed or carried off by order of Rostopchin.

Still Napoleon flattered himself that these fires were occasioned by incidental occurrences, or too prevalent irregularities. He entertained no suspicion that it was the initiative of a systematic conflagration, planned with the most daring conception, and executed with a persevering audacity unparalleled in history. On the next morning, the 15th, he therefore transferred his head quarters to the Kremlin.

The Russian army had marched on the 14th twelve miles upon the Kolomna road, and its head-quarters were placed at Pauki, where it remained on the 15th, and on the 16th fell back across the Moskwa, and took post near Borowskoi, on the right bank.

The rear guard on retiring from Moscow stopped at Wiesowka, five miles from the Kolomna barrier.

Winzingerode was detached with a small corps of

observation on the S. Petersburg road; and a strong body of infantry and cavalry escorted on the Wladimir road, on the way to Niznei Nowogorod, a convoy of the most precious effects saved from the capital.

Murat's advance posted itself at Koraegorowo.

The hourly, almost momentarily, increasing spread and intensity of the crimson canopy of the sky over Moscow impressed an awful feeling; but there was universal satisfaction at the thought of the enemy's discomfiture.

All hoped, all prayed, that Moscow might be a city of ashes, and the tomb of its invaders.

Sebastiani, who commanded Murat's advance, had sent word to Raeffskoi, " that being ordered to occupy Wiesowka, and a height or a hill beyond, he wished that possession might be yielded without useless conflict."

The proposition was accepted, but Sebastiani's parties, after reaching the point indicated, attempted to press farther. Vasiltchikoff, who had been left with some cavalry and twelve guns, disputed the progress towards Pauki, and leisurely at nightfall established himself at Ostrowtsi.

The enemy's cavalry was so much exhausted and enfeebled that it was able to make but very languid movements.

Kutusow had at length become sensible of the mischiefs that must result from a continuance of retreat in the direction of Riazan, and of the advantages which would ensue from a lodgment of his army on the Kalouga road. He saw that he was delivering up the Emperor, and at all events his European empire, to the enemy, and at last acquiesced in the proposal to make a change in the direction of the retreat, which, the longer it was delayed, became more perilous, and which might by another march or two be rendered impracticable.

Early in the morning of the 17th the army withdrew from Borowskoi, and changing a south-east course into a south-west, remounted the Pakra, and bivouacked on the road to Konstantinowskoi, not far from Nekitsh.

A rear guard of infantry was left on the right bank of the Moskwa, upon the heights near the bridge of Borowskoi, and the cavalry in front kept the enemy employed during the day in active skirmishes.

At night the cavalry retired over the bridge, which was destroyed.

The whole of the rear guard then followed the track of the army, excepting two Cossack regiments which were left on the Kolomna road, with orders to allure the enemy in that direction; orders most ably executed by the Cossack colonel Jasfremoff, for Sebastiani did not discover that he was only following shadows until he reached Biemel, above thirty miles beyond Moscow.

On the 18th the Russian army continued to remount the Pakra, and bivouacked near Podolsk, with its headquarters at Koutousowi; on the 19th it crossed to the left of the Pakra, and took post at Krasnoi Pakra.

Milaradowitch, with the advanced guard, was pushed on the 20th to Dessna; Raeffskoi covered the right flank of the army at Loukounia, near the confluence of the Dessna with the Pakra; and Dorokoff was detached with a corps of cavalry, consisting of a regiment of dragoons, a regiment of hussars, and three regiments of Cossacks, with a small proportion of flying artillery, to watch and operate on the high road from Mojaisk to Moscow. His head-quarters were established at Scaranowo, whence his detachments made with great success continued incursions on the enemy's main line of communication.

On the 21st the Russian army recrossed the Pakra, and occupied a position selected by Beningsen.

The Russian army, favoured by fortune and the suspension of energy and vigilance in the enemy, was thus safely established, with its flag waving defiance, in a position within twenty-five miles of Moscow, and its advance within fifteen; a position which rested on the Oka as its basis, and in direct and easy communication with Kalouga, and with all the resources and reserves in the yet unoccupied governments of the empire.

The humblest soldier recognised at once the value, and it may be said the dignity, of this position.

There was no more despondence,—no more drooping—no more muttering of discontent: the hour of imagined shame and degradation had passed; confidence was restored. The soldier again exulted in the prospective grapple with his enemy, and planted his foot, and handled his arms, as if he were about to charge, and penetrate the hostile ranks, and recover his burning lares.

The conflagration of Moscow had continued till it had embraced the whole city in its devouring wrath, making of it one flaming pile, and spreading over the vast space an ocean flood of fire. All the houses of the nobility—all the warehouses of the merchants—all the public establishments—all the shops—all combustible materials without and within were ignited as if by enchantment.

Of forty thousand houses in stone, only two hundred escaped; of eight thousand in wood, five hundred: of sixteen hundred churches, eight hundred were consumed, and seven hundred damaged; of twenty-four thousand persons, wounded and sick, more than twenty thousand were burnt alive.

Between two and three hundred Russians suspected as incendiaries were executed by the enemy; but the fires continued to break out with undiminished activity.

On the 16th the Kremlin itself, although not on fire, became so uninhabitable from heat and showers of fiery particles, that Napoleon was obliged to withdraw, and transfer his head-quarters to the château of Petrovskoi, on the road to S. Petersburg; nor could he return till the 20th, when heavy rain extinguished the flames, which left unconsumed only one tenth of the city, and such stores of provisions as were secured in the cellars of the houses that had escaped injury: these, however, afforded a very scanty support to his army.

Napoleon had marched on Moscow in the full confidence that he should find therein not only all necessary provisions, but a luxurious redundance, with repose until peace could be made; but *that* hope, even for a temporary respite, was terminated when the Russian army appeared in the quarter which he knew to be most favourable to harassing operations: he at once saw that its occupation was incompatible with the quiescence so much coveted by him in the interest of his forces.

The question has often been mooted, and never satisfactorily resolved, " to whose advice and direction should the burning of Moscow be ascribed?"

It was useful at the time to be silent and to suffer the enemy to be charged with the atrocity, that public indignation might be incensed to the highest degree against them; and, on the other hand, it was equally desirable not to deprive Russian patriotism of that title to the admiration of the world.

Rostopchin, the Governor, was placed in a false position. He could neither deny nor adopt the act; but his previous announcement of that intention, his demand of Kutusow "for three days' notice," the removal or destruction of all the fire-engines and apparatus, the release of several hundred malefactors, and the organization of their bands under directing superiors, impress conviction that Rostopchin was the author and abettor of the transaction. He never forgave Kutusow for the infraction of the promise—a promise which he publicly declared Kutusow "swore by the white hairs of his head" to keep, and the breach of which compelled him to make clandestine preparations, and take measures as if he were instigating an offence against his countrymen and country; whereas, if it had been kept, an occasion would have been presented to him to assume the avowed responsible lead in an act of public virtue enhancing national fame.

It has also been asked whether the nobility and commonalty flying from Moscow approved the destruction of their houses and property?

Dispersed over the country, all afforded the most generous and noble examples of disinterested patriotism. There was not one of either sex, old or young, who did not disdain to mourn over or complain of any personal loss; and when the English General assured any of them of the Emperor's plighted resolution "to continue the war whilst a Frenchman remained in arms on the Russian territory," many wept—many kissed him in their joy, as those might have done who were told that their own griefs were now to be soothed, and that the miseries of an expatriation were about to cease.

The same sentiments had animated the Russian military; the same greetings had welcomed Sir Robert Wilson's report of the interviews with the Emperor, and it was then that he wrote to Constantinople, Vienna, and London,—"The capture of Moscow is but the prelude to the destruction of the captors and the triumph of Russia. With the means of such an empire—with the spirit of such a people—with the example and energy of such a sovereign—with such a basis as this valorous and faithful army provides, ultimate victory cannot be a matter of doubt or of long delay."

On the 23rd Murat had found out the true direction of the Russian army, and moved on Podolsk, where he arrived on the 25th, and united with Poniatowski, whilst Bessières reached Dessna, whence the Russian advance retired.

During these marches partial cavalry affairs occurred, in which the Russians manifested increasing superiority.

The enemy's horses were daily growing weaker, and those taken were valueless from their sore backs as well as their low general condition.

On the 23rd of September the Russian partisans

took fourteen carts and fifteen hundred ducats on the Podolsk road. In another direction sixty powder waggons were blown up by the enemy to prevent their seizure, and one regiment of Cossacks made such booty of horses, watches, melted silver, and louis d'or, that each individual of it subsequently received as his own share eighty-four pounds sterling: but the Cossacks discriminated with much generosity between those articles which belonged to the State and those which belonged to themselves as captors; for when they took possession of melted silver which they had reason to believe was the produce of the sacred vessels of the churches, they invariably gave it up to the Hetman, representing "that they should think its retention a sacrilege."

Napoleon, on being informed "that Kutusow showed some inclination to continue in the camp of Krasnoi Pakra, as he was throwing up works," ordered dispositions to be made for marching from Moscow with his whole force to attack him. Indeed, the removal of the Russian army from so close a contiguity to Moscow was indispensable; for the Cossacks and light cavalry invested all the environs close to the barriers, intercepted the communications with the different corps, and rendered foraging impossible except in very large bodies.

Dorokoff had also contributed much to the distress of Moscow by cutting off detachments and convoys so frequently, that Napoleon issued an order that "no detachment should be sent on the Smolensk and Mojaisk road unless composed of fifteen hundred men;" and this order had become necessary notwithstanding that Junot with his whole corps occupied Mojaisk, and

Victor with thirty thousand men had reached Smolensk.

It was, moreover, found expedient to establish a strong post of infantry and cavalry at Bezouka, twenty miles from Moscow, to form the chain with Mojaisk, and another post between Bezouka and Moscow, composed of a division of infantry, of light cavalry, and chasseurs of the Viceroy's Guard.

Such a fretful investment and harassing defensive became every day more intolerable and prejudicial.

Beningsen had proposed to attack Murat and Poniatowski, still on the right bank of the Pakra, and whilst their communications with Bessières on the left bank were interrupted by the Russian partisan corps; but his suggestion was not approved. The temptation was great, and the success to a considerable extent certain; but it was perhaps more prudent to forbear a few days longer from rousing the enemy disposed to slumber, and awakening him to a desperate effort or precipitate retreat prematurely.

Murat and Poniatowski continuing to approach Krasnoi Pakra, Kutusow withdrew to Babenkowo, leaving Milaradowitch and Raeffskoi at Krasnoi Pakra. When Napoleon received that intelligence, he thought his object was accomplished, and desisted from his intended movement.

On the 27th there was an alerte in the Russian camp, and various dispositions were made to oppose the enemy.

On the 29th Murat and Poniatowski having advanced on Czerikowo and Winkowo from Podolsk, Milaradowitch attacked him, and recovered Czerikowo: this was an incident of importance, as it lay five miles in rear of Krasnoi Pakra, and consequently behind the greater part of the Russian army.*

Beningsen again proposed to accept battle if the enemy should advance; but Kutusow, being informed that Taroutino on the Nara offered a better position, retired on the 1st of October upon Spass Kouplia, and Milaradowitch fell back on Babenkowo.

On the 2nd the army entered the position of Taroutino, and the rear guards of Milaradowitch and Osterman (henceforth the advanced guards), which had united at Woronowo, retired about half a mile.

On the 3rd Osterman having been recalled to the army with his corps, Milaradowitch thought it expedient, as the enemy seemed disposed to break in again upon his rear, to approach nearer to Taroutino, and therefore took post at Spass Kouplia.

On the 4th, at ten o'clock in the morning, Murat made a strong reconnoissance, and Milaradowitch selected a position on the Czernicznia, which he firmly maintained.

In the combat the Russian artillery and cavalry again obtained distinction and considerable advantage.

Murat, finding the Russian main army disposed to support the advance, withdrew, and took up a position near Winkowo and behind the Czernicznia, where he "piled his arms," desisting from all hostilities, and indulging the pleasing illusion "of uninterrupted rest."

The Russians, who had been retiring before the advancing enemy from post to post, first set their

---

* In the various affairs which had occurred during the first four days of the Russian occupation of Krasnoi Pakra, no less than thirteen hundred and forty-one prisoners were brought into head-quarters by the Cossack parties.

foot on the certain ground to arrest his progress at Krasnoi Pakra, but did not fix themselves permanently until they entered the camp of Taroutino.

At Woronowo, Rostopchin and his serfs afforded another remarkable proof of patriotism, and of their horror (not dread, in the common acceptation of the word) at the advent of the enemy.

The village of Woronowo belonged to Rostopchin, and there he possessed a palace-residence of great magnificence.

The very stabling was of rare grandeur, surmounted over the gateways by colossal casts of the Monte Cavallo horses and figures which he had brought from Rome, with costly models of all the principal Roman and Grecian buildings and statues that filled a large gallery in the palace, the interior of which was most splendidly and tastefully furnished with every article of luxurious use and ornament that foreign countries could supply.

Rostopchin had possessed another palace at Moscow, and a country residence in the neighbourhood. These, contrary to his directions, had escaped the general conflagration, and even an order of Napoleon's for their being burnt, as some Generals who occupied them preferred their own accommodation.

During the night preceding the retreat from Woronowo, Rostopchin, Beningsen, Yermolow, and various generals and officers, with the English General and Lord Tyrconnel his aide-de-camp, bivouacked round a fire in front of the palace stabling. Rostopchin had prevented all sleep by his bitter complaints against Kutusow "for his evacuation of Moscow without giving him the '*covenanted notice*,' and for having thus deprived the authorities and inhabitants of an occasion to display, *not Roman, but more than Roman—Russian dignity* by a municipal and popular ignition of their city before it had been contaminated by an invader's presence." He declared that "he never would forgive the Marshal for deceiving him" (and he kept his word), "but that he would now fire with his own hands the palace we all so much admired, if the enemy pushed on; and he only lamented that it was not manifold more worthy of preservation." All dissuasion was useless; his resolve was inflexible.

At the morning's dawn, a deputation of elders from the village appeared, stating that "they had all made their dispositions to retire with the troops, and soliciting to be permitted to go to an estate of their suzerain's in Siberia, as they preferred to be removed there, or to any other province of the Empire, rather than to be subjected to French dominion." The permission being granted, the whole colony, seventeen hundred souls, began their march, and presented one of the most affecting sights ever beheld; but not a plaint was heard: "*God give our Emperor and Russia victory,*" with "*Benedictions on their lord,*" were the only exclamations or expressions that escaped their lips. Having posted their declaration on the church doors in three languages, Rostopchin, on hearing the picquets commence skirmishing, and seeing the enemy in movement, entered his palace, begging his friends to accompany him. On arriving at the porch, burning torches were distributed to every one. Mounting the stairs, and reaching his state bed-room, Rostopchin paused a moment, and then said to the English

General, "That is my marriage bed; I have not the heart to set it on fire; you must spare me this pain." When Rostopchin had himself set on fire all the rest of the apartment, then, and not before, his wish was executed. Each apartment was ignited as the party proceeded, and in a quarter of an hour the whole was one blazing mass. Rostopchin then proceeded to the stables which were quickly in flames, and afterwards stood in front contemplating the progress of the fire and the falling fragments.

When the last cast of the Cavallo group was precipitated, he said, "I am at ease;" and as the enemy's shots were now whistling around, he and all retired, leaving the enemy the following alarming and instructive lesson affixed to a conspicuous pillar:—

"I have ornamented during eight years this mansion-seat, where I have lived happy in the bosom of my family.

"The inhabitants of this property, to the number of seventeen hundred and twenty, quit it at your approach, and I voluntarily set the house on fire, that it may not be polluted by your presence.

"Frenchmen, I abandoned to you my two houses at Moscow, with their furniture and contents worth half a million of roubles. *Here* you will only find *ashes*."

Napoleon, on his return to the Kremlin, had persuaded a director of the establishment of the 'Enfants trouvés,' under the special protection of the Empress-mother, to write Her Majesty a letter, "announcing the fact of its preservation," and in this letter " to insinuate Napoleon's wish for an amicable transaction."

No answer arriving, Napoleon grew impatient, and prevailed on an individual whose brother had been diplomatically employed, to proceed direct to the Emperor with a letter, "in which he proposed a definite arrangement."

This mission also remaining unnoticed, Napoleon determined on opening a communication in a more accessible quarter. For this service he selected Lauriston to be his agent and negotiator.

The prior experimental attempts at a pacification which might extricate the French army from the toils, had transpired, and confirmed all the Russians in the assurance that it was lost if not relieved by some diplomatic convention—that in truth it was in the very state of embarrassment in which Napoleon in his bulletin had described the Russian army as being, when he wrote that it was "unwilling to go, but unable to remain." So universal and so well warranted was this conviction, that the English General had despatched a courier, after the combat of the Czernicznia, to Mr. Liston, with the intelligence that this result was certain "if the Marshal willed it:"—to which Mr. Liston replied, "Your account was necessary, for aught I know, to save this empire;" alluding to the growing influence of Andreossi, who had succeeded in deposing the Vizir* by whom the peace with Russia had been signed, and with whom the English General had negotiated its maintenance.

So impressed was every one, even at a remote dis-

---

* His head was cut off, as well as the hands of the two Princes Morusis the assistant negotiators.

tance, with the inevitable fate of the enemy's army if not saved by treaty, that Count Woronzow (who in consequence of his wound at Borodino had been obliged to retire to one of his estates) wrote from his bed to the English General, " Let me implore you to prevent by every means in your power any negotiation whatsoever, as Napoleon must be destroyed when he attempts to retreat. The frost will render his army an easy prey. The Russians will have only to plant their guns on the elevations commanding the ravines and roads, whence they may mow down the enemy without any risk; for the cavalry probably is not rough shod, and their infantry will not have strength and time to attack, or to leave the road to forage for man or beast. The Russian horses may even be removed from the guns; for if the guns were taken, they could not be carried off by the enemy."

There was, however, a general suspicion that Kutusow did not wish to push the enemy to such extremity; and a corresponding vigilance was exercised over his transactions.

The English General had gone on the preceding evening to Milaradowitch's bivouac, when early in the morning of the 4th of October a Cossack at speed brought him a summons from Beningsen, in his own name and in those of others, " to return instantly to head-quarters, as the Marshal had agreed, *not merely proposed, but actually agreed in a written note*, to meet *Lauriston at midnight beyond the Russian advanced posts.*"

Having communicated with Milaradowitch, the English General hastened to Beningsen, whom he found with a dozen generals, anxiously awaiting his arrival.

They afforded him proof that Kutusow, in answer to a proposition made by Lauriston on behalf of Napoleon, had agreed to meet him this same night at a station several miles from his most advanced videttes, on the road to Moscow, there to confer on the terms of a convention "for the immediate retreat of the whole invading army from the territories of Russia, which convention was also to serve as the basis of a peace, to which it was to be the preliminary."

They added that "Napoleon himself might be expected at the interview, as Lauriston had stated that he would be accompanied by a friend."* They therefore required from the English General "that he would act as commissioner of the Emperor under his delegated authority," and "as an English commissioner charged with the protection of the British and allied interests;" adding "the resolve of the chiefs, which would be sustained by the army, not to allow Kutusow to return and resume the command if once he quitted it for this midnight interview in the enemy's camp." They declared that "they wished to avoid extreme measures, but that their minds were made up to dispossess the Marshal of his authority if he should inflexibly persevere."

It was a critical commission to execute—perhaps more critical than the mission to the Emperor himself; but the English General felt that he had a duty to perform from which he could not shrink with honour.

---

* Although Napoleon, in his note to the Marshal in favour of Lauriston, had only asked for him full confidence by the phrase—"Ajoutez foi à tout ce qu'il dira sur des affaires très importantes."

The Marshal, on seeing him enter, looked already embarrassed, but asked "whether he had brought any news from the advanced guard?" After some slight conversation on that subject, the English General intimated a wish to confer with the Marshal alone.

An officer or two present having withdrawn, the English General said that "he had returned to headquarters in consequence of a report, an idle one he trusted, which had reached him that morning." That "it was, however, a mischievous report, causing much excitement and uneasiness; and therefore that it was desirable at once to put an end, under the Marshal's own authority, to the scandal."

The Marshal's countenance confirmed the allegation; but the English General proceeded with as much courtesy as possible to communicate the rumour, and afford opportunity for the voluntary cancel of the arrangement, without any humiliating or irritating eclaircissement.

The Marshal was confused, but in a tone of some asperity replied that "he was Commander-in-chief of the army, and knew best what the interests confided to him required; that it was true that he had agreed to give General Lauriston, at the request of the French Emperor, an interview during that night, under the circumstances reported, in order to avoid notice which might be accompanied with misrepresentation or misunderstanding of motives; that he should keep his engagement, hear the propositions which General Lauriston was empowered to offer, and determine his future proceedings according to their nature."

He then added that "he would admit that he already knew those propositions to be of a pacific character, and perhaps they might lead to an arrangement satisfactory and honourable for Russia."

The English General having patiently listened to all the explanations of the Marshal, asked him " if such was his final determination?" He said, " Yes—irrevocable;" and he expressed his hope that the English General would on reflection acquiesce in its propriety; and after taking into due consideration the state of the empire, and the fact that although the Russian army was becoming numerous, it was still far from being efficient in proportion, that he would in this instance suffer his affection for the Emperor and Russia to prevail over his well known hostile feelings to the Emperor of France."

These last expressions were uttered in a very sarcastic tone, and he seemed to think, or to desire, the conference terminated; but the English General was equally tenacious of his purpose, and commenced his reply by assurance of his deep regret at the discharge of a most painful duty which necessity imposed; but he had no alternative—no means of evasion.

He then reminded the Marshal "of the Emperor Alexander's last words to himself, the Marshal, on quitting S. Petersburg, relative to the rejection of *all negotiation whilst an armed Frenchman was in the country*; and of the renewal of that solemn pledge to him, the English General, with instructions to *intervene when he saw that pledge and connecting interests endangered by any one, of whatsoever rank he might be.*"

He then said that " the time was now come when unfortunately his intervention, in conformity with that instruction, had become necessary."

That "his, the Marshal's, project of meeting an enemy's general and envoy beyond his own advanced posts at midnight, was unheard of in the annals of war, except when illicit communications had been intended—so illicit as not to admit of a third person being employed; that the army would believe, and would be authorised to believe, that the Marshal on quitting the Russian lines was about to make a treaty, or enter into some transaction with the enemy, in defiance and contravention of their Emperor's promises and orders; that the interests of Russia and the honour of the Imperial army would *be compromised by any treaty, however speciously framed; and that the des ruction or capitulation of the enemy was the only 'point de mire' which should be entertained by the Marshal.*"

That "he had under his command already a hundred thousand men and upwards, stationed on the enemy's principal lines of communication, of which force there were thirty thousand horse, with seven hundred pieces of cannon, perfectly equipped; whilst the enemy's army was scarcely equal in number, with a ruined cavalry and an inadequately horsed artillery, and both arms were daily becoming enfeebled from want of forage; that the whole force was in dismay at the prospect of a retreat through an exasperated and ruined country, with the hazards, difficulties, and terrors of an approaching wintry season. That under such circumstances the Russian generals and army (for he had been made acquainted with their feelings on the subject) might and would feel themselves under the terrible necessity of withdrawing his authority until the Emperor's decision could be known; and that he, the English General, would be obliged to despatch instantly couriers to Constantinople, to Lord Walpole at Vienna, to London, and S. Petersburg, communicating these proceedings, which intelligence would have the most injurious effect by suspending all the succours in preparation, and breaking off the negotiations in progress."

That "Russia might now have the glory and advantage of redeeming Europe by the capture or annihilation of Napoleon and his army; but, abusing this opportunity, that she herself in a short time would be replaced in her former jeopardy, and being justly abandoned by every friend, would be overwhelmed with discredit and self-reproach."

The Marshal manifesting increasing pertinacity, the English General left him for a moment to call into his presence Duke Alexander of Wurtemberg, the Emperor's uncle; the Duke of Oldenburg, brother-in-law to the Emperor; and Prince Wolkonsky, aide-de-camp general to the Emperor, who had just arrived from S. Petersburg with despatches, and who was to return the same evening: these personages had been previously selected to support the English General's remonstrance, as being most likely to exercise a salutary influence, and as being less liable to objection on the ground of subordination than any of the other chiefs under the Marshal's orders.

The English General, on re-entering, stated that "he felt it right in a transaction of such magnitude to make another appeal to the Marshal, and endeavour to change his resolve. He had therefore requested these personages, so immediately connected with the Emperor and acquainted with his most intimate feelings, to co-operate with him, as he trusted they would, in pressing his views and entreaties."

He then recapitulated at large, and as nearly as possible word for word, "*the admission of the Marshal, his own remonstrances, and his declarations as to the course he must pursue.*"

The Duke of Wurtemberg with urbanity and tact expressed "his full confidence in the Marshal's loyalty, patriotism, and judgment; but recommended, under the considerations urged and the suspicious temper of the army, to which he could testify, that the Marshal should annul the proposed interview out of the Russian camp, and invite General Lauriston to one at his own head-quarters, as a more becoming and less disquieting proceeding." The Duke of Oldenburg followed, and concurred. Prince Wolkonsky, resting his arguments chiefly on his knowledge of the Emperor's determination to carry out the pledge he had made, and which he had renewed in the proclamation published after the capture of Moscow, also recommended revocation of the appointment with Lauriston.

The Marshal, after much controversy and an expression of dissent which, however softened by phrases, conveyed strong disapprobation of the proposed counteraction of his measure, began to give way, but still argued the impossibility of breaking an arrangement to which his signature was affixed. The English General answered, "that it was better to break than keep such a promise; that in breaking it he committed no public wrong, whilst in keeping it he would render inevitable many and grave mischiefs."

At length the Marshal submitted, and a note was

despatched to General Lauriston advising him that "the Marshal was unable to keep the appointment made, and inviting him to the Marshal's head-quarters at ten that same night."

General Lauriston wrote an urgent request that "the Marshal would adhere to his original rendezvous, as the deviation would cause much disappointment and inconvenience;" but on the Marshal's reply "that circumstances did not permit his acquiescence in that wish," General Lauriston understood that some unforeseen and insurmountable obstacle, which the Marshal could not control, had arisen.

On the arrival of General Lauriston, about eleven at night, and blindfolded, he was ushered into the Marshal's hut, and introduced to a circle of Russian generals and the *English General by name;* when, as General Lauriston afterwards said, "he immediately comprehended from what quarter the obstacle had come to the execution of the original agreement."

After some general conversation every one withdrew, and left the Marshal and the envoy together, who before his departure placed a letter from Napoleon for the Emperor Alexander in the Marshal's hands: a fact which the Marshal did not communicate, but which he acknowledged when he found that the delivery had been seen.

In the relation given by the Marshal of such parts of the conversation as he judged it expedient to make public, he stated that "Lauriston had at first complained of the barbarity of the Russians to the French," to which he, the Marshal, had replied, as he said, that "he could not civilize a nation in three months who regarded the enemy as worse than a marauding force of Tartars under Gingis Khan." Lauriston answered, "But there is at least some difference." "There may be," returned the Marshal, "but none in the eyes of the people; and I can only be responsible for the conduct of my troops."

Lauriston had no complaint to make against them; but adverting to an armistice said, "Nature herself would in a short time oblige it." The Marshal told him that "he had no authority on that head." Returning again to the subject of the armistice, Lauriston continued, "You must not think we wish it because *our* affairs are desperate. Our two armies are nearly equal in force. You are, it is true, nearer your supplies and reinforcements than we are, but we also receive reinforcements. Perhaps you have heard that our affairs are disastrous in Spain?" "I have," said the Marshal, "from Sir Robert Wilson, whom you just saw leave me, and with whom I have daily interviews."

"General Wilson may have reasons to exaggerate our reverses. We have indeed received a check by the bétise of Marshal Marmont, and Madrid, en attendant, is occupied by the English, but they will soon be driven out; everything will be retrieved in that country by the immense force marching thither." He then denied the burning of Moscow by the French army, and charged it as an act of the Governor's, adding, "It is so much at variance with the French character, that if we take London we shall not fire it."

In about an hour Lauriston withdrew.

At the time Kutusow determined to surrender Moscow, he had not been able to avoid the notification of that decision to the Emperor.

Alexander was deeply afflicted by this unexpected issue to a battle that had been described and celebrated as a victory that assured its safety.

He was sensible of the deception practised upon him, and wrote to the Marshal, "I will not reproach you, but posterity will severely judge you."

Unshaken, however, in his policy by a catastrophe that was spreading consternation through the empire, he wisely and bravely resolved on giving a manifest proof of his firmness, and published forthwith the following proclamation, which forms a document of great value in the history of this eventful period, and adds further titles to the Emperor's claim on the gratitude of his subjects then and for ever.

"Proclamation.

"The enemy entered Moscow the 15th of September.

"It might be expected that consternation should be general at this news, but let us disdain a pusillanimous despondency. Let us swear rather to redouble our perseverance and our courage; let us hope that, whilst combating in a cause so just as ours, we may direct upon the heads of our enemy the calamities he is heaping up for our destruction. Moscow, it is true, is in their hands, but our army is not disgraced or dispersed. The General-in-chief has yielded to a necessity, but only to reunite with advancing forces, and then to snatch from the enemy his ephemeral triumph.

"We know and feel how grieved all the hearts of the faithful Russians will be at the desolation of our provinces and the ancient capital of the empire, but the enemy occupies only its ramparts. Deserted by its inhabitants—stripped of its treasures—it resembles no more a peopled city, but a vast tomb, in which the merciless invader may erect his throne.

"This haughty destroyer of kingdoms on entering Moscow flattered himself that he was the arbiter of our destinies, and might dictate peace at his will; but his presumption is already foiled: he has found in Moscow not only no aid for his domination, but not even the means of subsistence.

"Our forces augment every day. They occupy all the roads, and destroy all the detachments of the enemy in search of food.

"He will soon be convinced of the fatal error which led him to consider the possession of Moscow as the subjection of the empire; and famine will compel him to attempt an escape through a country of which our intrepid warriors with closed roads will bar the passage.

"Look at the condition of this enemy: he entered Russia at the head of more than three hundred thousand men, but how is that force composed?

"Is there any national unity in this multitude?

"No! the different nations who march under his standards do not serve him from attachment or patriotism, but servile fear.

"Already the disorganising effect of his principle of fusion is apparent.

"Half the army is destroyed by Russian valour, by desertion, by want of discipline, by sickness and hunger!

"The pride of the conqueror is doubtless increased by the apparent success of his enterprise, but the 'end crowns the work.'

"Through the whole course of his invasion he has not found a spot where a Russian from terror has fallen at his feet.

"Russia is attached to the paternal throne of her Sovereign, who extends over her the guardian arm of his affection.

"She is not accustomed to the yoke of oppression. She will not endure a foreign domination. She will not surrender the treasures of her laws, her religion, and independence. She is ready to shed the last drop of her blood in their defence. This sentiment is ardent and universal.

"It has manifested itself by the prompt and voluntary organisation of the people under the banner of patriotism! Under such an ægis, where can there be any ground for a disgraceful fear? Can there be a man in the empire so base as to despair, when vengeance is the rallying word of the state?—when the enemy, deprived of all resources, sees his numbers daily diminishing, and a powerful nation environing him, with an army in his front and rear intercepting his supplies and retreat?

"Can a true Russian feel alarm? Has Spain not broken her chains, and menaced the integrity of the French empire? Does not the greatest portion of Europe, degraded and plundered by the ruler of France, serve him with a reluctant heart, and turn an impatient regard on us for the signal of general deliverance?

"Does not France herself sigh for the termination of a sanguinary war, in which she has been involved by a boundless ambition?

"Does not an oppressed world look to us for example

and encouragement, and can we shrink from such an honourable mission as is confided to us? No; let us rather kiss the hand that has selected us to act as the leaders of nations in the struggle for independence and virtue.

"Too long has humanity been afflicted by the calamities of war, and the cruelties of this horrible ambition; but we will brave it, for our freedom and the interests of mankind.

"We will enjoy the noble sentiment of a good action; immortal honour shall be the recompense of a nation enduring all the ills of a savage war, and contending with courage and constancy to obtain a durable peace, not only for herself, but for those unhappy countries which the tyrant is now forcing to fight in his quarrel.

"It is glorious—it is worthy a great people to render good for ill.

"Almighty God! is the cause for which we are battling not just? Cast an eye of compassion on our holy church. Preserve to this people its courage and constancy. Suffer it to triumph over its adversary and Thine. May it be in Thy hand the instrument of his destruction—and in delivering itself, redeem the freedom and independence of nations and kings.

(Signed) "ALEXANDER."

Every word of this proclamation told on the hearts of the people to whom it was addressed. It electrified them with corresponding animation and confidence.

The reinforcement and provisioning of the assembling army was one of the most extraordinary efforts of national zeal ever made. No Russian who possessed any article which could be rendered serviceable to the state withheld it: horses, arms, equipment, provisions, and in brief every thing that can be imagined was poured into the camps.

Militia performed the most remarkable marches, even for Russians, to reach the head-quarters.

Old and young, under and over the regulated ages, flocked to the standards, and would not be refused service. Fathers of families, many seventy years of age and upwards, placed themselves in the ranks, and encountered every fatigue as well as peril with all the ardour of youth. Governors of distant provinces, without waiting for orders or requisitions, urged forward every supply they could collect; and so many cannon were despatched by relays, that a hundred and sixty beautiful new guns were in one day sent away as superfluous.

When the army amounted to a hundred and ten thousand men, not only were they regularly fed, but fifty thousand horses received full rations of hay and corn without the extension of the foraging range above twenty miles.

The camp resembled a bee-hive in the activity of its swarming hosts. The whole nation was solicitous to fill it with stores and useful largesses.

Nor did Alexander confine the assurances contained in his proclamation to declaratory phrases, but sent vigorous instructions to the three chiefs commanding the corps destined to act in the rear of the enemy, to assist in working out the results predicted. Of these instructions the following are principally important:—

To Count Steingell.

"*Article* 5. If the troops assembling at Tilsit do not compel different measures, pursue the direction of your march through the governments of Wilna, on Widzy and Swentziany, where you should arrive by the 15th of October. Press on Oudinot defeated by Wittgenstein, and push him beyond the Wilia and the Niemen. Defend the Niemen against the Prussians, cover Riga, and act as a reserve to the three armies when united at Minsk and on the Beresina."

To Count Wittgenstein.

"*Article* 6. Attack Polotzk in the rear, then unite with Prince Jachwill at Dunaburg, fall on Oudinot with the greatest rapidity, cut him off from the main army. Throw him on Steingell, who about that time, after defeating Macdonald, will have reached Widzy and Swentziany, and give him up the command to pursue the enemy."

"*Article* 7. Having executed the above orders, reach Dokchitzy by the 27th of October, open communication through Minsk with Tchichagow, pass the Beresina, occupy Lepel, and the whole course of the Oula from Beresino to its confluence with the Dwina. Fortify all defiles on any and every road the enemy may take after passing the Dnieper."

To Admiral Tchichagow.

"*Article* 1. From Ostrog march on Pinsk: arrive there by the 7th of October.

" One of the principal objects of the operations is to cover your march by the corps lately under Tormanssow, and to gain some marches on Regnier and Schwarzenberg in your march from Pinsk to Neswige and Minsk; that, arriving at Minsk before them, you may prevent their junction with the main army on its retreat. Reach Neswige by the 13th of October at latest—sooner if possible."

"*Article* 2. Establish communication by the 15th of October with the army lately under Tormanssow; reinforce it if necessary, to enable it to push Schwarzenberg and Regnier out of the duchy of Warsaw into Gallicia."

"*Article* 3. On the 21st of October, or sooner if possible, occupy with principal force Minsk, where you will be joined the same day by the detachment from Mozyr; then occupy Borisow, and the course of the Beresina; form an entrenched camp, securing all the woods and defiles on the road from Borisow to Bobr.

" Fortify all points defensible, so that the enemy, pursued by our main army, may be checked at every step in his retreat.

" On the 7th of October you will be reunited by your left at Dokchitzy with Wittgenstein; assure the communication with Kiew by your right."

"*Article* 4. Forming thus the centre of three united armies, with a fourth in reserve at Wilna under Steingell, you will hold yourself in readiness for any unforeseen opportunities that may offer to annihilate the enemy, whether on the left or on the right side of the Oula, whether in your centre at Borisow and on the Beresina, or on your right flank at Bobruisk.

"Our united armies must act with the greatest promptitude and activity in the centre and on the flanks at any and every point wheresoever the enemy may present himself, not only to prevent any portion of the enemy's main army from escaping, but even its couriers and spies from gliding through the posts, so that the enemy, exhausted by marches and fatigues, may be entirely destroyed, even before reaching the frontier."

These instructions have been criticised as not being duly calculated with regard to time and distances of relative points, &c. They are also commented upon for not having designated the supreme Chief of the three corps when united, from which some inconvenience resulted; but those are points for future disquisitions. The instructions have been here inserted only as evidence, which they indisputably supply, of the sincerity of Alexander's convictions, and of the energetic measures adopted for the accomplishment of his purpose.

As Steingell's name appears in these instructions for the first time, it is necessary to state that Lieutenant-general Count Steingell commanded the army of Finland, which was released from that station by the treaty of Abo.

On the 9th of September Steingell disembarked at Revel with about twelve thousand veteran troops: they should have amounted to fourteen thousand, but five hundred perished in a tempest, and about fifteen hundred were detained from want of sufficient transports. On the 20th he reached Riga, where Essen commanded a garrison of about ten thousand, chiefly new levies, and where he was joined a few days afterwards by the absent detachment.

A battering train of one hundred and thirty pieces of cannon had been collected by the enemy for the siege of Riga at the villages of Reenthal and Brounswende, situated about a mile and a half from each other beyond the Aa, and three short marches from Riga. General Yorck, with a corps of sixteen thousand Prussians, and a brigade of three thousand in reserve, covered this depôt in a position about two marches distant.

Essen determined on an attempt to get possession of the depôt, and moved on Mittau with six thousand men, whilst Steingell marched on Eckau with ten thousand men, but neither had cavalry or artillery equal to their adversary.

Essen entered Mittau on the 29th of September, made some prisoners, destroyed some valuable magazines, and retired the next morning with several pieces of heavy ordnance which he had found there.

Steingell, although he had made himself master of Eckau where he killed, wounded, and took several hundred Prussians, and had reached the Aa within less than two miles from the depôt of artillery, was unable to accomplish his object; for General Yorck passed the river and attacked his left flank.

The action was feebly sustained till night, when Essen and Steingell, on hearing that Macdonald was advancing, retired on Riga, which they re-entered on the 30th.

Perhaps the enterprise might have been more successful if conducted with greater activity and vigour, but the loss had been inconsiderable.

Russian Main Army.

Since the Russian main army had taken up its position at Taroutino, and Murat at Winkowo, conversations had daily been held at the advanced posts by the principal Russian officers with Murat and his generals. They had commenced with the cessation of daily morning skirmishing; mutual courtesies followed as the lines of videttes were visited; and finally such civilities were interchanged that the intervening ground was respected as neutral, where both parties might meet and confer in security at pleasure.

Murat, on one of these occasions, expressed a wish to meet Beningsen the next day, who inconsiderately (for it was contrary to the Emperor's orders) kept the appointment.

After some personal compliments Murat said, "Peace is necessary—I wish it as King of Naples, who have a country to govern." Beningsen answered, "As much as you wish it, insomuch do we prefer war: besides, if the *Emperor would*, the Russians *would not*; and, to speak frankly, I belong to that party."

Murat observed, "National prejudices might be overcome." "Oh no," replied Beningsen, "not in Russia; the Russians are a terrible people, and would kill any man instantly who even talked of negotiation."

Korf on the same day met General Amande at another post; the conversation also turned on peace. Amande said, "We are really tired of this war: give us passports and we will depart." Korf answered, "General, you came without being invited; when you go away you must take *French leave*." Amande smiled, but replied gravely, "Is it not a pity that two nations who esteem each other should be carrying on a war of extermination? We will make our excuses, our apologies if you insist, for having been intruders, and shake hands upon our respective frontiers." "Yes," said Korf, "we believe you have lately learned to think us more worthy of your esteem than you did; but would you, General, continue to do so if we suffered you to withdraw with arms in your hands?"

On another occasion Murat, at an interview with Milaradowitch, asked him "to let his cavalry forage to the right and left of his camp without being disturbed." "Nay, would you wish," said Milaradowitch, "to deprive us of the pleasure of taking your finest cavaliers of France, comme des poules?" "Oh then, I shall order due measures of precaution," said Murat, "and march foraging columns, with infantry and artillery on their flanks." "That is what we desire," replied Milaradowitch; "we are impatient for an encounter:" and the next night, the 8th of October, forty-three cuirassiers and carabineers, and fifty-three on the morning of the 9th, were made prisoners, and notice of the capture sent to Murat by Milaradowitch.

Some of the French writers affirm, and indeed the charge was made in one of the bulletins, that an armistice was actually concluded; and they accuse the Russians of a subsequent treacherous infraction; but the armistice never existed: it was an invention *ex post facto*, to cover or palliate want of due discretion and vigilance. The facts which led to the intercourse amongst the chiefs were strictly as above stated. There was no authority for it—no arrangement—no written or verbal agreements of any kind, only that tacit one which individuals at their own peril ventured to act upon from day to day and moment to moment, but which afforded no protection under the laws of war against sudden resumption of hostilities, or even seizure and detention by higher authority of the parties communicating.

Murat himself told the English General in Italy, during the campaign of 1814, "that he always had a misgiving on the subject—that he feared he might be lulling himself into too much security, especially when he found him, the English General, notwithstanding invitations on his part, and advances more than half-way on the neutral ground to meet him, still pertinaciously refusing to approach him, or to accompany the Russian Generals." He said "he felt sure that there was no personal discourtesy intended, as both had so often met, and learned to respect each other in honourable conflict; also that there could be no want of usual English curiosity and desire to extract information on an infinity of subjects, *European as well as Russian:* he, therefore, could not help ascribing his keeping aloof to a cause which he very soon afterwards had reason to know was but too well grounded; but," he added, "my evil star prevailed, and like Napoleon I was blinded by a dazzling phantom of peace."

The intelligence of the proposed midnight conference beyond the advanced posts, and the reception of Lauriston by Kutusow, which Prince Wolkonsky conveyed to the Emperor, and which the English General had also been obliged to communicate in a despatch with full detail to His Imperial Majesty, severely displeased Alexander, who felt how much his word and interests had been compromised and endangered by that proceeding. The interviews between the enemy's officers and his own, of which Kutusow had made report in order to implicate others in the responsibility of communications contrary to His Imperial Majesty's orders, also distressed him, and therefore the following reproof was sent to Kutusow:—

"Prince Michael Larionowicz,

"The report brought from you by Prince Wolkonsky has made me acquainted with your interview with the French aide-de-camp General Lauriston.

"In the interview I had with you at the very moment of your departure, and when I confided my armies to your command, I informed you of my firm desire to avoid all negotiations with the enemy, and all relations with him that tended to peace.

"Now, after what has passed, I must repeat with the same resolution that I desire this principle *adopted by me to be observed by you to its fullest extent, and in the most rigorous and inflexible manner.*

"I have also learned, to my extreme displeasure, that General Beningsen has had an interview with the King of Naples, without any motive to instigate him to it.

"After making him sensible of the impropriety of

this step, I require from *yourself* an active and severe superintendence to prevent other generals from having interviews with the enemy, and holding similar conferences.

"All the opinions and suggestions you have received from me—all the *resolutions which I have expressed in the orders addressed to you, should convince you that my determination was unalterable, and that at this moment no proposition of the enemy can induce me to terminate the war, and by that to weaken the sacred duty that I have to perform in avenging my injured country.*

" S. Petersburg, 4th of October, 1812.

(Signed) " ALEXANDER."

It would not have become the Emperor to have referred more directly to the proposed meeting "beyond the advanced posts." He could not with propriety and prudence have so much humiliated the commander of his armies as to have adverted in a public despatch to his rebuke by a foreign general; and it was desirable on every account to keep the transaction as much confined as possible to the parties acquainted with it: but he wrote a letter of acknowledgment to the English General for the watchful care he had shown; and in his conversation with him afterwards at Wilna it will be seen how justly he appreciated the discomfiture of the Marshal's intentions in that transaction.

The daring and success of the Cossacks and partisan corps around Moscow continued increasing, and the enemy's weakness became daily more apparent.

Already four thousand horsemen were dismounted, and no remount could be procured.

The artillery was in a better state, but deteriorating sensibly.

Every morning several hundred prisoners were brought into camp, who had chiefly been taken in attempts to forage; and all concurred in the statement "of general starvation, suffering, and decay."

Amongst other misfortunes which befel the enemy at this time, Wereia, that had been occupied by a Westphalian battalion, and palisaded, was carried by assault on the 10th of October.

Four inhabitants of Wereia, who had escaped out of the town, had assured Dorokoff of the practicability of the attempt, in which the whole population would assist.

Collecting his troops, Dorokoff suddenly appeared before the place; and assisted, as promised and pre-arranged, by the Russians within, he gained an entrance into the town. Not an individual of the enemy's force escaped: four hundred were made prisoners; the rest were killed. Some considerable magazines were also secured.

The inaction of the Russian main army was becoming the subject of dissatisfaction, the strength of which was growing uncontrollable; for, as winter was drawing on, it was feared that the enemy would retire suddenly from Moscow, and rescue, by a timely withdrawal, the detached corps exposed in vulnerable positions. It was therefore earnestly desired that a blow should be struck without further delay, to cripple the enemy, and so impair his remaining strength that he might fall an easier—no one doubted of his being a certain prey.

Murat and Poniatowski presented the occasion for this offensive experiment.

Kutusow, incessantly urged by Beningsen, the Quartermaster-general Tol, and others, at last gave a reluctant assent.

A little rivulet, with very steep banks which form a difficult ravine, called the Czernicznia, taking its source near Spass Kouplia, on the high road from Moscow to Taroutino, runs in a southern direction parallel with the road for about five miles, when it takes a sharp bend to the west, crosses the line of road, and flows into the Nara. The distance from the bend to its confluence is about three miles and a half.

The enemy's right and centre were posted behind this rivulet and ravine, with the right on the Nara, and the centre left extending to the bend of the rivulet. Another streamlet flowing into the Czernicznia at that bend covered the left, which was separated from the centre by the before-mentioned Czernicznia main stream, that descended from Spass Kouplia, which was the only point of retreat for the whole force. Behind the right of the enemy lay a range of woods that reached to Spass Kouplia, through which the high road ran, and formed a close defile. In front of the right lay the village of Winkowo, and of the left Teterinki; in advance of which there was a plantation of woods that the enemy did not think of occupying, or even watching.

Between twenty-five and thirty thousand men occupied the position, of about six miles in extent, intersected, as stated, by the ravine and rivulet, and without any security for its rear, by natural or military obstructions, against a hostile approach and lodgment.

Poniatowski's corps was stationed on the right and in the centre, where the principal corps of cavalry was also posted. Sebastiani, with his division and some light cavalry, was posted on the left beyond the Czernicznia.

The 16th was the day first appointed for the attack, but some of the troops not having arrived in time at their appointed stations, the army after a short march returned to its camp.

Fortunately the enemy had not perceived the movement.

On the morning of the 17th the columns again passed the Nara, and proceeded to their respective destinations.

To enable a just comparative estimate to be formed of the force employed, and the results which were obtained, it is necessary to give an exact programme of the order of battle.

Orloff Denisoff, with ten regiments of Cossacks, including the Cossacks of the Guard, a regiment of chasseurs, and twelve pieces of artillery, had orders " to turn the left of the enemy, gain their rear, and seize the defile of Spass Kouplia." His support was composed of the light cavalry of the Guard, a regiment of dragoons, and six pieces of flying artillery.

Bagawouth, with the 2nd and 3rd corps and sixty pieces of cannon, was directed to attack the enemy's left and connect with Orloff Denisoff.

Osterman, with the 4th corps and twelve pieces of cannon, was instructed to form the intermediate link between Bagawouth and the rest of the army.

Beningsen was charged with the command of these columns, and it would have been well if he had been left to employ them, without further check or control.

Doctorow, with the 6th corps and twenty-seven pieces of cannon, formed the 4th column.

The 7th and 8th corps under Raeffskoi, with forty-eight pieces of cannon, composed the 5th column.

These two columns were directed to pass the Nara at Taroutino, move by Winkowo upon the Czernicznia, and engage the enemy along his front, from right to centre, that he might be unable to detach any aid to his left.

The reserve, composed of two divisions of cuirassiers, and the 5th corps (the Guards), with all the artillery of the reserve, formed behind the 5th column, on the great Moscow road.

Milaradowitch commanded the advanced rd of the whole of these columns, having under his orders the 2nd and 4th regiments of cavalry, four regiments of Cossacks, with several battalions of chasseurs, and twenty pieces of light artillery; but he was ordered to remain stationary until the action had begun on the enemy's left.

The whole force thus arrayed could not have mustered under arms fewer than ninety thousand combatants, with a hundred and eighty pieces of cannon, exclusive of above four hundred in the reserve park— a force from numbers, valour, and every requisite, sufficient to have annihilated the enemy immediately opposed.

On the 18th, about seven o'clock in the morning, instead of at day-break as proposed, a brigade of Bagawouth's column advanced out of the wood in

MURAT. 18TH OCT. 1812.

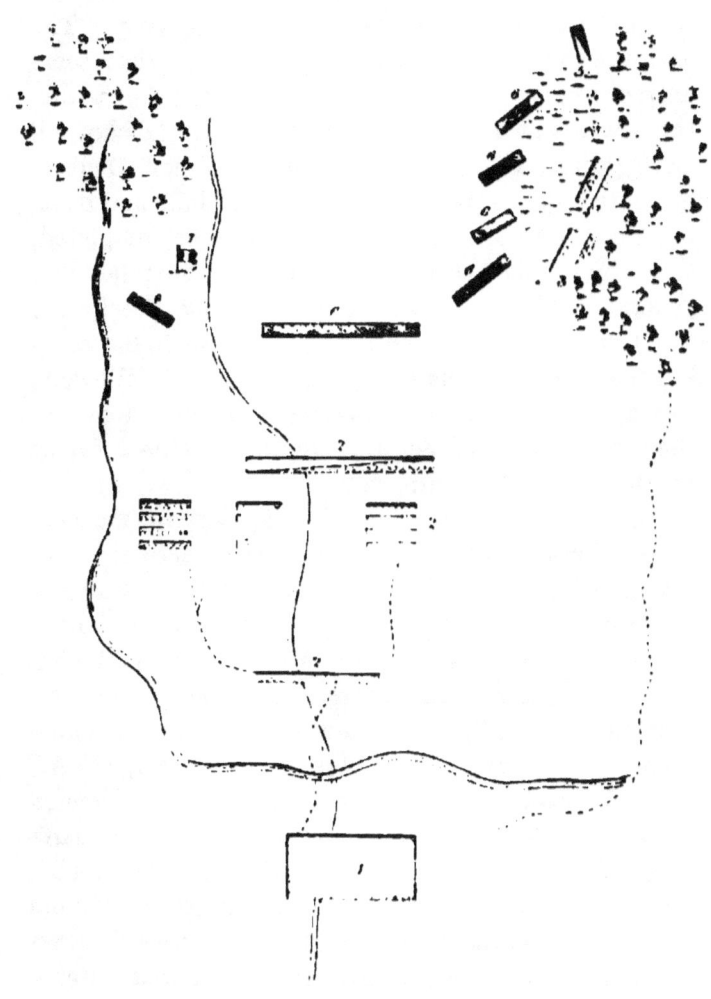

1 Russn Camp
2 Russn Army
3 Ostreman
4 Benningsen
5 Cossaques
6 French Camp
7 Murats Head Quarters
8 Moscow Road

front of Teterinki, and opened a brisk cannonade from six pieces of cannon on the enemy's left wing. The enemy's cavalry, who had just discovered that some extraordinary movements were in progress within the wood, was beginning to mount when the shot fell among them, and at the same instant Orloff Denisoff presented himself behind their extreme left, and dashing upon it before any formation could be completed, threw not only the cavalry but the whole left into general confusion. An immediate and precipitate flight behind the Czernicznia to unite with the corps beyond and find shelter from their pursuers followed; but all the artillery and material were abandoned as they stood, and in addition to many killed, fifteen hundred were made prisoners.

This success obtained, the English General was sent to the Marshal with Beningsen's urgent entreaty " for the advance with energy of all the columns." " Beg the Marshal," said Beningsen, " to give no time to the enemy to rally or make any new disposition; he has only to roll him back 'au pas de charge' in his present disorder on Spass Kouplia, whilst I am hastening there to intercept his passage, which I will effect." But Kutusow coldly checked this ardour, directed Beningsen to stop his movement, as Osterman's column, the third, had not yet taken up its ground, ordered away the third corps from the second column to fill up the vacancy, and arrested the forward movement of all the other columns, except Milaradowitch's, which he allowed to advance on Winkowo, pass the rivulet, and engage the enemy, still maintaining a wood on the right of their position to cover the retreat.

Murat had been completely surprised. He had not

risen when the first shots gave the alarm. With difficulty he gained his horse before the Russians were in possession of his quarters; his baggage, silver canteens, and cooking utensils, in which were found cats and horse flesh preparing for food, were taken. Desperate by a sense of the misfortunes menacing his comrades (for he always was regarded, and sought to be regarded, by his troops as a fellow-soldier), and by the discredit that would attach to his neglect of due precaution, he exerted to the highest degree all his energies and activity: his plume was seen waving in the thickest of every fray—now he was rallying the fugitives; now restoring order in the columns; now charging on the pursuers; now covering his line of retreat by the most energetic defensive measures and personal daring.

No chief could more devotedly endeavour to repair a fault—for fault there had been, and that he himself acknowledged—or display more brilliant courage in the midst of the most anxious and distracting peril.

If, however, Orloff Denisoff had been duly supported,—if Beningsen had been permitted to sustain him at Spass Kouplia, which point his Cossacks had reached,—and the other columns had been advanced in time, not all Murat's talent, courage, and exertions would have been able to preserve a single individual of his whole force; not a man would have escaped the sword or captivity.

The Cossacks, especially those of the Guard under Orloff Denisoff, intrepidly attacked even the cuirassiers endeavouring to form a screen for the columns gliding along the skirts of the wood to gain Spass Kouplia.

Charges were mutually given and repulsed, and

there never was a cavalry combat in modern warfare where the antagonists continued so close and commingled for such a length of time. Had it not been for the cuirass before and behind, the Cossack spear would infallibly have pierced every horseman.*

At length the enemy's infantry, pressed on its rear by Milaradowitch's advance as vigorously as his means and orders allowed, gained and filed through the defile of Spass Kouplia, when the cuirassiers suddenly broke, rushed into it, and escaped under the fire of some chasseur battalions posted at the entrance.

The Russians did not proceed farther; for Kutusow sent an order to desist from pursuit, as he received and believed information given by the prisoners taken (which, however, proved erroneous), "that a strong French reinforcement sent by Napoleon was approaching."

Murat did not halt his flying force until it reached Arrinowo.

The Russian army returned to Taroutino, leaving Milaradowitch with his advanced guard at Winkowo.

Two of the enemy's generals, Dery and Fisher, had been killed, also two thousand men; a general and two thousand prisoners were taken, with an eagle, thirty-eight pieces of cannon, forty tumbrils, all the baggage, and a considerable number of wretched horses.

The trophy, however, which gave the most satisfaction was the rescue of three hundred wounded

---

* During this combat the Cossacks were never distant more than half pistol shot from the squadrons, which kept as close formed as possible; and each party during the whole time not only dealt blows, but pelted hard words at each other. The English General had rejoined the Cossacks after carrying back Kutusow's "negative" to Beningsen, and was a witness of this extraordinary mêlée.

prisoners in a church which the enemy had just fired.

The loss of the Russians had not exceeded five hundred men; but the death of General Bagawouth, who had been struck by a cannon ball, greatly aggravated that loss, for he was an excellent officer, and much esteemed.

It has been already stated that skinned cats and horse-flesh had been found in the kitchen of Murat.

All the cooking pots left at the bivouacs—for the enemy were surprised whilst cooking their breakfast—contained bouillons of horse-flesh; and the carcases of butchered horses strewed about the bivouacs were numerous, and most offensive from their putridity.

The vast superiority of Kutusow's force and the defective position of the enemy rendered the success obtained very incommensurate with the means employed. Kutusow was master of the enemy's fate, when he suspended the offensive and changed it to a timid defensive, as if desirous of averting the catastrophe of his enemy; and his conduct in this affair would only be explicable by that suspicion, unless the relation of subsequent proceedings should prove that his motive was to be ascribed with more truth to a rival jealousy of his second in command.

The result nevertheless, imperfect and unsatisfactory as it was to the army, operated most beneficially on Europe as well as Russia, and favoured many interests requiring this irrefragable proof of the enemy's weakness and hopeless condition.

Napoleon had at length ascertained his error in expecting Alexander's entertainment of his pacific proposals; and aware that the unusual mildness of the weather then existing could not be of long duration, made his dispositions to evacuate Moscow.

Recalling his corps, which had been detached in an opposite direction to his intended line of march, and ordering the necessary preparations to be made, he vindictively resolved to blow up the Kremlin—an useless, Vandal, and exasperating act, which Mortier was commanded to carry into execution.

On the 15th all the sick and wounded that could be conveyed, spare artillery, trophies, and baggage, which had been directed to move on Smolensk, commenced their march in a column that contained nearly seven hundred pieces of cannon, two thousand five hundred tumbrils, and six thousand public and private carriages of all descriptions.

On the 16th the Viceroy, charged with the advanced guard of the army under Napoleon, passed the Pakra at Gorki, and bending to the right reached Ignatowo.

The news of the defeat of Murat greatly disconcerted Napoleon; but it exposed the jeopardy of his situation in a more manifest light than any in which he had heretofore contemplated it, and accelerated his arrangements.

On the 19th he quitted Moscow with the Old Guard, the corps of Ney and of Davoust, the divisions Delzon and Pino of the Viceroy's army, and proceeded to Watinlenka, establishing his head-quarters at Troitskoie, where he was joined by Murat and Poniatowski.

On the 21st the Viceroy reached Fominskoie, and united with Broussier's division.

Napoleon, who had halted on the 20th, moved on the 21st to Ignatowo.

On the 22nd he proceeded to Fominskoie, and Poniatowski was directed to advance on Wereia, that he might cover, on the side of Medynsk, the great convoy moving on the route by Mojaisk to Smolensk.

On the 20th Berthier, by Napoleon's orders, despatched the following letter to Kutusow :—

"PRINCE KUTUSOW, "Imperial Head-Quarters, 20th October, 1812.

"General Lauriston was commissioned to propose to you an arrangement that might give to the war a character more conformable to established rules, and which might avoid all evils not indispensable for its conduct.

"In fact, the devastation which pains the Emperor is still more injurious to Russia, as it is her own country that suffers.

"You will readily perceive, General, the interest I take in knowing the definitive determination of your Government.

(Signed) "PRINCE OF NEUFCHATEL."

To this letter the Marshal sent the following reply :—

"MY PRINCE,

"Monsieur de Berthemy, whom I have received in my own quarters, has delivered the letter which your Highness addressed to me.

"All that relates to this new demand was immediately submitted, as you must know, my Prince, to the Emperor my master, by Prince Wolkonsky.

"Nevertheless, considering the distance and the difficulty of the communications at this season, it was physically impossible that I could yet have received an answer.

"I therefore can only refer you to what I had the honour to state to General Lauriston.

"I will, however, repeat a truth of which, my Prince, you will doubtless appreciate all the force and extent, namely, that it is difficult, notwithstanding every desire, to check a people irritated by all it sees—a people who for three hundred years have not known an internal war, who yet are ready to immolate themselves for their country, and who are not susceptible of these distinctions, which define what should be done and what ought not to be done, according to the modern customs of warfare.

"As to the armies which I command, Prince, I flatter myself that all the world will recognise in their conduct the principles which distinguish a brave, loyal, and generous nation.

"I have never practised any other in a long military career, and I flatter myself every enemy has always rendered my measures that justice.

(Signed) "KUTUSOW."

Napoleon's letter was a mystification of the real object of the mission of Lauriston, and the present communication was made to ascertain whether any answer had been received to the letter for the Emperor Alexander sent by Prince Wolkonsky.

The expression of Napoleon's wish "to humanize

the war" was not consistent with some of his own acts and instructions; for he had at the same instant "ordered the destruction of the Kremlin;" and in a note to Berthier of the 18th of October he had thus expressed himself:—

"Order the ten Russian soldiers" (proved to be unfortunate sick, and for that reason saved by Berthier) "found in a cellar of the 11th quarter (arrondissement) to be shot as incendiaries: let the execution take place at four in the morning, without drawing attention to it (sans éclat).

(Signed) "NAPOLEON."

In another note of a few days' earlier date, also to Berthier, he observes—

"COUSIN,

"The Duke of Treviso must establish the most severe police. Let every Russian soldier *found in the streets be shot*: therefore give those in hospital warning not to go out again.

(Signed) "NAPOLEON."

On the 23rd, at two in the morning, Mortier, who had been left in Moscow with a public order to collect provisions for a month, and make various demonstrations as if he were to remain in garrison there, evacuated the Kremlin under the instructions of a secret order; and as the last guard was withdrawn, the mines were sprung which had been some days preparing.

The palace, the church of San Nicholas, the arsenal, and adjoining buildings, were thrown down or set on fire by the explosion: an ignoble monument of resentment, which, honourably for the Russians, and beneficially for civilisation, was not followed as an example at either capture of Paris.

Mortier left about fifteen hundred sick in Moscow, and marched on Wereia with an immense train of carriages, that had not been ready to accompany the first convoy to Smolensk. Before his departure from Moscow, Winzingerode, with some Cossacks, had entered the city by the S. Petersburg barrier; but incautiously approaching the Kremlin, was made prisoner, with his aide-de-camp, Nariskin. On finding that he had ensnared himself, he waved a white handkerchief as a flag of truce; but that stratagem was of no avail, and the general was lawfully detained, with his aide-de-camp, as good prize.

It had been an original error to leave Winzingerode with so small a force, composed of one regiment of dragoons, one of hussars, some Cossacks of the Guard, and three regiments of Cossacks.

Had he been in greater strength, he might have harassed the enemy seriously, and contracted their foraging range in a district full of supplies; or had the enemy moved on Witepsk, which events showed would have been the safest line of retreat for Napoleon, Winzingerode could have done little more than have hovered on the flank of a column. His means would not have permitted any attempt to oppose a firm and efficacious resistance.

A few hours after Mortier had quitted Moscow, General Ilowaiskoi, who succeeded Winzingerode in his abdicated command, entered the Kremlin, where he found eighteen Russian and twenty-four French pieces of artillery.

According to the most accurate return of the enemy's total force retiring from Moscow, it consisted of ninety thousand effective infantry, fourteen thousand feeble cavalry, twelve thousand armed men employed in the various services of artillery, engineers, gendarmerie, head-quarter staff, equipages, and commissariat, and more than twenty thousand non-combatants, sick, and wounded—altogether about a hundred and forty thousand individuals.

The "impedimenta belli et fugæ" were never more embarrassing, nor was prospect ever more fearful; and yet no terrified imagination could picture to itself the real horrors that awaited this multitude.

The march, however, had begun auspiciously: the weather was fine; and the Russian information as to the enemy's proceedings, which had heretofore been most continuous, rapid, and accurate, was at this important moment completely intercepted.

When therefore intelligence was received on the 22nd at the Russian head-quarters that an enemy's corps had arrived, and was established at Fominskoie on the Nara, forty miles from Moscow, and about twenty from Taroutino, it was presumed that the corps was hazarded without support to collect provisions, and that it had not been duly admonished by Murat's disaster that the Russian army was able and disposed to assume the offensive.

Doctorow, with a corps of three thousand cavalry, twelve thousand infantry, and eighty-four pieces of cannon, was ordered " to march on Fominskoie, and surprise the enemy, if practicable; but if he should be found supported by any other corps, or in a position, with due precautions taken, to defend himself until reinforcements should arrive to his succour, on no account to engage in a combat which might require further aid from the main army to extricate his own corps so compromised, and perhaps to bring on a general battle under disadvantageous circumstances."

The Chief of the staff, Yermolow, and the English General accompanied Doctorow.

This general, who afterwards commanded the Russian army on the frontiers of Persia, was the best administrative officer in the service, but he did not entertain any presumptuous opinion of his own qualifications; for when complimented after the war "on the distinguished situation he had held under the Marshal," he said, quaintly, "You are mistaken—it was God and San Nicholas who did Kutusow's duty and mine; and it must be owned we gave them enough to do in repairing our errors."

As the operations of this detachment influenced very materially the fate of the enemy by disconcerting his plan of egress out of Russia, it is of importance to give an accurate detail of its proceedings, and of the incidents which guided its movements.

The corps marched early in the morning of the 23rd of October, and Milaradowitch was directed "on the same day to push a reconnoissance on Woronowo, to attract Murat's attention," it being supposed that he still held that position.

About four o'clock in the afternoon Doctorow reached Aristowo, twelve miles from Taroutino, and a few from Fominskoie.

As this station lay in a wooded dell, and the country beyond seemed open to observation from a very considerable distance, the corps was halted to refresh, and to await information from the exploring parties.

In a short time several officers and Cossacks arrived, bringing the intelligence "that the enemy was in a position about five miles distant, which was in itself strong and well guarded: that the picquets were all on the alert, and that a concealed approach was impossible."

These reports being confirmed by the staff officers sent to reconnoitre, a council of war was held at the request of Doctorow, and the English General was required to assist as a member.

Doctorow first stated his orders, and then "that the enemy was twelve thousand strong, with objects unknown, and that he had taken up defensible ground."

The Council called on the English General to give his opinion, and insisting, the English General observed "that if he commanded under similar orders and circumstances, he should suspend any further advance until more information was obtained from parties sent to reconnoitre the enemy's line of communication; that in his opinion the enemy's corps was not isolated, and *en l'air*, but an advanced guard or wing of some considerable body in movement.

"That if this were found not to be the case, a night attack might be attempted under cautious dispositions; but he should for the present keep the Russian corps where it was, to avoid giving alarm to the enemy by exposing the contiguity of a force which he probably did not expect to be in his neighbourhood."

This opinion was unanimously adopted, and orders were issued in accordance.

Doctorow, Yermolow, and other generals then thanked the English General for the honesty of his judgment, since they said, " Although we were of that advice, *au fond de cœur*, before the council met, none of us would have ventured in the temper of the troops, especially after the late affair at Taroutino, to take upon himself the initiative of such a temperate course of proceeding. We must have voted by acclamation, 'en avant, coûte qui coûte,' without any regard to conditional orders; but as your anti-French zeal is known to the soldiery, every one will be satisfied with your decision, and await with patience the issue."

In the course of an hour afterwards Colonel Sislavin, a celebrated and gallant partisan, galloped into Aristowo, and communicated the news " that he had seen the French army on march from Ignatowo to Fominskoie:" other Cossacks followed, who reported that " they had seen the enemy enter Borowsk in great force;" and a French officer, brought in prisoner, admitted that " Moscow was evacuated; that Napoleon was with the column at Ignatowo," but stated that " he, the officer, knew nothing of the destination of the army except that it was leaving Russia."

Messenger after messenger then poured in from all quarters with confirmatory intelligence, and the greatest and most joyous animation prevailed in the camp.

It was clear that Malo-Jaroslavets was the point on which the enemy was moving; and whilst the corps was getting under arms, advice was received " that the enemy from Fominskoie was already on march in that direction."

Not a moment was lost: by seven o'clock the corps of Doctorow was straining every nerve to reach Malo-Jaroslavets before the enemy, whose lights were frequently visible during the night, as the columns occasionally approached within a mile or two of each other.

Doctorow had despatched advice to Kutusow " of the intelligence he had acquired, and of his own movement on Malo-Jaroslavets;" urging that " reinforcements might be sent as fast as possible to that point, and expressing a hope that the whole army soon after daybreak might arrive to take up a position on the roads to Kalouga and Medynsk, and thus bar them against the enemy's progress in either direction."

Yermolow, and the English General by his aide-de-camp, sent similar accounts and solicitations both to the Marshal and Beningsen.

These despatches reached Kutusow's head-quarters on the evening of the 23rd; and as Doctorow advanced, officers were successively sent from different stations on the route to make the report of progress.

Milaradowitch, during the day, had also sent Kutusow notice " that Murat had withdrawn from Woronowo, on the new road to Kalouga and Fominskoie."

Thus Kutusow was in full possession of the requisite information for the government of his proceedings by nine o'clock in the evening, and his army had but to march ten miles, whereas Doctorow, when at Aristowo which he left at seven, was distant from Malo-Jaroslavets twelve miles, without any regular road, but having to wind and make his way through a flat meadow-

MALO JAROSLAVETS. 24TH OCTH. 1812.

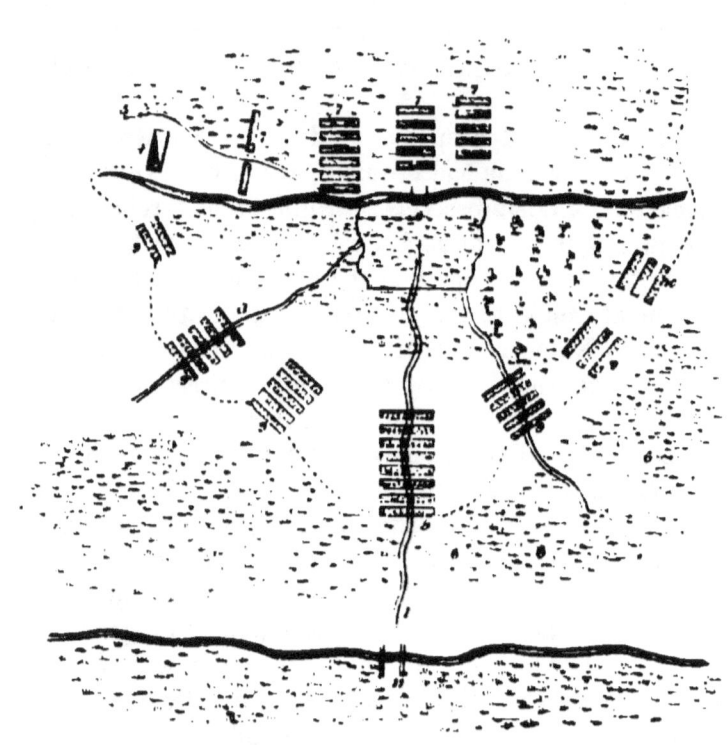

1. Kaluga Road
2. Tula Road
3. Mulin Road
4. Cossaques
5. Wiazma &c Road
6. Boggy
7. French
8. Town taken & retaken 11 times
9. Russians
10. Doektorow
11. Causeway

country full of streamlets and large ditches, unprovided with any bridges for the passage of his artillery, without any pontoons or means except such as could be found on the spot; and yet before day dawned he had crossed the Protwa at Spasskoie, and gained the plain which lay in front of Malo-Jaroslavets.

Every one was ignorant of the locale, and therefore the only disposition that could be made during the imperfect light was to post columns on the different roads leading from the town, and of which there were, including the Spasskoie road, five principal ones, to resist the egress of the enemy (who it was supposed would endeavour to move forward at daybreak), and to confine him within the town until the main Russian army or sufficient reinforcements could arrive to frustrate his project. Doctorow then ordered two regiments of chasseurs, supported by two more, to dash into the town, and drive the enemy (whom some fugitive inhabitants reported to have reached and entered it) out of the place, and over the river Lougea, which ran immediately below, and to destroy his bridge.

Malo-Jaroslavets is built upon the side and summit of a lofty hill, rising immediately above the Lougea (which the enemy called the Lutza), and over which river is a bridge distant about a hundred yards from the ravine, already described as forming its screen and protection.

The ground on both flanks of the town, ascending from the river, is woody and steep, and the ground on the left is intersected with very deep fissures and ravines, so as to be impracticable for artillery movements from the bank of the river.

The whole town is built of wood; near the summit of the hill there is an open space like a Grande Place; and near the ravine, at the bottom are a church and a couple or more of houses that command the approach.

The semicircle occupied by Doctorow, from Terentiewa close to the Medynsk road on his left, and to the Spasskoie road on his right, within which space he also secured the road to Kalouga and Serpoukow, extended about two miles and a half along flat uncovered land; but there were some considerable woods behind and not more than a mile distant, through which the Medynsk and Serpoukow roads ran.

The intervals between the columns were of course very great.

The chasseurs charged forward and quickly dislodged the enemy in the town; but at the bottom of the hill on which it is built ran a deep ravine, the opposite side of which covered the bridge, and behind this ravine the enemy found inassailable shelter.

The English General having gone upon the right flank of the town to reconnoitre this embankment and the position of the bridge, perceived, as day dawned, a large body of the enemy descending the lofty hill on the left bank of the river to pass the bridge and enter the town: this dense body was flocking forward as if quite at ease and unconscious of any serious opposition being designed to the passage and occupation.

The English General having reported this incident to Doctorow, galloped with a battery of light artillery placed under his directions to an elevation which he had selected for its site, and opened its fire almost within grape shot of the mass. At the first discharge there was a general halt, on the second a wavering, on the third a total dispersion, and every one flew forward or scrambled up the hill to get out of the reach of this unexpected cannonade.

The movement of the advanced guard was thus checked, and nearly an hour gained before the Viceroy (who afterwards told the English General at Mantua "that the first shot made him start with more alarm than he had ever felt in his life, as he foresaw at once the fatal consequences") could arrive in person, bring up his artillery, and re-establish order: an essential hour for the Russians.

In about an hour the enemy (Delzon's division), under cover of a heavy fire, recommenced the descent of the hill; and joining the two battalions defending the bridge, pushed up through the streets of the town to the skirts, when the battle began with a violence which corresponded with the magnitude of its objects and the resolute determination of each party to achieve its own.

The enemy was infuriated by despair; the Russians by "the Moscow cry of vengeance."

The very militia who had just joined (and who, being armed only with pikes, formed a third rank to the battalions) not only stood as steady under the cannonade as their veteran comrades, but charged the sallying enemy with as ardent ferocity.

Doctorow, under cover of his powerful artillery, which poured shot, shells, and grape on the advancing columns, re-entered and repossessed himself of the whole town as far as the ravine, except the church and adjoining houses which the enemy had garrisoned, and which commanded the ground beyond, so that the Russians could not remain under their fire to contend for the ravine and seizure of the bridge.

In this attack Delzon was killed, and fell into the arms of his brother, who also received a mortal wound.

Guilleminot succeeded to the command, and resumed the offensive. After various attempts he at last regained the Grande Place; but, though reinforced by the division Broussier, he could not establish any lodgment beyond.

About ten o'clock the corps of Davoust and Ney had reached the heights opposite Malo-Jaroslavets; and every instant it became more manifest that the enemy had resolved to force his passage through the Russian circumvallation.

Officer after officer had been despatched to hasten the arrival of the reinforcements, and of the main army under Kutusow.

Every regiment of Doctorow's corps had been already engaged, and the killed and wounded exceeded five thousand.

The troops, exhausted by their previous marches and seven hours' combat, could scarcely continue the action.

At that anxious moment the corps of Raeffskoi arrived within view; and, as soon as it reached the position, was ordered "to penetrate into, and carry the town by storm."

The "huzzas" of the columns announced to the enemy that they were about to be assailed by fresh troops, whose impulse they quickly found they were unable to resist.

The Russian grenadiers carried all before them; and for the sixth time the Russians became masters of every post but the fortified church and buildings adjacent.

The Viceroy, alarmed for the safety of the troops left within them and in the ravine, as well as for his bridges, a second one having been constructed, urged forward the division Pino to rally the fugitives and lead to another onset.

This division had joined the army the day after the battle of Borodino, and was considered therefore a maiden corps which had to establish a fellowship of reputation. This it most deservedly acquired; but the Russian grenadiers, notwithstanding its impetuous efforts and the flames raging around them (for the town was on fire in all parts), tenaciously maintained their position: and the Viceroy was compelled to send across the river all his corps, except the cavalry, to preserve his têtes du pont.

The Russians in their turn, yielding to the new pressure, retired from the town, and took post at half-cannon shot distance from the outskirts.

The enemy, elated, presented heads of columns at the several outlets, as if they were about to advance on the Russian alignment; but they were unable to face the artillery that swept the esplanade in front, and the Russian chasseurs repossessed themselves of the nearest houses yet unburnt.

At three o'clock another reinforcement arrived, consisting of some battalions of Raeffskoi's corps that had not joined in time from an out station to march with it, and this reinforcement, small as it was, revived the spirit of all.

Napoleon, who had passed the night at Borowsk and reached the heights opposite Malo-Jaroslavets about one o'clock in the afternoon, was enabled thence to watch the road of Spasskoie, and the march of the Russian reinforcements.

He had been highly satisfied with the exertions of the Viceroy to maintain Malo-Jaroslavets, but he was sensibly depressed at the manifold difficulties in which this obstruction involved him and the whole army. Still he flattered himself that Kutusow might not sit down before Malo-Jaroslavets to dispute the passage, since if he did, he was not prepared to hazard a general battle for his removal, as several of his corps were absent and could not be recalled.

This hope, however, was weakened when, about four o'clock, he saw the main Russian army arrive before the town to take up the position for its investment.

Kutusow had perseveringly turned a deaf ear to every messenger and entreaty, founding excuses for delay on the absence of the foragers, and other frivolous pretexts.

The thunder of the cannonade had shaken the very windows of his quarters; but it was not until after his dinner meal that he ordered his droska, and five o'clock had passed before the army occupied its already selected stations.

The corps of Borosdin and the third division of the third corps relieved the sixth corps, and joining the remains of the seventh corps, entered the town, obtaining at first some partial success; but the army of the Viceroy had been so reinforced within it, and the flames of the burning houses had so extended and raged with such violence, that retention of any portion but the skirts was impracticable.

The enemy had also established considerable batteries that swept the whole interior; and spreading to the right and left of the town, had extended his right nearly to the village of Terentiewa, and his left to Czerikowo on the road to Spasskoie.

The Russian chasseurs, however, continued to occupy the gardens, hedges, and ruins, whence they kept up an active musketry fire till eleven at night. The vigour of the cannonade had ceased at nine, but shells were thrown till nearly midnight.

The enemy in this sanguinary conflict must have lost nearly ten thousand men: the Russians somewhat less.

About the same number of troops had been actually engaged on each side, and might amount to twenty-two thousand or twenty-three thousand men.

The Russian general Dorokoff was mortally wounded. On the enemy's side, Delzon and Levie were killed, and Pino, Gefflenga, and Fontana wounded.

The town had been consumed to ashes, and with it all the severely wounded.

After sunset the spectacle had been indescribably magnificent and interesting. The crackling flames—the dark shadows of the combatants flitting amongst them—the hissing ring of the grape as it flew from the licornes—the rattling of the musketry—the ignited shells traversing and crossing in the atmosphere—the wild shouts of the combatants, and all the accompaniments of the sanguinary struggle formed an ensemble seldom witnessed, and which made a greater impression from the decisive consequences which attached to the issue.

The Italian army had displayed qualities which entitled it evermore to take rank amongst the bravest troops of Europe. It had confronted and sustained in the earlier period of the day a superior and concentrated weight of artillery that might have daunted and subdued the firmness of the most resolute veterans; and throughout the whole action, and under all its vicissitudes, had evinced an elasticity and energy that never drooped or relaxed.

Doctorow might perhaps have reached and destroyed the enemy's bridge, if, instead of making his attack with only four battalions of chasseurs, he had in the first instance thrown into the town, and brought to bear on the flanks, all his force; but he arrived in the dark, knew nothing of the locality or of the enemy's numbers, and, as there were several fords between Spasskoie and the town, he had every reason to fear an attack on his rear from that side.

When the Viceroy brought up his artillery and planted his batteries to sweep the ground leading to the bridge, approach was no longer practicable, nor could the bridge be reached by the Russian shot from any point; for the river towards the town made a rentrant bend, in which the bridge lay, and thus concealed and protected it by the circumjacent ground.

Had Kutusow sent forward a corps by a forced march as soon as he received the first information of the enemy's movement (he ought to have sent forward three thousand horse and as many infantry, by rapid conveyance for which he had abundant means, with some flying artillery), and advanced the next morning at daybreak with the army, he might have anticipated the enemy's arrival or effected their dislodgment before the Viceroy was reinforced; but by not taking any measure to aid Doctorow, he threw a cruel weight upon his corps, and he afforded the enemy an opportunity for nearly twelve hours to effect a passage* and take a position beyond the town, from which he might have checked the approach of the Russian army whilst filing his remaining columns and artillery on the Kalouga or Medynsk roads.

At eleven o'clock at night Kutusow summoned all the generals to his bivouac in front of the town, and issued an order of battle, as he said that "he had made up his mind to resist the advance of Napoleon, and that he was prepared to decide the fate of the enemy by a general action." On which the English General went up to him, and shaking his hand, "congratulated him upon the decision as one worthy of the Marshal's character, and the great cause confided to his charge." He at the same time "begged that all former misunderstandings might be obliterated, and in the transactions of the ensuing day he hoped for opportunity to render him useful service." The Marshal said "he had determined to finish the war on that spot—to succeed or make the enemy pass over his body,"† and requested the English General "to keep up constant communication with him from every point of the field where he might be moving during the combat," and

---

* After Kutusow's arrival in the field, the Prince of Oldenburg rode up to the English General and asked him "if he had seen the Marshal?" He said, pointing to a distant tree, "He may be in that direction." "No," replied the Prince, "that cannot be, for I have just seen a shell pass beyond."

† He then expressed himself with a solemnity of devoted patriotism that would have become Leonidas at the pass of Thermopylæ; but, alas! his subsequent conduct did not confirm the belief of his sincerity.

authorized him " to use his name on every emergency as bearing an order from himself."

Above eighty thousand men were placed in position, with nearly seven hundred pieces of cannon, pointing their muzzles on all the sallying points of the town.

The enemy could not be more than seventy thousand strong; for a large force had moved with the great convoy on the Mojaisk road, and Poniatowski with his corps had been detached to Wereia, with instructions to reconnoitre the road to Medynsk.

The state of the enemy was moreover calculated to put the Russian commander at ease with regard to the result of the intended obstruction.

It was now indisputable that the enemy was not proposing to entangle his adversary by a series of complicated operations, but that his sole object was "transit," without the passport he had been so long expecting. That in case of success he could not afford time to pursue his advantage, and deviate from this sole point de mire of his movement. That should the enemy even penetrate the Russian semicircle of investment, and gain the Kalouga or Medynsk line of road, the Russian divided wings would have nothing to apprehend from separation, but might immediately act as distinct corps to harass his flank and rear.

The enemy had neither provisions nor ammunition for protracting manœuvres.

About a mile and a half from Malo-Jaroslavets on the Kalouga road ran the rivulet of Koricza, through a very deep and broad ravine: this rivulet formed a boggy soil and marsh: over this marsh a narrow causeway was constructed, and extended a good quarter of a mile.

' Beyond the causeway rose a high hill, which ran parallel with and commanded the whole ravine.

A division stationed on this hill, with a due proportion of artillery, would have been able to resist the advance of any enemy, however numerous, and would have rendered return very difficult for that portion which might have descended into the ravine.

The Russian commander therefore could apply the mass of his force to guard the Medynsk road, and cover the Serpoukow road. Whichever way the enemy turned, he was in a position to head, flank, and pursue him without exposing his own attacking columns to any pressure beyond their means of counteraction.

Three hours had elapsed in busy and zealous preparation, when, about two in the morning, the generals were again summoned by Kutusow.

All assembled, as each afterwards admitted, with concurrent misgivings as to the object of their meeting.

Kutusow, sitting in the midst of the circle, shortly acquainted them that " he had received information which had induced him to relinquish the intention of defending the ground in front of Malo-Jaroslavets, and determined him to retire behind the Koricza to secure the road to Kalouga and communication with the Oka."

This announcement was a thunderbolt that caused a momentary stupor. It was, however, represented to him, " that such a movement, in such a moment, and under the circumstances of darkness and the narrow causeway on the line of retreat, could not be executed without perilous confusion; and that the enemy, seeing this, would doubtless endeavour to increase it by an attack; that the whole army would be placed in jeopardy, and the rear guard inevitably lost, if the enemy availed himself of his advantage."

The English General enforcing these considerations was told by the Marshal, "I don't care for your objections. I prefer giving my enemy a 'pont d'or,' as you call it, to receiving a 'coup de collier:' besides, I will say again, as I have told you before, that I am by no means sure that the total destruction of the Emperor Napoleon and his army would be such a benefit to the world; his succession would not fall to Russia or any other continental power, but to that which already commands the sea, and whose domination would then be intolerable."

The English General only replied "that the occasion was one for the execution of military duty, not for political altercation, which he should postpone; and that the Marshal ought in the discharge of that duty always to respect the maxim, 'Fais ce que dois, advienne que pourra.'"

All further argument was a waste of time, and minutes were precious.

The retreat was instantly begun, and conducted with a vigour, a rapidity, and success that were scarcely credible even to the eye-witnesses.

Before day-break the causeway had been passed by the greater part of the artillery, but still an immense number of carriages and troops were battling to gain entrance upon it.

Fortunately the enemy could not perceive what was passing beyond the table-land; and Ouwarrow, who with a considerable body of cavalry formed the rear guard, made such a disposition as to render the enemy uncertain as to the movement of the army.

It was nevertheless a most critical moment.

The English General had returned to the rear guard to report the confusion in the ravine, and the necessity of tenacity for some time to permit its clearance.

The débouchement of the enemy's columns was anticipated with great anxiety.

A shell thrown at the cavalry from the skirts of the town indicated the commencement of the sally; a second confirmed the assurance; and the burst of a furious cannonade was expected from instant to instant.

Ouwarrow said to the English General, "We will hold to the last, and at least save our honour out of the wreck; but we are lost."

Happily, and inexplicably, the enemy's fire ceased, and no forward movement was made from the town. Time rolled on—the rear guard remained undisturbed, and the shells which had been thrown had usefully assisted, by the alarm they had occasioned, to clear the passage of the causeway; so that about eleven o'clock Ouwarrow quietly retired with his rear guard, and entered the new position.

It was a most unaccountable inaction on the part of the enemy, and altogether another Providential escape for the Russian army.

Napoleon's star no longer guided his course, for after the rear guard had retired, had any, even the smallest reconnoissance, advanced to the brow of the hill over the ravine—had the slightest demonstration of a continued offensive movement been made, Napoleon would have obtained a free passage for his army on the Kalouga or Medynsk roads, through a fertile and rich country to the Dnieper; since Kutusow, resolved on falling back *behind the Oka, had actually issued the orders " to retire there in case of the enemy's approach to his new position."*

Such is that so-called *destiny* which is supposed occasionally to assume the government of human transactions, and to shape them to desired and prescribed ends; the idea of which destiny made Napoleon exclaim after the battle of Culm—

> " J'ai vécu, commandé, vaincu quarante années ;
> Du monde entier j'ai eu les destinées ;
> Et j'ai toujours connu qu'en chaque événement
> Le destin des états dépend d'un moment."

Whilst Kutusow was preparing to fly from shadows, Napoleon was deliberating on his environing dangers.

When the combat had ceased he had returned to his head-quarters at Gorodnia, and called Berthier, Bessières, Murat, and Lobau to his council. Spreading a map of Russia before them, as General Gourgaud states, "he submitted the following question:—

"It appears that the enemy keeps his ground: in the situation of the army, is it advantageous to give him battle or not?"

Murat and Bessières were against it; Lobau agreed with them, and said decidedly, "My opinion is in favour of retreat by the shortest and best known route, that is by Mojaisk, and with the greatest expedition."

After an hour's discussion Napoleon broke up the council without expressing his own views or intention, but sent orders to Davoust " to take the command of his advanced guard;" and to Ney "that he should move from Fominskoie to a position between Borowsk and Malo-Jaroslavets, but leave a division at Borowsk to guard the great artillery park, and an immensity of baggage which had there been collected."

On the 25th, at daybreak, as Napoleon was proceeding with his usual escort of three squadrons towards Malo-Jaroslavets, and had advanced above a mile on the road, he was alarmed by a Cossack "hurrah," which burst suddenly on his right, and in a moment the plain was covered with ten regiments of Cossacks that had passed the Lougea at a ford left unguarded, and had ambushed themselves in a contiguous wood.

The escort formed and advanced to check their onset, but it was compelled to give way, and Napoleon would have been overtaken in his flight to Gorodnia, if a corps of grenadiers à cheval and of dragoons had not presented themselves to cover his escape.

The Cossacks dispersed, part taking to the interior, part recrossing the Lougea at a bridge, near a mill, four miles above Malo-Jaroslavets; they carried off eleven cannon belonging to the park of the Imperial Guard, the whole of which they had surprised; but want of draught-horses, as the enemy's had been taken to water, prevented them from removing the remainder.

During the day another regiment of Cossacks had hovered round Borowsk, making various successful attacks on flying detachments, which yielded them much booty and many prisoners.

This encounter delayed Napoleon's arrival at Malo-Jaroslavets till near mid-day, when he examined the ground which the Russian army had occupied, and then returned to Gorodnia, thus losing another irreparable twenty-four hours.

On the 26th Napoleon again set out for Malo-Jaroslavets, but on receiving intelligence that the Russian army had fallen back, instead of taking advantage of the roads that were in consequence laid open to his uninterrupted march, he ordered the retreat of his own army by Mojaisk and Wiazma on Smolensk.

Before Napoleon could come to such a conclusion he must have been very conscious of the extreme weakness of his army, for the march he now decided on undertaking was one of two hundred and sixty miles through a devastated country, whose towns, sacked and burnt, offered no shelter or supply against the inclemency of winter and the pressure of want; whilst the fact of a compulsory retreat by such a line tended to discourage his troops, and disqualify them still more for the exertions they would be required to make.

Napoleon had to reproach himself in some measure for the obstruction he met with at Malo-Jaroslavets; for he had employed six days in making the march from Moscow, not eighty miles, including the day lost at Fominskoie. He should have raced to gain Malo-Jaroslavets, and might have occupied it on the 21st, and then three roads would have been open for his selection:—

1st. The road to Kalouga.

2nd. On Mohilew by Metchovsk, Gisdra, Roslaul, and Mstislaw.

3rd. On Smolensk, by Medynsk, Joukhnow, and Jelnia.

All these roads were good, and ran through sufficiently provisioned country ; the last route, by Kutusow's retreat, still remained free for his use.

On the 26th Napoleon slept at Borowsk—on the 27th at Wereia: the weather that night first turned cold, the thermometer falling four degrees below freezing point, but the days still continued sunny and fine.

On the 28th Napoleon passed through Mojaisk, and received intelligence from Davoust that "in the night of the 26th and 27th he had evacuated Malo-Jaroslavets, and had reached Borowsk, only followed by some Cossack detachments."

On the 29th Napoleon proceeded with his Guard over the "superb field" (as he had termed it when a conqueror) of Borodino, and on which thirty thousand bodies still remained unburied.

What must have been the reflections of the fugitive chief, not on that which was to come, but on that which he was relinquishing? His courage might find support in the excitement of its impending ordeals, but from what source of consolation could he soothe the anguish of his baffled aspirations? On that same day he arrived at Gjatsk, and on the 31st at Wiazma ; on this day also all his corps d'armée had reached the high road to Smolensk.

The Imperial Guard, Murat's cavalry, Mortier, and Junot had passed Wiazma.

Poniatowski, who had fallen back from Wereia, had arrived at Gjatsk, and the Viceroy had moved a march beyond.

Davoust had gained Gridnewa, between Wiazma and Borodino; but the Cossacks had taken from him twenty-seven cannon, two eagles, and several hundred prisoners, also various convoys of sick and wounded with much baggage.

When Napoleon entered Mojaisk, he found fifteen hundred of his sick and wounded collected there on their way from Moscow, and his published orders show that he enjoined their removal in earnest terms; but the carriages of every description were overloaded, and they as well as whole columns of hospitals were successively abandoned to their pitiless fate.

Happy were the first victims!

Whilst the enemy was making his arrangements for the retreat from Malo-Jaroslavets, Kutusow on the same day, the 26th, had retired fifteen miles on the road to Kalouga, thus totally uncovering and abandoning the Medynsk road, and making a chemin d'or for the enemy.

This retrograde movement on Gouczarowo was so inexpedient, so unwarrantable, so inexcusable, that no palliator has been found, even amongst the most friendly Russian commentators on Kutusow's campaign.

Kutusow pretended that the rear of his left was menaced by Poniatowski, who had been ordered to reconnoitre the Medynsk route from Wereia; but so far from any danger being to be apprehended from that quarter, Colonel Ilowaiskoi, with three regiments of Cossacks, had attacked the reconnoitering detachment sent forward by Poniatowski under General Tickewitz, taken him prisoner and two hundred men, with five guns, all he had, and killed five hundred out of one regiment of infantry, and five hundred horse;

moreover, Poniatowski himself, with his corps, had already been ordered by Napoleon to unite with the main army at Mojaisk.

The retreat on Gouczarowo was in truth a scandal, which it is still galling to reflect upon.

On the 27th the Russian army was directed on Polotniangin Zaworty, it being understood that the enemy had taken post at Borowsk.

On the 29th it moved to Adamoskoie, as the evacuation of Borowsk was announced.

On the 30th it proceeded to Kremenskoie through Medynsk; and thus five days had been consumed in a horse-shoe sweep of fifty miles, whereas the distance in a direct line and by a good road did not exceed twenty-five.

On the 31st the direction of the army was changed: the two preceding days it had pointed on Mojaisk, whereas now it made a sharp turn to the left, as if to gain Wiazma; and it was given out to the troops, on authority, that the enemy's line of retreat was there to be pierced. A proclamation of Kutusow's was also circulated, in which, after adverting to the enemy's flight from the capital, he called on all Russians "to extinguish the flames of Moscow in the blood of the fugitives;" and concluded with an appeal to the military in the following words: "Peace and glory await you! God is our guide."

On the 1st the march was continued on Kousowy.

On the 2nd to Souleiko.

On the 3rd to Doubrowa.

On the 4th to Biskowo, distant about seven or eight miles from Wiazma, with a good road and favourable intervening country for the movement of the army.

Milaradowitch had been permitted to follow the enemy's movement from Malo-Jaroslavets with his own corps and Passkewitch's.

Platow was ordered to co-operate with a corps of cavalry and his Cossacks.

On the 2nd of November Milaradowitch with an advanced guard of cavalry had reached the defile of Tsarewo Zalomich, on the Mojaisk and Wiazma road, at the very moment the Viceroy's columns were passing. Milaradowitch saw that they were in great disorder, but having no infantry with him, he prudently forbore a partial advantage, which by giving alarm might precipitate the enemy's march.

Whilst making his dispositions for the attack on the ensuing morning, he despatched an officer to Kutusow, to advise him of the enemy's situation, and of his intended attack; also to urge a simultaneous one by the Marshal in the enemy's rear behind Wiazma.

In consequence of this information Kutusow at daybreak did march his army from Doubrowa to Biskowo, and there halted!

Early in the morning of the 4th the cavalry of Milaradowitch moved to reach the high road leading from Fedorowskoie to Wiazma: when it arrived near Moksimowa, about eight in the morning, the Viceroy and Poniatowski had already passed this point, but the advance of Davoust was only approaching.

Milaradowitch charged down upon it, threw the enemy into confusion, formed à cheval upon the road, and opened his guns, which he had established on the heights, upon the broken column.

Platow, hearing the cannonade, commenced his

attack upon the rear guard in Fedorowskoie, and in this attack he was supported by the cavalry of Passkewitch.

The enemy maintained Fedorowskoie for some time, but was at last overpowered and vigorously pursued by the cavalry.

The Viceroy, informed by the cannonade of the danger to which Davoust was exposed, immediately faced about and returned with two Italian divisions and the Poles to extricate him, for in need he never deserted a friend. On arriving near Messoidowo he formed his troops on the high adjoining ground, and opened a fire from his guns which enfiladed the Russian left.

The rest of his corps, consisting of the division Pino and the Guards, had been left at Wiazma "to co-operate with the corps of Ney in resisting the Russian army, if it should advance from Biskowo on that city;" and they were ordered " to make the best disposition that their means might permit for that object, and to secure the ulterior retreat of the Viceroy and Davoust."

The whole force of the enemy amounted to at least forty thousand combatants.

Milaradowitch with the Cossacks could not bring more than twenty-five thousand into action.

Davoust, on seeing the Viceroy prepared to assist him, threw forward a cloud of tirailleurs, and moved on with his main body. The Russian cavalry, posted on the road and on each side, could not withstand the united cross fire of the Viceroy, of Davoust's artillery, and of the light troops; but one of the batteries was withdrawn with great difficulty. The regiment of Kharkow's dragoons that had passed beyond the main road was also obliged desperately to cut its way through the enemy to rejoin the Cossacks.

It was not until near ten in the morning that Prince Eugène of Wirtemberg arrived with his infantry division to take part in the action—always a most conspicuous part. Without pausing he attacked the enemy ascending the heights to carry a Russian battery, which still continued its fire, though in the most imminent jeopardy.

The enemy fled; the tirailleurs disappeared, and the main body of Davoust's corps, quitting the road and passing through the open field, filed behind the Viceroy's left to re-form on his right, and compose a consolidated body near Messoidowo.

On the remainder of the Russian infantry coming up, Milaradowitch renewed the attack under the protection of a superior and admirably served artillery. The enemy fell back on a second position, between Rjawets and the farm of Ribeaupierre, and thence, when menaced on both flanks, to some heights in front of Wiazma, where they were reinforced by the two Italian divisions, the Italian guards, and the corps of Ney.

The Russian army had arrived at Biskowo about the time the cannonade began; the soldiers with reluctance piled their arms, and impatiently awaited the beat of drum to resume them.

Every Russian discharge seemed loaded with the censure of their Emperor, the indignation of the country, and the reproach of comrades at their absence and the protracting delay.

Beningsen and all the other generals implored Kutusow to march, or detach a portion of his force.

The English General represented "that even a division of cavalry with some flying artillery must embarrass the enemy, and perhaps might achieve a 'coup-de-main' in his rear of influential importance." Kutusow remained inflexible, only saying "the time was not yet come."

The English General immediately required a courier's passport, and despatched one of his aides-de-camp, Baron Brinken, of the Russian dragoons, to the Emperor, at S. Petersburg, with a statement of the transactions that had occurred since the combat of Malo-Jaroslavets, the present refusal to move against the enemy hotly engaged by Milaradowitch, and the discontent of the army, which felt dishonoured, if not betrayed. He then proceeded with Beningsen, General Sabloukoff, a gallant general of cavalry, and a party of Cossacks, to the scene of action.* On reaching it they found Milaradowitch pressing the enemy back on the town with so much vigour, that they had been obliged to deploy and bring under fire their whole force.

The ground between the two armies was open, but undulating on the flanks, and behind the town it was wooded. After some time the English General, wishing to ascertain what natural obstacles, if any, would have opposed the operations and lodgment of a force from Biskowo on the road from Wiazma to Dorogobouche, and also being desirous of alarming the enemy in his rear, proceeded with five hundred Cossacks, placed under his direction by Milaradowitch, to execute these objects: with them he not only

* Baron Brinken also accompanied him so far, as Wiazma lay on the route by which he was to pass for S. Petersburg.

gained without any interruption the road he proposed to reconnoitre, but actually entered Wiazma with a detachment and made some prisoners, from whom he learned "that a general retreat was being made over some bridges which had been thrown across the Wiazma river, on the left of the town already evacuated except by irremovable sick and wounded; that the baggage and artillery had been retiring all day, and that Napoleon with the Imperial Guard had passed, the preceding day but one."

This was about four o'clock in the afternoon: had the Marshal therefore marched at eight o'clock, or even ten or twelve, Wiazma might have been seized, the bridges destroyed, and the corps of the Viceroy, Poniatowski, Davoust, and Ney would have had no alternative but dispersion, ensuring destruction or surrender.

About two o'clock Kutusow did direct Ouwarrow with three thousand cavalry to proceed to Milarado-witch; but he only arrived in time to open some guns on the left of the enemy retiring in front of Wiazma, and which left was covered by the Ulitza before its confluence near the town with the Wiazma river.

If such might have been the results of a co-operation on the 4th from Biskowo, how much greater advantages had been thrown away by the circuitous march on Aristowo involving a loss of four days, which permitted Napoleon to pass on the second through Wiazma without molestation, and which left Wiazma free for the retreat through it of the following and then distant corps!

The English General having returned to report to Milaradowitch his information, "and that there was

WIAZMA. 3ᴿᴰ NOVʀ

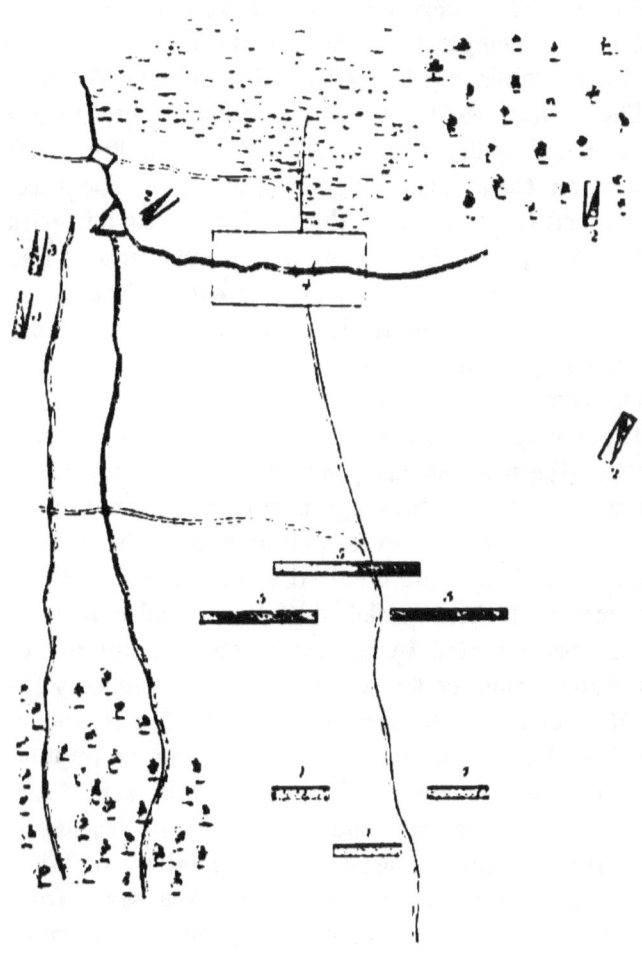

1 Miloradowitch
2 Cossaques
3 3000 Horse Afternoon
4 Wiazma surrounded by old Rampart
5 Ney, Davoust, Beauharnois

no supporting or reserve force on the other side of Wiazma," Milaradowitch pressed forward to precipitate the enemy's retrograde movements, and prevent his establishing himself for the night in Wiazma.

The enemy, fearing to be compromised by a longer defence, and suffering intolerably from the fire which poured on them, made a general retreat. The Viceroy gained the town, and the bridges on its left, with some order; but the corps of Davoust broke, and rushed to the points of passage in great confusion.

Ney steadily covered his retreat; but a regiment of Russian grenadiers charged his rear guard into the town, bayoneting all who resisted.

The enemy, to facilitate their escape, set fire to such parts of the town as had been preserved from former conflagrations, and thus again consigned numbers of their wounded comrades as well as sick to the flames: in one church several hundred were consumed alive, and many of them perished the more miserably by being first mangled by an explosion of a number of live shells; whether left accidentally, or designedly (as the Russians thought) for the destruction of Russians, could not be ascertained. This suspicion or imputation of treachery increased the general horror of the too prevalent ferocity and indiscriminate carnage; but a Swiss family, consisting of a mother, with her two daughters most beautiful girls, was saved from the sanguinary fury which raged, and honourably conducted in safety to a sheltering post.

The enemy had lost in this deadly combat above six thousand killed and wounded; two thousand prisoners, including General Pelletier; a standard, and three cannon.

The Russians had above two thousand killed and wounded, but no prisoners except General Swiczin, whose horse had run away with him in a charge.

Ney, writing to Napoleon at Slavkowo, two days' march from Wiazma, immediately after the action, stated, "Better dispositions might have produced a more favourable result: the most unfortunate event of the day is, however, the circumstance of my troops having been eye witnesses to the disorder of the first (Davoust's) corps. It is a fatal example, impairing the *morale of the soldier*. I am obliged to tell the truth to your Majesty, and I cannot be responsible as if I commanded alone the retreat. I occupy the defile of the wood behind Wiazma, and I will retire during the night. The enemy's cavalry and artillery are numerous, and I calculate that their infantry amounts to twenty thousand men."

Davoust, writing the next day to Berthier, reports, "On this day order has been restored on the march; but there are four thousand men, belonging to all the regiments of the army, who will not move with regularity: on the slightest attack on the part of the enemy they fly, and endanger the steadiness of my columns."

On the 5th the enemy continued their retreat, harassed by the Cossacks and raked by their cannon; but a more formidable destroyer than shot, spear, or sword now declared against Napoleon and the remnants of his army. *Snow* fell from the troubled sky, and Winter assumed her dominion " to smite him and all his devoted host with its wrath."

The enemy's army marched in the following order:—

Advanced Guard, Junot.
General Gerard.
2nd and 4th Corps of Cavalry.
Old Guard.
Poniatowski.
Viceroy.
Davoust.
Ney.
Rear Guard.

Ney and the other corps d'armée on the night of the action at Wiazma had, as he stated in his report to Napoleon, bivouacked in a great forest.

On the 5th Ney reached Semlewo, on the 6th Dorogobouche, during which marches he lost several cannon and fifteen hundred men.

Napoleon had projected an ambuscade for the Russians, but the state of his army obliged him to relinquish that design.

On the 6th Napoleon's head-quarter guard reached Mikailouka, where he was overwhelmed with distressing intelligence.

From Paris he received advice of the attempt of Malet to make a revolution, and from Victor an account of the combat of Czasniki,* whilst every moment the increased falling and freezing snow added to the perils of his situation.

Berthier, under Napoleon's dictation, wrote to Victor, "Unite your six divisions and attack the Russians, drive them before you to the Dwina, and retake Polotzk; in a few days your rear will be inundated with clouds of Cossacks.

"The army and the Emperor to-morrow will be at Smolensk, but greatly fatigued by a march of a hundred and twenty leagues without a stop. Resume the

* Or Tchasniki.

offensive: our safety depends on it. Every day's delay is a calamity.

"The cavalry of the army is already unhorsed: the cold has killed all the horses. March! it is the order of the Emperor, and necessity."

On the 7th the head-quarters of Napoleon's army were established at Sloboneva, on the right bank of the Dnieper.

On the 8th they were transferred to Bredechino.

Junot, with the advanced guard, passed six miles beyond Smolensk on the road to Mstislaw.

On the 9th Napoleon re-entered Smolensk, and, as "grief never comes but in battalions," he there learned that the Russians had taken Witepsk; that the Viceroy had suffered great loss on his way to Witepsk, to which he had been ordered to march on leaving Dorogobouche; that he had been obliged to give up the prescribed movement, and was falling back on the main army; and that Baraguay d'Hilliers, with a brigade, had laid down his arms at Linkowo.

The Viceroy's route on Witepsk had been traced by Doukouchina and Poreczie; but on the first day's march from Dorogobouche the road was intersected by a little river called the Vop, with very steep rough banks, and which river flowed at no great distance into the Dnieper. The surface was frozen, but not sufficiently to bear. On the 8th an attempt was made to throw a bridge across; but as the troops were about to pass on the morning of the 9th, from want of proper timbers to support, it gave way and fell. At this moment the Cossacks appeared, and some of them, dashing through the icy river, gained the opposite bank.

The Viceroy, forced to attempt a similar passage, directed the Guards to wade; the water and broken ice reached their breasts, but they passed.

The Viceroy, with his staff, followed; then the artillery and cavalry, amidst the greatest confusion, were advanced for the same purpose.

The foremost guns reached the opposite slopes, which had been cut out of the banks by the pioneers to favour the ascent, but the wet soil of the slopes being soon covered with an icy surface, the foremost horses could not find footing to drag up the guns; the following guns stuck in the mud, and, as they stood in the bed of the river, were soon frozen fast.

The impossibility of saving any carriage being now manifest, a general pillage of them by the troops remaining behind could not be prevented: no orders were obeyed, no property was respected. Amidst this scene of lawlessness, violence, and terror, the Cossacks, eager for their share of the booty, had charged upon the multitude, and, had not some gunners turned the artillery that was being abandoned on them, they would have destroyed or swept off the whole. The river was soon full of dead horses and drowned men, whom the intensity of the cold had benumbed, whilst the situation of the Guards who had passed, with wet clothes frozen to their bodies, with no fuel to dry themselves, and no food for their support except such as they happened to be carrying in their own havresacks, was deplorable in the extreme.

The division Broussier had continued on the left bank during the whole of the 9th to aid the passage of the crowd and prevent a general rush and massacre from the still hovering Cossacks; but on the morning of the 10th it was also obliged to wade through the river, leaving behind above sixty cannon, all the tumbrils and carriages containing much plunder, and the ground strewed with baggage wreck.

Out of fourteen thousand combatants who had commenced the march, not above six thousand men stood under arms; and of ninety-two pieces of cannon only twelve remained: but all admitted that "the Viceroy had, during this distressing trial, displayed that spirit, presence of mind, and activity which became the 'Chevalier sans peur et sans reproche.'"

Platow, who had gained the right bank to head the shattered corps, opened his artillery as it entered the plain on which Doukouchina is situated, and in which town Colonel Ilowaiskoi, who had been under the orders of Winzingerode at Moscow, was stationed with two regiments of Cossacks.

The Viceroy, advancing in close columns, succeeded in gaining the town, in which he found supplies: these were much needed, for his troops were quite exhausted, and unable to move again till the 12th, when, setting fire to the town, the Viceroy began his march on Smolensk, for he could not attempt to reach Witepsk.

On the 12th, at night, he halted at Wlodiminowa, and on the 13th he arrived at Smolensk, losing on his way two more guns and some hundred prisoners taken by the pursuing Cossacks.

The preservation of any part of the corps was nevertheless a meritorious, almost a marvellous, achievement.

The brigade of Baraguay d'Hilliers, taken at Linkowo, had been one of a division composed of four demi-provisional brigades lately arrived from France.

Napoleon, when he had intended to move on the Kalouga road, ordered this general to take up a position between Jelnia and Smolensk; but when he relinquished that intention, he had omitted to send, or could not convey, fresh instructions for this isolated force.

Orloff Denisoff, Davydoff, Sislavin, and Figuer, uniting their partisan detachments, attacked, on the 9th, the brigade posted at Linkowo.

The enemy, surprised, attempted to secure a height that covered the village, but, being twice driven back by the Russian batteries, exposed to a destructive fire from which they could find no shelter, and despairing of succour, Brigadier-General Augereau, sixty officers, and two thousand men laid down their arms.

Some cavalry, which was marching to their aid, was charged and cut to pieces. The remainder of the division, hearing of these disasters, retired from their stations at Dolgoumestre and Jaquina, and fell back on Smolensk.

On the morning of the 4th, the snow, as has been noted, had first fallen in large flakes so as to cover the soil.

On the 5th the quantity increased considerably.

On the 6th rose that razor-cutting wind which hardened the snow and made it sparkle as it fell like small diamonds, whilst the air, under the effect of its contracting action, was filled with a continual ringing sound.

The atmosphere seemed to be rarefied till it became quite crisp and brittle.

The enemy, already afflicted by hunger, fatigue, sickness, and wounds, were ill prepared for this new, though always certain calamity. From this time a state of feeling prevailed that denaturalized humanity —a general recklessness pervaded all—a callousness to every consideration but selfish momentary relief, with one *honourable exception* in favour of the French, who, *when captive, could not be induced by any temptation, by any threats, by any privations, to cast reproach on their Emperor as the cause of their misfortunes and sufferings.* It was "the chance of war," "unavoidable difficulties," and "destiny," but "not the fault of Napoleon."

The famished, dying of hunger, refused food rather than utter an injurious word against their chief to indulge and humour vindictive inquirers.

With this excepted trait, rage appeared to madden all. Everything that could be fired was set in flames, and the same ruthless violence was directed against helpless comrades as against foes.

The maniacs tore away the clothing of their own companions when they were to be abandoned.

If any food was found, they turned their arms against each other. They repulsed with force every one who endeavoured to share their bivouac fire when one could be lighted, and they mercilessly killed every prisoner.

Nor was the Russian peasant, victim of the enemy's fury in his advance as well as retreat, less ferociously savage.

A demoniacal frenzy infuriated Russians and French alike.

On coming to the first enemy's bivouac on the morning of the 5th, some Cossacks accompanying the English General, seeing a gun and several tumbrils at the bottom of a ravine, with the horses lying on the ground, dismounted, and taking up the feet of several, hallooed, ran, and kissed the English General's knees and horse, danced, and made fantastic gestures like crazy men. When the delirium had somewhat subsided, they pointed to the horses' shoes and said— "God has made Napoleon forget that there was a winter in our country. In spite of Kutusow the enemy's bones shall remain in Russia."

It was soon ascertained that all horses of the enemy's army were in the same improperly-shod state, except those of the Polish corps, and the Emperor's own, which the Duke de Vicenza, with due foresight, had kept always roughshod, as is the usage of the Russians.

From that time the road was strewed with guns, tumbrils, equipages, men, and horses; for no foraging parties could quit the high-road in search of provisions, and consequently the debility hourly increased.

Thousands of horses soon lay groaning on the route, with great pieces of flesh cut off their necks and most fleshy parts by the passing soldiery for food; whilst thousands of naked wretches were wandering like spectres, who seemed to have no sight or sense, and who only kept reeling on till frost, famine, or the Cossack lance put an end to their power of motion. In that wretched state no nourishment could have saved them. There were continual instances, even amongst the Russians, of their lying down, dozing, and dying within a quarter of an hour after a little bread had been supplied.

All prisoners, however, were immediately and invariably stripped stark naked and marched in columns in that state, or turned adrift to be the sport and the victims of the peasantry, who would not always let them, as they sought to do, point and hold the muzzles of the guns against their own heads or hearts to terminate their suffering in the most certain and expeditious manner; for the peasantry thought that this mitigation of torture " would be an offence against the avenging God of Russia, and deprive them of His further protection."

A remarkable instance of this cruel spirit of retaliation was exhibited on the pursuit to Wiazma.

Milaradowitch, Beningsen, Korf, and the English General, with various others, were proceeding on the high-road, about a mile from the town, where they found a crowd of peasant-women, with sticks in their hands, hopping round a felled pine-tree, on each side of which lay about sixty naked prisoners, prostrate, but with their heads on the tree, which those furies were striking in accompaniment to a national air or song which they were yelling in concert; while several hundred armed peasants were quietly looking on as guardians of the direful orgies. When the cavalcade approached, the sufferers uttered piercing shrieks, and kept incessantly crying " La mort, la mort, la mort!"

Near Dorogobouche a young and handsome Frenchwoman lay naked, writhing in the snow, which was ensanguined all around her. On hearing the sound of voices she raised her head, from which extremely long black, shining hair flowed over the whole person. Tossing her arms about with wildest expression of agony, she kept frantically crying, "Rendez moi mon enfant"—Restore me my babe. When soothed sufficiently to explain her story, she related, "That on sinking from weakness, a child newly born had been snatched away from her; that she had been stripped by her associates, and then stabbed to prevent her falling alive into the hands of their pursuers."

Even amongst the Russians there were also instances—and those not rare—of benevolently disposed and highly-educated men adopting measures of equally unjustifiable character to terminate protracted sufferings.

When General Beningsen and the English General, with their staffs,* were one afternoon on the march, they fell in with a column of seven hundred naked prisoners under a Cossack escort; this column, according to the certificate given on starting, had consisted of twelve hundred and fifty men, and the commandant stated "that he had twice renewed it, as the original party dropped off, from the prisoners he collected en route, and that he was then about completing his number again."

Amongst this wretched convoy was a young man who attracted notice by his appearance, and by his keeping a little aloof from the main group. One of General Beningsen's staff, of high titular rank,† after entering into some conversation with him

---

* The Hon. Captain Dawson Damer, who had just joined the English General as an aide-de-camp, was present on this occasion—a most gallant officer and gentleman.

† The Grand Duke Constantine.

about his country, rank, and capture, asked him "if he did not under present circumstances wish for death?" "Yes," said the unhappy man, "I do, if I cannot be rescued, for I know I must in a few hours perish by inanition, or by the Cossack lance, as I have seen so many hundred comrades do, on being unable from cold, hunger, and fatigue to keep up. There are those in France who will lament my fate—for their sake I should wish to return; but if that be impossible, the sooner this ignominy and suffering are over the better." The questioner then said that "from the bottom of his heart he pitied his fate, but that aid for his preservation was impossible: if, however, he really wished to die at once, and would lie down on his back, to give proof of the interest he took in him, he himself would inflict the death blow on his throat."

General Beningsen was some little distance in advance, but the English General, who had stopped to hear the conversation, on finding that such a cruel issue was proposed, remonstrated against the idea, urging the necessity "of saving the unfortunate officer,"—for so he proved to be,—"coûte qui coûte," after having excited hopes by engaging in a discourse with him.

Finding that there was no inclination to abandon the intention, the English General spurred forward to overtake and bring back General Beningsen; but happening to turn round before he could reach him, he saw the Russian officer, who had dismounted, strike with his sabre the fatal blow that severed the head nearly from the body! nor could this officer afterwards be made to think that he had done a reprehensible act. He defended it "by the motive, and the relief afforded to the sufferer, there being no means to save him, and if there had been, no one daring to employ them."

The slaughter of the prisoners with every imaginable previous mode of torture by the peasantry still continuing, the English General sent off a despatch to the Emperor Alexander " to represent the horrors of these outrages and propose a check." The Emperor by an express courier instantly transmitted an order " to prohibit the parties under the severest menaces of his displeasure and punishment;" at the same time he directed "a ducat in gold to be paid for any prisoner delivered up by peasant or soldier to any civil authority for safe custody." The order was beneficial as well as creditable, but still the conductors were offered a higher price for their charge, and frequently were prevailed on to surrender their trust, for they doubted the justifiable validity of the order.

Famine also ruthlessly decimated the enemy's ranks. Groups were frequently overtaken, gathered round the burning or burnt embers of buildings which had afforded cover for some wounded or frozen; many in these groups were employed in peeling off with their fingers and making a repast of the charred flesh of their comrades' remains.

The English General having asked a grenadier of most martial expression, so occupied, " if this food was not loathsome to him?" " Yes," he said, " it was; but he did not eat it to preserve life—*that* he had sought in vain to lose—only to lull gnawing agonies." On giving the grenadier a piece of food, which happened to be at command, he seized it with voracity, as if he would devour it whole; but suddenly checking himself, he appeared suffocating with emotion: looking at the bread, then at the donor, tears rolled down his cheeks; endeavouring to rise, and making an effort as if he would catch at the hand which administered to his want, he fell back and had expired before he could be reached.

Innumerable dogs crouched on the bodies of their former masters, looking in their faces, and howling their hunger and their loss; whilst others were tearing the still living flesh from the feet, hands, and limbs of moaning wretches who could not defend themselves, and whose torment was still greater, as in many cases their consciousness and senses remained unimpaired.

The clinging of the dogs to their masters' corpses was most remarkable and interesting. At the commencement of the retreat, at a village near Selino, a detachment of fifty of the enemy had been surprised. The peasants resolved to bury them alive in a pit: a drummer boy bravely led the devoted party and sprang into the grave. A dog belonging to one of the victims could not be secured; every day, however, the dog went to the neighbouring camp, and came back with a bit of food in his mouth to sit and moan over the newly-turned earth. It was a fortnight before he could be killed by the peasants, afraid of discovery.*

---

* A similar anecdote is related by Pliny.—"Sed super omnia in nostro ævo actis pópuli Romani testatum, Appio Junio et P. Silio Coss., cum animadverteretur ex causa Nerouis Germanici filii in T. Sabinum et servitia ejus, unius ex his canem nec a carcere abigi potuisse, nec a corpore recessisse abjecto in gradibus Gemoniis, mœstos edentem ululatus, magna populi Romani corona circumstante; ex qua cum quidam ei cibum objecisset, ad os defuncti tulisse. Innatavit idem cadavere in Tiberim abjecto, sus-

The peasants showed the English General the spot, and related the occurrence with exultation, as if they had performed a meritorious deed.

The shots of the peasantry at stragglers or prisoners rang continuously through the woods; and altogether it was a complication of misery, of cruelty, of desolation, and of disorder, that can never have been exceeded in the history of mankind. Many incidents and crimes are indeed too horrible or disgusting for relation.

Milaradowitch had continued his pursuit with activity, causing the enemy much loss at the passage of the Osma, and again at Dorogobouche, where he took four guns and four hundred prisoners; but finding the high road too destitute to afford any supply, he quitted it to move through cross roads, leaving only the Cossacks under Ibedorowskoi with two regiments of dragoons to follow the enemy, from whom he took at Solowirewo, where they passed the Dnieper, twenty-one guns, sixty tumbrils, four hundred soldiers, and many stragglers.

The Russian detachment that scoured the country and hovered on the enemy's flanks, also obtained numerous successes, and seized various depôts. At Khamanstrewo thirteen hundred prisoners were made by them, and as many at Kuraziwo.

Milaradowitch on the 14th of November reached Raquilowra and Ladorozie; and on the same day Count Ojarowski, who had been detached with a flying

tentare conatus, effusa multitudine ad spectandum animalis fidem."—*Plin. Nat. Hist.*, lib. viii. cap. xl.: De Canibus.

corps, entered Krasnoi; but on the arrival of the Old French Guard he withdrew a league to Putkowa.

Napoleon had been employing his time in re-organising his army, consisting now of scarcely forty thousand effective infantry and five thousand cavalry, thus distributed:—

Infantry of the Guard	16,000
1st corps	10,000
4th „	5,000
5th „	8,000
7th „	700
Total	39,700
Cavalry Guard	3,000
4th corps of Cavalry	700
Light Cavalry	1,900
Total	5,600

In addition to this force, there were three thousand dismounted cavalry doing duty as infantry.

Arms were distributed to those who wanted them, and such equipment as the magazines could supply; hand-mills to grind grain, recently arrived from Paris, were also issued, to be thrown away immediately, as useless; but no frost-nails were to be found amongst the stores, and that was the article most wanted for the efficiency of the artillery and cavalry.

Up to this period three hundred and eighty guns had been lost.

Flour and spirits for fifteen days were distributed to the Guards, and for six days to the other corps as they arrived; fifteen hundred oxen had been collected near Krasnoi, and many herds had been sent by the route of Mstislaw to that point for the use of the army, but all had been taken by the Russian light parties, except two hundred head, which the Guards appropriated to themselves; and it is asserted by the French historians that there were at this time thirty thousand sick, wounded, stragglers, followers, and drivers, who had reached Smolensk from Moscow, to whom no rations were issued, and who killed and eat three hundred horses in good condition, belonging to the military equipages.

The cold had now become excessive.

On the 9th of November Réaumur's thermometer had fallen to twelve degrees below zero, and on the 13th to seventeen degrees.

Many men were frozen to death, and great numbers had their limbs, noses, and cheeks frozen.

To add to the distress that prevailed in Smolensk, the Cossacks who had arrived on the 11th, surrounded the city and cut off all communication.

On the 12th Ney was attacked by Yurkoff at Isowickowo.

The action was sanguinary, and lasted the whole day.

Ney preserved his position.

On the 13th Claparède, with a division escorting the military chest, the trophies of Moscow, and the baggage of the head-quarters' staff, set out for Krasnoi.

In the afternoon the Viceroy arrived with the remains of his corps, which began immediately to pillage the stores yet in magazine.

Napoleon, who had retarded his departure until the arrival of the Viceroy, left Smolensk on the 14th, preceded by Mortier. The following instructions were issued by Napoleon through Berthier for Davoust and Ney before he quitted the town:—

"To Marshal Davoust. "Smolensk, 14th of November, 7 o'clock, A.M.

"The Emperor directs you to support the Duke of Elchingen in his retreat: you will therefore relieve the Viceroy, who is to march to-morrow for Krasnoi, in such posts as you may judge it desirable to hold.

"Your corps and that of the Duke are to march on the 16th or 17th, and General Charpentier, who forms the garrison, with three battalions of Poles, will then also quit the city.

"Before you leave, you will blow up all the towers of the walls of Smolensk. The mines are prepared. You will burn all the ammunition, and you will destroy all the tumbrils you cannot remove, &c.

"You will cut the tourillons of the cannon you are unable to take away [there were no workmen or instruments to execute the order]. You will only leave in the hospitals the smallest number of sick possible.

(Signed) "Alexander Berthier."

In a letter addressed to Victor, Berthier also wrote:—

"His Majesty is about to march with a part of the army on Orsza, but this movement can only be made slowly: it is therefore more necessary that you should attack Wittgenstein with the troops you have. The Emperor cannot doubt of your success, and if obtained quickly the result will be most important, as the Emperor may then occupy Witepsk, and take winter quarters between that city, Orsza, and Mohilew, and also along the Dwina on Polotzk.

"These winter quarters will either assure peace during the winter, or prepare for a certain success in the ensuing campaign, by a decided demonstration against S. Petersburg.

"The two great armies, French and Russian, are fatigued; they may take possession of posts by marches, but neither one nor the other can fight a great battle to gain a post.

"Communicate with the Duke of Reggio, and concert together to give battle, which is of the greatest importance for the Emperor's operations.

"Winter quarters, and superiority in the next campaign, depend upon its promptitude as well as issue.

"ALEXANDER BERTHIER.
"Smolensk, 13th of November."

In the same letter Berthier acquainted Victor that "Kutusow was moving on Witepsk."

It would have been an useless interruption of attention engaged in more interesting narrative, if it had been before this point called to the diary of Kutusow's marches after leaving Biskowo.

It suffices to give merely the march routes, for during that period his operations in no way disturbed the enemy's movements.

5th	November		Wiazma.
6th	„		Gawziokowo.
7th	„		Beloi Cholm.
8th and 9th	„		Elna*.
10th	„		Battutino.

* Or Jelnia.

11th and 12th November	.. ..	Labkowo.
13th .. „	.. ..	Tchelkarowo.
14th and 15th „	.. ..	Zaurowo.
16th and 17th „	.. ..	Chilowa.
18th and 19th „	.. ..	Dobroia.

During these marches, leisurely made, the army had suffered such little comparative privation and loss, that when it reached Chilowa, the position in front of the enemy at Krasnoi, the regiments were nearly as effective as when they set out.

The Russian army which had now collected round the ruins of the once colossal enemy, after deducting every corps detached, and estimating the diminution from casualties of all descriptions, amounted to at least eighty thousand combatants. Every arm of these was in high order, with six hundred pieces of well-horsed cannon.

Had Kutusow pressed his march, he might have arrived in Krasnoi on the 13th, or 14th at the very latest; but that was an advantage which Kutusow disdained to take of a flying and failing enemy.

On the 15th Napoleon entered Krasnoi.

Milaradowitch, who had reunited his corps and taken post at Merlino, about five miles from Krasnoi, had cannonaded from commanding ground the enemy's column, which was obliged to abandon in every ravine guns and baggage; about two thousand prisoners were also made, for the rear-guard, driven by a charge from the road, was dispersed in the adjoining woods.

Napoleon, on the night of his arrival, being incommoded by the Russian light parties established too near Krasnoi, ordered an attack to be made on

Count Ojarowski, who had posted himself, on being driven out of Krasnoi, at Putkowa.

General Roguet, with a division of the Young Guard, executed the attack two hours before day break, and expelled the Russians; but on reinforcements being brought up, he was compelled to retire.

Napoleon's situation at Krasnoi was momentarily becoming more critical; but he could not withdraw and abandon the Viceroy, Davoust, and Ney; nor had he sufficient force with him to secure his own retreat on Liady and Orsza.

He therefore resolved to trust to the boldness of his dispositions for suspension of the aggressive movement menaced by the main Russian army, then stationed unexpectedly in view.

With the Young Guard he presented a front to this mass.

With the Old Guard and Claparède's division he occupied the ground in and about the village, and posted his cavalry under Latour Maubourg on the Liady road to cover his line of retreat.

In the middle of this anxious night he was joined by the Viceroy, whose force was reduced to three thousand five hundred combatants, without one gun or an article of baggage.

The Viceroy had quitted Smolensk early on the 15th, and halted at Lubna. Towards evening (having preceded the main column with his staff and the corps of sappers to reconnoitre the road) he was approaching Merlino, when suddenly he saw the route before him fill with a swarm of fugitives driven by a body of Russian cavalry; and immediately afterwards Milaradowitch appeared with his corps on the crest of a hill rising above a ravine, in which he had till then concealed his troops.

The Viceroy directed Guilleminot to assemble the fugitives, and make what stand he could, whilst he galloped back to bring up his column.

This promiscuous crowd, composed of about twelve hundred individuals, amongst whom were eight generals and a motley mass of armed and unarmed stragglers, huddled together in utter disorder, having united with the sappers' staff, the whole fell back in a compact body, which suffered severely under the active fire of the pursuing Russian light artillery.

This herd kept together until it found itself covered by the fire of the Viceroy's advancing battalions, when, as if with one accord, it broke and sought shelter behind their line.

The Viceroy's troops steadily resisted the contagion of this disorder, and even gave animating welcome cheers to the runaways.

Milaradowitch, seeing the forlorn state of the enemy, sent in a flag of truce to propose a surrender, which was rejected.

The enemy had only two guns left—two having been taken already, and during the march eighteen having been abandoned; the corps had also been reduced to five thousand combatants; still the Viceroy was able to maintain himself on some advantageous ground until nightfall, when, leaving the high road, he pushed across the fields by Fomino, Titurnowo, and Menokowo, and reached Krasnoi, saying with Francis the First, "I have lost every thing but our honour."

Napoleon, becoming more alarmed for the safety

of Davoust and Ney, and yet bolder as the danger increased, determined to attack Milaradowitch, lodged on the high road between Katowa and Merlino (where he was hourly making prisoners of the detachments trying to gain Krasnoi), and thus to reopen the communication for the passage of the separated corps.

The disposable force at Napoleon's command only amounted to fifteen thousand infantry, two thousand cavalry, and thirty guns; for the Viceroy with his three thousand five hundred men had been ordered to march on the morning of his arrival on Liady, to secure that point of retreat to the Dnieper.

Mortier commanded the advance; but the combat was of short duration, for Kutusow, on receiving notice of the movement, had directed Milaradowitch to fall back on Chilowa, and leave only some Cossacks on the route.

Davoust had left Smolensk on the 16th, and halted three miles beyond Korytnia to arrest Ney's arrival; but hearing of the Viceroy's disasters, and that the Russians still occupied the road, he despatched advice to Ney "of the necessity he was under to join Napoleon without delay;" and at three o'clock on the morning of the 17th he put his corps in movement.

He had already arrived within two miles of Krasnoi, as Milaradowitch had been withdrawn from the line of route, when Kutusow, on an officer being sent to him, permitted Milaradowitch "to re-advance from Jesskowo, where he had stopped, and open his guns on the left and rear of Davoust's column."

Napoleon, to favour Davoust's junction, had formed his little army in two parallel lines to cover the main road.

The right was thrown on Krasnoi, the left on the ravine of the Lossncia; and as two Russian battalions in Ouwarrowo incommoded the front and left of his position, he made an attack, which dislodged them. Prince Galitzin, to whose corps they belonged, was not allowed to send them any support; nevertheless the Prince opened a destructive cannonade on the enemy's alignment to favour their retreat.

Davoust having effected his junction, and Milaradowitch having approached Prince Galitzin's right, Galitzin, under the authority of Beningsen, determined to recover Ouwarrowo, when a column of the voltigeurs of the Imperial Guard attempted to oppose the march of the division.

This column, charged by two regiments of cuirassiers, formed squares and beat off the assailants; but two pieces of cannon being brought up to play on an angle which they perforated, the attack was renewed, when the whole were either killed or taken.

Ouwarrowo was immediately evacuated, and the enemy's first line, which had moved forward to support the voltigeurs, fell back on seeing their fate; but in its retreat it was shattered by the grape of a company of flying artillery directed by the brave Colonel Nitchin.

Kutusow, who had declared as he was marching from Biskowo that "he would at Krasnoi no longer act the part of Fabius, but draw the sword of Marcellus," had reached this limit to his Fabian policy about two o'clock in the afternoon of the 16th, and there received the intelligence "that Napoleon was in Krasnoi" (not two miles off the spot whence he was surveying it)

KRASNOI, 17TH NOVR.

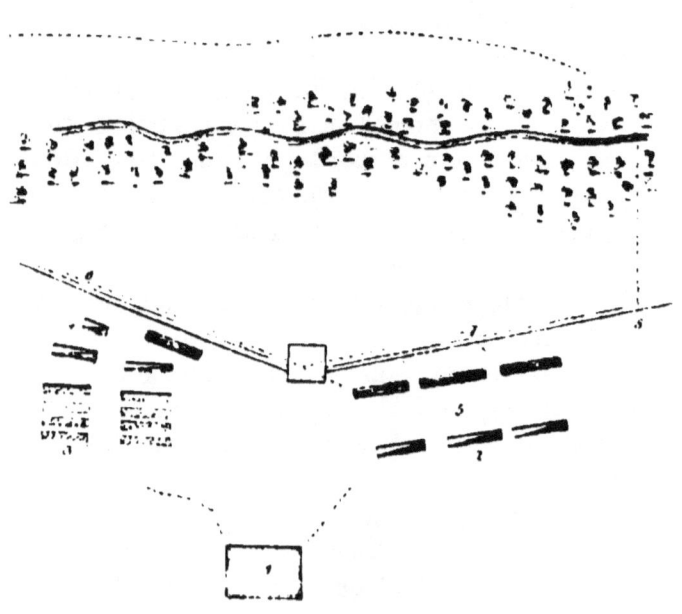

1 Grand Army
2 Benningsen Cavalry
3 Tormanzou
4 Cossaque attack, afternoon
5 French Guards cut down
6 Orsa Road
7 Smolenske Road
8 Ney's combat & line of Retreat

with Claparède's division and his Guards, the remainder of his army being still at Smolensk, or en route to Krasnoi.

There was a loud and general demand by the troops, as they stood in column of march, to advance instantly on Krasnoi; and the cry of "Moscow!" "Moscow!" ran along the ranks; but Kutusow had courage enough to refuse inflexibly his permission; and he ordered the army to bivouac round Chilowa, in full sight of Krasnoi and of every movement made by the enemy.

Nevertheless, apprehending some outbreak of feeling from a too determined opposition to the wish of the army, so vehemently and significantly expressed, he gave out an order of battle " for the attack of the enemy on the *ensuing morning*;" thus wilfully and designedly, as will be shown hereafter, affording to the enemy a whole evening and night for an unmolested retreat on Liady, and the reunion of the corps on march from Smolensk.

Tormanssow had orders to march from Chilowa at seven in the morning, with thirty thousand men and a hundred and fifty pieces of cannon. Rosen had the command of his advanced guard, composed of a regiment of Cossacks, a regiment of chasseurs of the Guard, and another of Friedland, the cuirassiers of the Emperor and of the Empress, with a company of the Guard artillery. This advanced guard was to begin its movement at six, and proceed by Zoumakowo, Sielenowicze, and Koutkowa, on Sorokino, and there establish itself, so as to cut off the enemy's retreat from Krasnoi.

Galitzin was directed to attack Krasnoi from

Achramiewo, and Milaradowitch was to connect with and support Galitzin.

The detachment of Ojarowski was instructed to act, as circumstances might require, on the rear of the enemy.

Kutusow kept the direction of the reserve under his immediate control.

The two armies in presence of each other (if the enemy's force opposed, as compared with its own former and the present Russian strength, could properly be called an army) preserved during the evening and night most perfect stillness; but much movement of carriages had been heard and observed on the road to Liady, to the great vexation of the Russians.

When the morning of the 17th dawned, the enemy was seen stationed in his position: hour after hour successively rolled away, and the orders that had been given by Kutusow the preceding afternoon remained in suspension along the whole line.

The disgust at this inaction was universal.

The troops within reach of the enemy could not and would not any longer remain passive; and Galitzin, under Beningsen's authority, only yielded to the general impulse when he directed the attack to be made on the voltigeurs of the Guard, as has been already related.

Beningsen, after that attack, sent an aide-de-camp to report to Kutusow "its *success, and the certain destruction of the enemy if he would permit the movement to be made as originally proposed.*" "Who sent you?" said Kutusow. "General Beningsen himself, from the field; and we are waiting but your Excellency's order to take by ourselves Krasnoi and all without and within."

"Tell your General," replied Kutusow, as he turned in his droska, "*je m'en-f—*"

Well might Beningsen ascribe the failure at Taroutino (for so it was, compared with the means, the occasion, and the possible result) to the cause of jealousy which he then assigned.

To the English General, who had also quitted Beningsen "to implore his consent to the advance of the army," and who had represented to him "that Napoleon, his Guards, and what remained of his invading force were now in his power—who had pledged himself from his own observation, *that by the single word* MARCH *the war would be finished within one hour*," he only dryly observed, " You had my answer at Malo-Jaroslavets."

Nor was it till about two o'clock in the afternoon that Kutusow gave assent to the march of Rosen and Tormanssow; so that it was near four o'clock before the advanced guard reached the main road at Dobroia, about a mile and a half from Krasnoi; but Napoleon and his Guards had then already passed, and also all the troops except a rear guard of Davoust's, which, attacked on all sides, was obliged to take to the woods that lay on the right of the road, and between it and the Dnieper.

General Kikin and the English General had preceded with some Cossacks the columns of Tormanssow and the advanced guard under Rosen. Before descending into the village of Dobroia they saw the road covered with swarms of fugitives, in such apparently helpless condition that one of the Cossacks said " Is

T

it not a shame for the Marshal to allow these spectres to be walking thus quietly away from their graves?"

On entering Dobroia, which Colonel Nitchin and Galitzin were attacking in front after forcing Krasnoi, they found themselves in the midst of a mass of the enemy, abandoned cannon, tumbrils, carriages, horses, &c.

The bewildered throng offered no resistance, though the greater part had arms. They were too feeble and exhausted to make any exertion. They merely moved on as it were mechanically, like so many automatons.

The Cossacks had rushed at the carriages, each seizing one with four or six horses as his prize.

The third carriage seized proved to be Davoust's, in which the Marshal's bâton was found; another was a fourgon, in which were the maps and plans, not only of Russia and Turkey, but of Central Asia and India; for Napoleon had projected the invasion of Hindostan as one of the articles of peace with Alexander, in a treaty of offensive and defensive alliance.*

On leaving Dobroia, the English General saw another mass moving from the road towards a wood. A Russian officer, who had just arrived with two licornes, and was unlimbering them, agreed that it

---

* Alexander, speaking afterwards with the English General on the subject of this prize, said to him, "England owes me a greater service than she imagines; for by my rejection of peace her Eastern empire has perhaps been preserved." On which the English General observed, "To complete the act of grace and remove all temptation, your Majesty had better send her the whole fourgon taken at Krasnoi." "No, no," answered Alexander jocularly, "the contents are in very good keeping in my chancellerie; but I confess I wonder that you did not contrive to blow up the fourgon when you had it in your possession, on finding that you could not carry it off. Tell me, have you and Cathcart not orders to burn all manufacturing establishments when we get into Prussia and Germany?"

would be an ignoble massacre to fire into it; but he fired two rounds "a-head," which "brought-to" the whole body, and they patiently waited some minutes for the arrival of a few Russian dragoons to conduct them back to Krasnoi.

Such was the impotent state of the enemy before whom Kutusow had so ignominiously held back.

It must appear incredible in after times that this escape of Napoleon was permitted under the circumstances here represented. It is natural to presume that there was some latent cause influencing Kutusow's forbearance — that *fear alone of discomfiture* could not have operated to this extent of pusillanimity.

Let then Colonel Boutourlin, the aide-de-camp of the Emperor Nicholas and champion of Kutusow, in his work on this campaign — let him here state the defence, and by that defence be the Marshal judged for his conduct at Krasnoi.

EXTRACT.

"The enemy's army, anticipated in his line of retreat by the column of General Tormanssow (according to the stated dispositions of the evening), would have been cut off and reduced to the cruel alternative of cutting their way through, sword in hand, or of throwing themselves on the Dnieper. It is probable that if Napoleon had taken this direction, as the means of passage of the river were very scanty, he could have escaped" [where, and for how long?] "with only a small number of men, and the main body must have been entirely destroyed; but unfortunately, the Marshal had made his dispositions in the persuasion that a considerable part of *the enemy's troops would have filed during the night on Liady*, and that he would only have to contend against a force very inferior to his own; and he then found himself in error, when he learnt that Napoleon, with his whole army excepting the corps of Ney (not thirty thousand combatants), was still in Krasnoi. He therefore delayed Tormanssow, to give a free passage to a *part of Napoleon's force (and Napoleon himself), and then he would have only to attack Davoust, which would assure the Russians a victory less brilliant, but more sure, and less dearly bought.*"

Surely this must be irony in every language but the Russian, even if it passes in Russia as a vindication.

Every drop of Russian blood subsequently shed—every Russian life lost in the pursuit from severity of climate—every soldier wasted in subsequent toils and privations—every rouble expended in the protracted contest—all Russian property afterwards destroyed—every injury inflicted by the flying enemy on a Russian inhabitant, forms an item of accusatory charge against Kutusow, and warrant for his condemnation "by that posterity" to which Alexander consigned him " for judgment."

The enemy had lost in the combats of Krasnoi two eagles, forty-five guns, two generals, and above seven thousand killed, wounded, and prisoners.

The Russians had not lost more than five hundred.

Still it was a day of honour for Napoleon, who had shown great presence of mind, dauntless intrepidity, and consummate practical skill in the dispositions made of his handful of troops to impose on the Russian commander, in the judicious selection of the moments, and in the whole conduct of the retreat.

The Russian army, instead of pursuing the enemy, remained immovable in and about Krasnoi; because, according to the reason assigned, "Ney's corps [a feeble corps of seven thousand combatants] was still at, or on the way from, Smolensk."

Early on the 16th Ney had received the despatch which informed him that Davoust for the reasons already stated "had been obliged to attempt an union with Napoleon forthwith at Krasnoi;" in which despatch he was recommended "to follow immediately;" but Ney could not, or as some say would not, evacuate Smolensk till day-break, as originally directed.

Soon after he had withdrawn from the town, the mines exploded with a thundering blast, which announced far and near that "the Holy City was restored to Russia."

Platow, who had endeavoured to get possession of the S. Petersburg suburb on the 15th, immediately entered, and dividing his force into two portions pursued the enemy on both banks of the Dnieper.

Denisoff commanded the moiety on the left bank, and found on his way, soon after quitting the suburbs, a hundred and twelve abandoned guns.

Ney's corps, as has been said, consisted of seven thousand combatants; and there were as many non-combatants and stragglers, the whole more or less armed, in bivouac at Korodnia.

On the 18th the advanced guard approached the village of Nikolino, about four miles from Krasnoi, where Milaradowitch was posted with twelve thousand men, on a hill that overlooked a broad and deep ravine, through which the Lossmiana runs, and on the opposite side of which was a corresponding elevation backed by a deep wood.

Considerable woods lay on the left of Nikolino, extending to the Dnieper, distant about six miles.

It was nearly three o'clock in the afternoon when the alerte was given of the enemy's approach, and the Russians stood to their arms.

A thick frost-fog rising from the low grounds about the Dnieper, indicating a tendency to thaw, obscured the view. On a sudden the enemy, who had descended and passed the bottom of the ravine unperceived, presented themselves near the summit of the ascent crowned by the Russians.

Forty pieces of cannon loaded with grape, simultaneously on the instant, vomited their flames and poured their deadly shower on the assailants.

The survivors intrepidly rushed forward with desperate energy—part reached the crest of the hill, and almost touched the batteries. The Russians most in advance, shouting their "huzza," sprang forward with fixed bayonets, and without firing a musket.

A sanguinary but short struggle ensued: the enemy could not maintain their footing, and were driven headlong down the ravine.

The Hulans of the Guard at the same time charged, swept through the shattered ranks, and captured an eagle.

The brow and sides of the hill were covered with dead and dying, all the Russian arms were dripping with gore, and the wounded, as they lay bleeding and shivering on the snow, called for "death," as the greatest mercy that could be ministered in their hopeless state.

Ney, still ignorant that Napoleon had retired from Krasnoi, and that the whole Russian army barred his passage there, attempted to renew the combat; and planting his only remaining twelve guns on the height above the ravine, he directed Colonel Bouvier to assault the Russian batteries with several companies of sappers and miners.

The grenadiers of Pawlask, who had steadily endured the enemy's fire, charged the storming column as it approached, and the whole perished, victims of their devotion and splendid daring.

Altogether, as the English General wrote to Mr. Liston, "It had been a combat of giants, hand to hand; and relatively to numbers one of the most slaughterous of the campaign."

General Ricard, two other generals, and Colonel Pilet (who had both legs shattered and an arm broken) being wounded, as well as many officers and men, Ney found himself obliged to desist, and fall back into the wood; but though not actively pursued, as the obscurity became great, his situation was fearfully desperate. Night had closed in—a Russian winter night, of more than usual Russian severity;* he was in a deep forest, in an unknown country, no food, no fire, no inhabitants to give information, no guide to conduct, no succour for the wounded, no possibility of safety from the efforts of despair, the ways full of foes, and misery in every direction!

* According to the thermometer there was a partial rise of temperature, but the atmosphere was not less chilly in consequence.

Colonel Pilet, notwithstanding the agony of his wounds, counselled still, it is said, "the retreat on the Dnieper, that Orsza and Napoleon might be reached." Ney adopted the suggestion, although there was scarcely a possible chance of preservation; but he thought it his duty to make the trial, and therefore recommenced his march with all who were capable of the exertion.

Milaradowitch, desirous of ascertaining the direction which Ney had taken and his intentions, sent two flags of truce to offer him a capitulation that should secure the lives of himself and his brave companions. The bearers of these flags of truce, however, were immediately detained, lest they should on return give the information wanted as to the position in which they had found the corps.

Passing in silence within half a mile of the Cossacks under Denisoff, whose lights served as beacons, they gained the village of Worickza on the Dnieper, and attempted the passage of the river; but the ice broke under the first gun, and it was necessary to abandon the whole train of artillery and every wheeled carriage. Before the entire body had passed, the Cossacks, attracted by the sound, had arrived, and were enabled to make several hundred prisoners.

The corps which now proceeded on its desperate enterprise was reduced to three thousand combatants and as many followers, who were an embarrassment, instead of an aid: the rest had been killed or taken.

In the village of Gorciroe some Cossacks were surprised, which capture supplied a few horses; but on the 19th, to the consternation of all, Platow with his swarm of Cossacks appeared on a plain that lay before them, and immediately opened his artillery fire. The column, unable to force its way in their direction, turned upon a wood that ran on its left; but as it was about to enter, a masked battery of several guns discharged a volley of grape on the advanced party.

Ney darted forward, followed by the drooping soldiery whom his example reanimated; but the guns which the Cossacks had mounted on sledges, since there were no roads through the wood for carriages, were withdrawn at speed.

The column, to avoid further annoyance and alarm from the Cossacks, kept in the wood; but Platow had already made several hundred prisoners before the whole of the stragglers could enter.

After a march which had continued the whole day, a village was reached where some shelter for a few hours and food were obtained.

On the 20th, at daybreak, the struggle through the woods was continued, for whenever any egress was attempted, the "hurrah" of the hovering Cossacks was heard; but they were less formidable than in the open space, as they could no longer find practicable routes for their guns, although the carriages were of the lightest possible construction.

At three o'clock in the afternoon the column arrived at Jackouchowo, twenty-five miles from Orsza, when two Polish officers offered to proceed on peasants' horses to acquaint Napoleon, if still there, with the approach and condition of the corps, which offer was accepted.

Half way from Orsza the forest protection ceased.

The night of this last march was, however, very dark, and a thick fog, whilst it afforded further shelter from observation, greatly impeded progress.

The way lay over a very steep hill, which was ascended with great difficulty. On arriving at the summit the fugitives saw, to their terror, a long line of bivouac fires illuminating an extensive plain beyond. It was indisputably a Russian corps established to intercept the march.

"We are at last doomed," muttered some of the boldest; but Ney, who was himself staggered at the first moment, again revived the general courage, and, exhorting them "to advance in speechless silence, and then make a resolute onset, in which, if they perished, their enemies might long remember that they had lived," the whole moved on, and when at the presumed charging distance, rushed upon *air* and the *bivouac fires* which Platow had lighted as a stratagem to prevent or delay progress.

The Polish messengers had reached Orsza, although their route had been beset by the Cossack parties.

The Viceroy, on hearing of Ney's distress, immediately flew to arms, and marched with his corps to aid his arrival. About eight miles from Orsza the union was effected amidst transports of congratulation.

When Napoleon heard of Ney's safety he exclaimed, with an emotion of feeling which he rarely expressed, "I have two hundred millions in the vaults of the Tuileries—I would have given them all for Ney's safety."

It is impossible to eulogize too highly the spirit, the energy, and the constancy exhibited by Ney through so many trials of these qualities. The whole achievement confers honour, not only on Ney and his meritorious comrades, but on the military profession at large, which derives general lustre from such transcendent exertions and exemplary valour.

Napoleon had halted at Lindy on the night of the 17th: on the ensuing night he had reached Dubrowna, where he learnt the capture of Minsk by Tchichagow.

He immediately directed Dombrowski "to defend the tête du pont of Borisow on the right bank of the Beresina, and ordered Oudinot to march instantly with his corps and another division on Borisow, and there uniting with the division Dombrowski and the troops of Bronekowski, to move on and retake Minsk."

The force thus collected he calculated would amount to forty thousand combatants.

Victor was instructed "to keep Wittgenstein in check, and mask Oudinot's movement as long as possible."

On the 19th there was a false alarm at Napoleon's head-quarters, and the panic cry arose "Aux armes!" The Guards formed, but there was no enemy.

Napoleon then set out for Orsza. After a march of about three miles he assembled the Old Guard, formed them into a square, and dismounting, thus harangued them: "Grenadiers of my Guard, you are witnesses of the disorganization of my army.

"The greater part of the soldiers, by a deplorable fatality, have even thrown away their arms.

"If you should follow this fatal example, all hope would be lost. The safety of the army is under your care. You will justify the good opinion I have of you. The officers must not only maintain a severe discipline, but the soldiers must exercise over one another a rigorous superintendence, and themselves punish those who separate from their ranks."

At mid-day of the 18th Napoleon reached Orsza.

No attempt had been made by Kutusow, at the

head of the main army resting inactively with superfluous force, to seize Orsza, in which were large magazines, or to cut the bridge, though both services might have been effected on the 15th and 16th, and even on the 17th, for the garrison was very weak, and the tête du pont indefensible against a vigorous attack.

It has been truly remarked that the Russians might have thrown bridges over the Dnieper at Khomino and Rasassna, and, by forced marches, have gained the route of Orsza to Borisow before Napoleon could have reached it; but this was an enterprise of too active and decided a character for a commander who had refused so many preceding opportunities to stop his enemy by which fortune had wooed him in vain.

On the 14th the weather had somewhat moderated; on the 19th a thaw commenced.

At Orsza Napoleon employed himself with great energy in reorganizing his forces. Arms were again distributed, with ammunition and provisions, to the troops.

With his thirty-six guns still remaining he completed six batteries; two of them were allotted to the Viceroy, who had acquired nine others, two to Davoust, who had preserved eight, and two to Latour Maubourg.

The most stringent order was then published " to incorporate all stragglers into the different corps; to punish *prévôtalement* all who again quitted their ranks; to give up all horses to the artillery; to burn all effects except a change of linen and shoes, as well as all carriages, except a certain number for the use of the emigrants from Moscow; to render all generals and others responsible for the execution of orders which the honour of the French and the safety of the army required."

The order was judicious, and the execution essential; but the disorganization was too great, the number of stragglers too considerable (the non-combatants exceeding the combatants), and the marches too continuous and harassing for due attention and compliance.

The enemy had been followed on the road to Orsza only by some Cossacks.

The Russian army and its detached corps did not quit Krasnoi till the 20th, when it marched to Romanowo.

On the 21st and 22nd to Lanika.

On the 23rd to Morosowo.

On the 24th and 25th to Kopys, where the Dnieper was crossed, and where a bag of French letters was brought in by the Cossacks, one of which, from the King of Bavaria, declared "the impossibility of furnishing another regiment of cavalry in addition to his contingent," adding, "if it were practicable, you might be sure I would do it, comme je ne voudrois pas me faire tirer par les oreilles pour un rien." This expression was peculiarly apposite to Napoleon's habit.

On the 26th the army proceeded to Staroselie.

On the 27th to Kroughoie.

On the 28th to Oukhwaly.

On the 29th and 30th to Mikhewiczi.

On the 1st of December to Joukowitz, where it passed the Beresina, which the advanced guard had only reached at Oukoloda the preceding day.

These marches were made as leisurely as possible, and did not average more than ten miles each.

On the 2nd the army advanced to Rowaritsa.
On the 3rd it halted.
On the 4th it advanced to Chipiany.
On the 5th to Doubowiki.
On the 6th to Gorodock.
On the 7th it again halted.

Kutusow left the army on the 4th to join Tchichagow, and on the same day arrived at Kossin.

On the 5th at Bielorouczie.

On the 6th at Radochkowiczi, where he fell in with the advanced guard of Milaradowitch.

RUSSIAN FLANK ARMIES.

It is now necessary to suspend the recital of Napoleon's further movements in order that the antecedent events, and the actual state and position of the co-operating armies and corps on which Napoleon relied for aid and extrication from his entanglement between the Niemen, Beresina, and Dnieper, may be brought into clear view.

It is, indeed, indispensable to give this key to Napoleon's dispositions for linking the Moscow remnant with their operations.

Army of Tchichagow.

Admiral Tchichagow, in conformity with the arrangements entered into with the English General, and instructions from the Emperor received the 6th of August "to expedite his march," crossed the Dniester at Choczim on the 6th of September.

His army consisted of twenty-seven thousand infantry and nine thousand cavalry, with a powerful artillery. The whole formed the finest martial spectacle that could be seen; and its general condition reflected great credit on the Admiral's administrative superintendence.

On the 18th the armies of Moldavia and Wolhynia united on the right bank of the Styr.

In consequence of Bagrathion's mortal wound, Tormanssow was soon afterwards recalled to assume his command in Kutusow's army; so that Tchichagow, after deducting his losses on a long march, found himself eventually at the head of sixty-four thousand men. On the day on which the Admiral joined his forces he received an order from Kutusow " to march with his whole force on Moscow;" but the Admiral was too far advanced, and the losses of Tormanssow's corps had been too great, to admit of this separation.

Schwarzenberg, with twenty-six thousand Austrians, twelve thousand Saxons, and six thousand Poles, retired on the night of the 22nd of September, as he had ascertained by a strong reconnoissance made on the 20th, that the union had been effected, and that the whole force had crossed the Styr on the day of the 22nd.

On the 23rd a Polish prisoner communicated to the Admiral the intelligence of the "battle of Borodino and the destruction of Moscow."

The same day an order from Kutusow, which had been much delayed on the road, directed Tormanssow "to withdraw his corps from the Moldavian army, and join the main army to defend the capital threatened by the enemy advancing from Smolensk." Even had this order arrived in due time, Moscow could not have been preserved by the co-operation, for there was an intervening distance to pass of seven hundred and fifty miles.

On the 27th another order was received from Kutusow, directing Tormanssow "to remain with his army in Wolhynia; and the Admiral to join, with his Moldavian force, the main army."

On the 29th Colonel Czernicheff brought a final order from Kutusow "for the Moldavian and Wolhynian armies to continue united under the Admiral, and for Tormanssow to repair in his own person to the Imperial head-quarters."

The caricature which was once exhibited in England of a personage on whose forehead was written "Order, Counter-order, and Disorder!" here found its archetype.

The confederate army, under Schwarzenberg, retired across the Boug at Opalin and Wladowa, losing in its retreat fifteen hundred killed, wounded, and prisoners. The pursuers lost about five hundred.

Between the 30th of September, the day on which Tormanssow actually resigned his command, and the 10th of October there had been various skirmishes and strategical movements and counter-movements, but of no particular importance except on the 8th, when Prince Lichtenstein was wounded in a sharp affair; and on the 9th, when both Commanders-in-chief drew out their forces to ascertain each other's strength and position.

In consequence of this demonstration the Admiral advanced in a thick fog at daybreak on the 10th, to attack the confederates; but they had retired across the Lenza, leaving only a rear guard strongly posted, which withdrew in the night of the 11th and 12th, and joined the army at Wingrod, behind Briansk; which retrograde movement uncovered Wilna, Minsk, and the whole right wing of Napoleon's army.

The Admiral, finding that his army required some repose, decided at a most unfavourable moment to put it into cantonments round Brest Litowski, and by so doing engaged in a stern chace after Time, of which he never more could gain and keep the lead.

He, however, scoured the duchy of Warsaw with his detachments, one of which under General Tchaplitz surprised at Slonim the 7th regiment of Hulans, which was cut to pieces, and its colonel taken. On the other hand, General Essen, who, with ten thousand men, had marched on Biala to check the 7th corps (Regnier's,) which had arrived there, was unexpectedly attacked by Regnier himself, and obliged to retire with the loss of a gun and six hundred men.

Being reinforced by succours which the cannonade had set in movement, Essen recovered his ground; and the Admiral on the 20th collected his army to dislodge Regnier; but finding Biala already evacuated, he returned with his troops into cantonments.

On the 27th of October the Admiral broke up these cantonments, and divided his army into two operative corps.

The corps placed under General Sacken's orders consisted of his own division—

Sacken	6,000
Essen	9,000
Bulatow	5,000
Lecevie	7,000
Total	27,000

Of these twenty-seven thousand eight thousand were cavalry, exclusive of Cossacks, and to this corps General Lieders, who was on march from Servia with three thousand men, was ordered to attach himself.

The Admiral's own corps consisted of—

Lambert	6,000
Langeron	11,000
Woinoff	5,000
Tchaplitz	6,000
Total	28,000

Of which twenty-eight thousand ten thousand were cavalry, exclusive of Cossacks.

To this army, General Ertel with twelve thousand men from Bobruisk, and Wittgenstein with his army, were (by the general instructions sent by the Emperor after the capture of Moscow, as already given) "directed to unite themselves."

Five thousand additional Cossacks of the new levy, who had just arrived, were left with Sacken to be duly armed.

The confederates under Schwarzenberg at this period consisted of—

Austrians	25,000
Saxons	8,500
Poles, Kossenki	8,000
Durutte's Division, leaving a rear-guard at Warsaw	9,000
Total	50,500

Of which five thousand five hundred were cavalry.

On the 31st the Admiral reached Prujany, where he received an order from Kutusow, written after the battle of Malo-Jaroslavets, "to march his army on Kiew" (a distance of four hundred and fifty miles), "and to cover that city, as Napoleon was moving by Kalouga in that direction."

The Admiral, bearing in mind the previous contradictory orders and the cancels which had reached him almost simultaneously with their receipt, not obeying this new instruction, directed fifteen thousand militia assembling on the borders of the Crimea, and destined for his army, to march on Kiew.

On the 3rd of November the Admiral reached Slonim.

On the 11th of November the Admiral, who had retarded his movement in consequence of a demonstration of the Austrians on the Niemen at Mosty, arrived at Neswige, and drove out several depôts of the enemy's cavalry. General Lieders from Servia here reunited with the Admiral's corps, bringing with him a regiment of infantry and one of Hulans. He had at first been directed to join Sacken, but the Admiral, finding that Ertel did not obey his order and move from Bobruisk, changed his destination.

The Polish Governor of Minsk continued to slumber

in presumptuous security, and could not be made to believe that the Admiral was moving on that city.

Well might Napoleon say, as he did on receiving afterwards the intelligence of the capture of Borisow, "We are doomed then to make nothing but blunders;" for at Minsk everything was done which ought not to have been done, and nothing done that exigencies required and means permitted.

The garrison of Minsk consisted of four thousand men. Dombrowski, who had been watching Ertel at Bobruisk, was on march to reinforce it with six thousand men; but he was not pressed to accelerate his arrival, and detachments from Victor's corps, which would have afforded a considerable additional strength, were daily allowed to pass through Minsk, and mostly to be taken by the partisan corps environing the city and infesting the country.

Besides these forces at the disposition of the Governor in such an extremity, and which were estimated as amounting collectively to fifteen thousand men, Loison was at Wilna with fifteen thousand fresh and unoccupied troops; and Oudinot was at Bobr with ten thousand men, whence he might have marched, if advised in time, to defend Borisow and the Beresina.

Bobr could have been left by Oudinot without hazard, for Victor with twenty-five thousand men had reached Chessacky from Smolensk.

The Governor of Minsk could not plead ignorance of the Admiral's intentions, for an officer charged with duplicate despatches ordering "the movement on the Beresina with the united armies of Wittgenstein and the Admiral," had been taken with his escort some time previously near Minsk.

The Admiral had sent Colonel Czernicheff with his regiment of Cossacks from Slonim to inform Wittgenstein "of his march on Minsk and the Beresina." Czernicheff was directed "to take the route of Novogrodok and Radochkowiczi to Lepel." In his progress he fortunately, on the 17th, fell in with the escort of gendarmes conducting Winzingerode and his aide-de-camp into France, and recaptured them.

On the 13th of November the Polish General Kossenki, who had been detached by the Governor of Minsk to Novoi Swerzenn, was surprised by General Lambert, defeated, and driven across the Niemen without having had time to destroy the bridge. One of his detachments on the road to Mir, and another on the road to Neswige, were all either killed or taken.

The Russians lost but few men in this enterprise; the Poles lost several hundred killed, and eight hundred prisoners.

Kossenki requested the Governor of Minsk "to be allowed to join Dombrowski with the three or four thousand men still at his disposition;" but he was directed to retire on Koidanow, about twenty miles from Minsk, with all his force, the Governor stating that "he felt confident that the Admiral had not left Wolhynia with his army, and that only some of his flying corps were menacing Minsk."

On the 15th Lambert again attacked Kossenki at Koidanow, and brought twelve guns to bear on his position. After a sharp action, in which a thousand of the enemy were killed, three thousand laid down their arms and also surrendered two standards and two guns.

Kossenki fled to Minsk with only five hundred men.

The Governor, notwithstanding these severe warnings, remained infatuated, and assured Dombrowski, who had preceded his corps to communicate with him in person, "that he had ample force to hold Minsk until Dombrowski should have reached Beresino, and established his connection with Oudinot."

Two hours after this assurance had been given, and Dombrowski had departed, the Governor, on the sudden appearance of the Russians in the environs, was himself *obliged to evacuate the city with his garrison!*

Lambert entered Minsk on the 16th, where he found five thousand sick, two millions of rations, immense magazines, a great quantity of powder, and a number of guns,—some of them Russian,—without carriages.

Altogether there were forty days' supplies of grain and cattle, beer and spirits, for a hundred thousand men, besides thirty thousand pairs of shoes, and twenty-seven thousand muskets, with clothing and equipment in proportion.

The loss of this city was a fatal blow to the enemy, and was equally advantageous to the Russians, not only on account of the value of the stores seized, but because it propitiated public feeling abroad as well as at home, and favoured the political transactions dependent on such decided proofs of the enemy's inability to keep a winter's hold in the Russian territory.

General Sacken, who was an able strategist, though not a fortunate executive officer, had endeavoured to mask the movement of the Admiral; but Schwarzenberg was not in this instance deceived, and therefore advanced on Slonim, where he arrived on the 12th, to menace the rear of the Admiral.

Regnier, to cover this march, had advanced on the 4th to Narewka, and on the 6th to Swislocq, leaving Kamenskoi at Wingrod with a brigade to protect Warsaw.

Sacken, having posted five thousand men at Brest Litowski and environs, had marched by Bielowa on Wolkowich, through which town Regnier had passed on his way to Rudnia; but hearing that Sacken was following, he reoccupied Wolkowich with a few hundred men to form a guard for his head-quarters and baggage, and took up a position on the heights behind the town with his troops, consisting of sixteen thousand infantry, including Durutte's division, and eleven hundred horse. As Sacken's force, composed of sixteen thousand infantry, six thousand cavalry, and five thousand Cossacks, was so greatly superior, Regnier sent an urgent request to Schwarzenberg "for his return and prompt combined operation against Sacken, who had seriously assumed the offensive."

On the 15th, about three hours after midnight, the slumbering garrison and generals in Wolkowich were roused by a discharge of small arms.

The Russian advanced guard had, unobserved, approached and gained entrance.

Regnier jumped out of window; others of the garrison escaped with more or less difficulty, but many were killed and wounded, and much baggage was taken.

At break of day the enemy descended in force from the heights, and repossessed themselves of the town.

Sacken in the mean time had pressed on, and, finding the enemy in order of battle, deployed also his whole force, but only actually engaged slightly with his right wing.

On the 16th, in the morning, Sacken, with two thousand men, attacked and carried Wolkowich.

At mid-day he renewed his attack on the enemy's left with more vigour, when about three o'clock in the afternoon the guns of an approaching enemy were heard in the rear of his centre.

Schwarzenberg had received at Slonim, on the 14th, Regnier's communication; and, leaving seven thousand men behind to watch that point, he immediately marched with eighteen thousand by Iwackewiczi on Izabelino.

Regnier, on hearing the cannonade, renewed the attack upon Wolkowich, from which the Russians withdrew; and as soon as night favoured, Sacken retired through cross roads to Swislocq, his direct route of movement through Prujany being cut off by the Austrians.

Sacken owed his successful escape to Regnier's justifiable unwillingness to hazard a night march through an extensive forest.

On the 24th of November the Russians reached Brest Litowski and Kobrin, whence they fell back on Lubolm and Kowel.

Regnier had reached Brest Litowski, and Schwarzenberg Kobrin, the same day with the Russians; but there they halted; and on the 27th Schwarzenberg, having received a despatch from Maret, the Duke of Bassano, "requiring his immediate return to cover Warsaw," fell back, and on the 1st of December Regnier followed his movement.

The loss of Sacken had amounted to seven thousand

men and several guns ; but he gained by what is usually reputed a loss, viz. the abandonment of much baggage.

The movement, though very disastrous to the corps, had operated beneficially on the issue of the campaign, for the Austrians were diverted by it from pursuit of the Admiral and check on his operations against Minsk, from which city they were on the 14th, when at Slonim, only distant five days' march, and the Admiral did but arrive there on the 17th.

They might not have saved the city, though that was not improbable; but they would at all events have prevented the subsequent movements and disasters on the Beresina. Even on the 17th, when Sacken withdrew from Wolkowich, had Schwarzenberg marched against the Admiral, he would have greatly embarrassed his operations.

During these transactions an unusual event had occurred. On the night of the 20th the Austrians had surprised the third regiment of Ukraine Cossacks at Prujany, and taken three whole squadrons; but as a balance to this rare occurrence and prize, Kossenki, who had been left with eight thousand Poles, having made an attempt to penetrate into Wolhynia by Oustilony, was driven across the Boug with heavy loss by General Moussin Pouchkin, who advanced from Wladimir to repel his incursion.

The governor of Minsk retreated on Borisow, where he gathered a motley force together, of about three thousand men.

Dombrowski, who had reached Semlo, on hearing of the Governor's flight and the capture of Minsk, returned to Beresino, that from thence he might secure a safe line of march on Borisow. His division only amounted to about five thousand men, General Kossenki having taken from it a Lithuanian regiment, which was lost with the Wurtemberg battalion at Koidanow, and the other regiment that had been detached on the Bobruisk road, which he intended to act as his rear guard, not having then rejoined; but he had with his column twenty guns.

The Governor of Minsk resumed his tranquillity at Borisow, and only placed in the unfinished tête du pont, which was of great extent, a battalion of the 95th French regiment.

Instead of urging Victor's arrival, he left that Marshal to believe that there was no reason to apprehend any attack being made on Borisow that he could not repulse; and even persuaded General Pampeluna, sent by Victor (who had misgivings) "to inquire into the real state of affairs," to remain with him, and take post with a detachment, at Wesselowo on the left bank of the river.

The Admiral, on the 19th, sent forward Lambert to Jouknowo; Tchaplitz covered his left on the route to Zembin; and Colonel Loukoffkin was detached with a regiment of Cossacks on the road to Igumen, where he fell in with six Russian battalions, four squadrons, and another regiment of Cossacks coming from Mozyr to join the Admiral. General Ertel had despatched this force instead of joining with his whole corps of twelve thousand men, as ordered: this disobedience so displeased the Admiral that he superseded him in his command by General Touchkoff.

Colonel Loukoffkin immediately marched his detachment in pursuit of Dombrowski's rear guard, formed by the regiment that had been stationed near Igumen.

The Russian colonel Paradouskoi had been sent from Minsk to Radochkowiczi, and had there collected and captured about two thousand fugitives from Minsk endeavouring to gain Wilna.

On the 20th Lambert reached Jodin, and pushed his advance on Ouperecoiczi; Langeron supported Lambert at Jodin, and Tchaplitz entered Zembin.

Dombrowski, with the greatest exertion, pushed on to garrison the tête du pont of Borisow, before which he arrived at midnight of the 20th and 21st.

There was no officer or guide to conduct him on his arrival to any point of the entrenchments, and therefore, passing somewhat beyond, he posted his troops, in the best manner the darkness permitted, on the right of the works upon the road to Zembin by Starnocha; but his left, instead of resting on the works, was separated from them by a spacious interval.

These works, as has been stated, were in a very unfinished state, with a redoubt on the right and left, and several in the centre, little more than traced.

At dawn on the morning of the 21st Lambert presented himself before the tête du pont.

The 14th regiment of Russian chasseurs formed the attacking column on the right, the 38th on the left, and the 7th on the centre; but the 7th was directed not to advance till the flanks were carried.

Two batteries of twelve guns each supported the assailants; two regiments of infantry and the cavalry of the advanced guard formed the reserve on the road of Jodin.

The French battalion of the 95th, stationed in the tête du pont, partaking of the confidence and neglect of the Governor, was completely surprised and driven to the bridge, and the 14th chasseurs gained the redoubt on the right of the works; but the 38th could not hold its ground against a Wurtemberg battalion, which had hastened from Borisow on the first alarm to the support of the French battalion.

The Russian General Engelhardt, who had advanced with the 7th to support the 38th, fell mortally wounded in the onset; but the regiment continued its movement, and regained the redoubt of the left.

Dombrowski, as soon as he perceived the danger to which the Russian occupation of the tête du pont exposed his corps, took ground to his left, and established a connection with the Wurtemberg battalion, that still maintained itself in the central works and covered the bridge.

About mid-day Dombrowski had succeeded by a lateral movement in establishing his whole corps à cheval on the great road leading to Minsk. He then filed his artillery park and baggage over the bridge, and planted six guns on the opposite side of the river to flank the bridge and cover his retreat, if forced.

Lambert also, selecting an advantageous site, opened his fire on the bridge. Dombrowski's artillery endeavoured to silence it, and a heavy cannonade continued till five in the evening.

Lambert being wounded in rallying the chasseurs, who had failed in an attack on the central works, Colonel Krussowskoi succeeded to the command; and bringing to the charge all his force, under cover of a fire of grape from twelve pieces of cannon which he had established in the redoubt of the left, he succeeded in carrying the whole line of the entrenchments, and consecutively both the bridge and the town.

Dombrowski in vain tried to rally and defend a mill on the Orsza road. It was stormed, and the enemy driven towards Lochnitza, leaving in the hands of the Russians fifteen hundred dead, and two thousand five hundred prisoners, two standards, and eight guns.

The Russian loss amounted to two thousand killed and wounded.

Langeron, on hearing the cannonade, had made the greatest efforts to arrive; but he could not join the advanced guard till nightfall, and not a soldier of his force was engaged in the combat.

The Admiral, who had also pushed forward with the division Woinoff, soon followed Langeron, and established his head-quarters the same night in Borisow.

During the day Colonel Loukoffkin had overtaken at Oucha the separated regiment forming Dombrowski's rear guard, and had driven it over the Beresina at Usza, making between two and three hundred prisoners.

On the 22nd Woinoff's corps and the reserve passed the Beresina, and took post on the road to Bobr; Tchaplitz returned from Zembin, and bivouacked near the tête du pont of Borisow; and Loukoffkin proceeded from Oucha to Chabachewiczi.

General Pampeluna, posted at Wesselowo, had sent intelligence to Oudinot of the loss of Borisow, who marched immediately on its receipt with his corps to Nemonitsa, where Dombrowski had posted himself with the remains of his force.

On the 23rd the Admiral directed Major-general Pahlen, who had succeeded Lambert in the command of the advanced guards, "to reconnoitre with his division the road towards Bobr." On the heights of Nemonitsa his advance met, without any forewarning, the advance of Oudinot moving on Borisow, under the command of Dombrowski.

The action commenced at the instant. Pahlen's column, taken unawares and allowed no respite to form and make an attempt to stand, was trundled back in extreme confusion into and through Borisow and over the bridge, with the loss of fifteen hundred prisoners and all the baggage of the head-quarters, as well as its own. Indeed it is unaccountable how any of the column escaped, for the bridge was six hundred yards long, and without a passage to right or left for artillery.

Three regiments of Russian chasseurs which were exploring the woods on the left of the road, as well as three thousand cavalry out foraging, unable to gain the town, were thrown upon Staroi Borisow, and saved by a peasant directing them to a ford near Brill.

The Admiral, who was at dinner when the enemy entered Borisow, effected by great good fortune his own retreat, but lost, with the greater part of his baggage, all his correspondence: he however succeeded in cutting the bridge, and in establishing batteries that prevented its repair.

The first loss of Borisow had been a fatal incident for Napoleon; the recovery offered some satisfaction to his arms, and usefully distracted the enemy's attention; but the Russians having retained the tête du pont, the passage of the river at this point was no longer practicable, for the circumjacent ground completely commanded the marsh, as well as that part of the river over which the bridge was laid.

Army of Wittgenstein.

Whilst the Admiral was thus still in a position to guard the right bank of the Beresina, Wittgenstein, driving Victor before him, was directing his march towards the left bank, and rear of the right of Napoleon's army.

Towards the end of September Wittgenstein had received considerable reinforcements; and having required Steingell to co-operate, commenced his march from Sokolisqui, in the beginning of October, on Polotzk, with thirty-six thousand men, one-third of which force was composed of militia.

Polotzk was held by S. Cyr, with twenty-seven thousand men, the remains of the second and sixth corps; but the sixth corps could only present under arms five thousand effectives, for the Bavarians, who composed it, had suffered more than any of the other confederates of the whole army from fatigue and climate.

On the 16th of October Steingell, with his corps twelve thousand strong, to which Wittgenstein added a regiment of hussars, passed the Dwina at Dessna, of which he had forced the occupation, and continued his march on Polotzk by the left bank of the river.

S. Cyr, who had entrenched Polotzk, doubly palisading it, and covering the approaches by strong redoubts, was aware of Wittgenstein's movement, and had made his dispositions of defence on both banks of the Dwina.

Corbineau with a light brigade, and the Bavarians, were sent to oppose Steingell; and S. Cyr's principal force was posted in front of the city behind the redoubts.

Verdier's division, commanded by Loison, occupied the right, which was prolonged to some distance by a body of cavalry.

Legrand's division joined Verdier's left, and rested its own left on the Pelota.

At day-break on the morning of the 18th, Wittgenstein commenced his attack in two columns.

The battery in advance of the division Verdier was assaulted with great bravery, and defended with equal obstinacy. During the action this battery was taken and retaken three several times.

The tirailleurs on both sides, incessantly engaged, held their ground with great tenacity; and the charges of cavalry, frequently made, were attended with alternate success.

At length, about four o'clock in the afternoon, Wittgenstein, seeing that the action was protracted without the prospect of any decisive issue, and disappointed of the co-operation he expected from Steingell by an attack on the enemy's rear which had been directed, determined on bringing up his reserve, and engaging at once the enemy's whole line.

The Russian militia, who had been chiefly employed as tirailleurs, on the order being given swept forward with the most daring intrepidity—the enemy said like madmen—and possessed themselves of the advanced works.

The enemy's cavalry made several attempts to charge upon the tirailleurs, but the Russian cavalry afforded them requisite protection.

The Russian mass then moving forward with exemplary steadiness, bore down all opposition.

A Swiss brigade with a battalion of Croats, who ventured to sally from the alignment, were in a moment overthrown and forced back on the Pelota.

The Swiss brigade saved itself after a brilliant display of highly disciplined valour, for its firing in retreat was as regular as if at an exercise; but the Croat battalion, though equally resolute, being completely surrounded before it could regain the works, was obliged to lay down its arms.

The Russians were at length in possession of all the enemy's exterior redoubts; but the fire that poured into them from the batteries and entrenchments of the town itself would not permit continued occupation.

Only the light troops therefore during the night lodged themselves within cannon shot of the town. The army took post at a greater distance.

Steingell, who had been delayed by the state of the roads, rendered almost impassable by a week's rain, advised Wittgenstein during the night "that his advance had reached the Ouchaz, about eight miles from Polotzk, and that he could be ready to attack the next morning."

Wittgenstein, who had intended, according to his instructions, to pass the Dwina at Goriany and attack Polotzk in the rear, had not been able to construct a bridge, the pontoons and materials not having arrived; but fearing that Steingell might be overpowered by S. Cyr if he remained inactive, he had resolved on bombarding Polotzk: Steingell's guns, however, being heard in the morning, he changed his intention, and made his dispositions to carry the town by storm so soon as opportunity might favour.

The next morning Steingell's advance drove Corbineau from the banks of the Ouchaz; but S. Cyr had contrived to withdraw, unperceived by Wittgenstein, a portion of his troops from Polotzk, and to pass them about mid-day across the Dwina at a point which enabled him to reinforce and head Corbineau, who was watching Steingell's advance in front of the defile of Brouonoia—a defile of three miles long, beyond which Steingell with his main force had halted.

At Polotzk the day had also passed in mutual observation; but about the close, Prince Jachwill, who had been directed " to watch the enemy's movements in the town, and open his guns on it so soon as he might see any indications of retreat," thought he perceived symptoms of withdrawal, in which suspicion he was confirmed by a fire breaking out in the barracks of the division Legrand: he therefore began to cannonade the corps on the skirts of the town, and the town itself; the enemy hastily retired from the camps behind the entrenchments, but then returned the cannonade, which continued with activity part of the night.

The town had been very soon set in flames, and at midnight the Russian storming parties had orders " to make their attack," in which they were exposed to view by a blaze of light from the burning houses.

The Swiss regiment behind the palisaded entrenchments fought gallantly, but after two hours' contest the Russian militia, passing over a bridge a hundred paces long, reached the ravine of the Pelota, and cutting down the palisades with their axes (which every Russian knows how to handle dexterously and forcibly) opened a way into the streets.

S. Cyr had already passed the Dwina with his cavalry, and the greater part of his infantry and guns; but that portion which remained disputed obstinately the advance of the Russians, breaking down the bridges after crossing, and opposing every impediment. A thousand men, with one gun, not being able to withdraw, laid down their arms.

The enemy's loss during the two days' combat had exceeded six thousand men, including two thousand prisoners; and S. Cyr himself was severely wounded.

The Russian loss was also severe: ten generals and chiefs of the S. Petersburg and Narva militia were wounded,[*] and five thousand men killed and wounded.

The enemy abandoned great magazines in Polotzk, the Russian prisoners taken in the battle of the 18th of August, and some wounded officers captured by the cavalry the preceding evening.

Before S. Cyr quitted Polotzk, he had further reinforced the corps opposed to Steingell by a Swiss and a Bavarian regiment; and on the 20th Wrede, who had taken the command of the whole, surprised Steingell's advanced guard, and made two colonels, one major, fifteen officers, and eighteen hundred men of its two chasseur regiments prisoners. This disaster, which chequered the success at Polotzk, was a great mortification to Wittgenstein, but he sent General Sagonoff with ten thousand men to Steingell's aid.

---

[*] Names of nine of the wounded Generals—Balk, Gusner, Prince Sabiesk, Mastow, Diebitch, Sagonoff, Rudiger, Mardanowo senr., Bibikow.

Wittgenstein had been instructed "to turn the right of S. Cyr, and cut off his communication with Victor;" but as he had not been able to pass the Dwina at Goriany, that object could not be accomplished.

S. Cyr had shown great firmness and prudence in his defence of Polotzk whilst the corps of Steingell and Wittgenstein were kept apart, and in his manœuvres to prolong that separation.

Much time was required to replace the bridges of Polotzk, the river being very rapid; but in order not to lose more than was necessary, Wittgenstein directed "two squadrons of the hussars of Grodno and two regiments of Cossacks to swim across," which they did, and cleared the left bank of the enemy's parties.

On the 23rd Steingell, reinforced by Sagonoff, passed the Dwina and pushed to Zaproudie, whence he detached five thousand men under Wlastoff "to watch Macdonald."

The bridges of Polotzk being repaired, Wittgenstein, leaving two thousand five hundred men in garrison, crossed to the left bank of the Dwina.

Legrand, having succeeded to the command of the 2nd corps in consequence of S. Cyr's wound, retired leisurely on the Oula to approach Tchasniki and Sienno. Wrede, with the 6th corps, followed his movement, but, after reaching Selitche, turned on Koubloutchi and Glubokoie to cover Wilna, the reverse of the Beresina, and the adjacent country to the Wilia.

A party of Steingell's at Selitche fell in with and captured the Bavarian baggage: in one of the fourgons twenty-two standards were found.

On the 26th an attack was made on the enemy's rear guard at Lepel, but it was repulsed.

On the 29th Steingell and Wittgenstein joined at Lepel. The united force, exclusive of the five thousand detached under Wlastoff, and the two thousand five hundred left in Polotzk, amounted to thirty-two thousand combatants.

These thirty-two thousand were then separated into four divisions, amongst which a hundred and ten pieces of cannon were distributed. Prince Jachwill, Steingell, Baz, and Fock were appointed to the commands.

Legrand, having been joined in his retreat by a division of Victor's, who was on march from Smolensk to join him with two other divisions, took up a position at Tchasniki.

On the 30th Wittgenstein reached Slobodka, scarcely two miles distant.

On the 31st, at seven in the morning, Prince Jachwill commenced the attack, from which the enemy did not shrink; but on the arrival of Steingell's force, Tchasniki was carried by the bayonet, and the enemy fell back on a parallel position between Tchasniki and the Scudeulia.

The Grodno hussars attempted to pierce through the enemy's cavalry in the centre, behind which his infantry was forming, but not being supported, were checked, and obliged to regain the general alignment; Prince Jachwill pressed on the enemy's right vigorously; Steingell attacked a wood occupied by their left, and soon forced it.

The cavalry pursued the left to the Loukolmia, and Legrand, withdrawing all his troops over it, re-formed on the left of Victor, who had taken post on the heights of Smoliantsy, where he was joined during the combat by another of his divisions.

The Russians, under cover of their guns, endeavoured to pass the bridge; this attempt was ineffectual, but after an action which had lasted ten hours, the enemy's batteries were silenced, and Victor retired on Loukolm.

Eight hundred prisoners fell into the hands of the Russians, and the number of killed and wounded was considerable.

The Russians lost about five hundred men.

On the 1st of November Victor retired on Sienno, and on the 4th to Czercia.

Wittgenstein continued at Tchasniki, but on the 6th detached General Harpe with two squadrons, some Cossacks, two battalions, and four guns, "to march on Witepsk by both banks of the Dwina." This general, in the first instance, to remove any suspicion of the enterprise, directed his movement on Bechenkowiczi, where he found a French hospital of several hundred wounded. Halting there a day or two, as if his expedition had terminated, he suddenly renewed his march, and moved on to the point of his true destination.

The surprise on both banks was completely successful, and an attempt to burn the bridge failed, the flames being quickly extinguished by the Russians.

After a short combat a part of the garrison fled on Liosna, and General Pougest and three hundred men were taken, with very valuable magazines.

Wittgenstein, finding that Macdonald was inactive, and that Wrede was menacing his right wing by a movement on Dokchitzy, recalled Wlastoff with his five thousand men, and sent Fock, with the reserve, to Lepel.

Victor, urged by the despatches received from Berthier, as already given, "to drive Wittgenstein back across the Dwina—the Emperor and necessity enjoining that attempt"—advanced on the 11th from Czereia to Loukolm; and Oudinot, who had recovered from his wound and joined his corps (the 2nd), marched with it on Bobr by Kholopeniczi, in conformity with the same orders, "that he might act as the advanced guard to Napoleon's army moving towards the Beresina."

Wittgenstein, becoming acquainted with these movements, carried his army to the right of the Oula, to occupy and defend the position of Smoliantsy.

On the 13th of November the enemy attacked the advanced guard of the Russians near Aksiouty, under Alexsief; and notwithstanding that Steingell sent three regiments of infantry to sustain it, the whole were driven back with much loss within less than two miles of Smoliantsy.

On the morning of the 14th Victor continued the movement on the route of Czereia to Smoliantsy.

At eleven o'clock the engagement began on the right of the Russian position.

The troops in front had been directed "to fall back and draw the enemy under the cross fire of a battery established on the high ground in front of the centre and behind the village of Smoliantsy." The lure succeeded. Several columns, one after another, endeavoured to force this point, but it was a fruitless expenditure of courage and life.

The enemy also tried to make an impression on the Russian left by a charge of cavalry en masse, but a masked battery discomfited that effort.

Victor then directed his principal attack against the village of Smoliantsy, and penetrated to the foot of the heights on which the battery that had already occasioned them so much loss was established; but the Russians charged down with the bayonet and regained the village, which was won and lost five times during the action.

The enemy at length, unable to endure the fire of the Russian guns, suspended for some time their attacks, but towards evening renewed them, and again recovered the village, from which they were as quickly driven by the regiment Sewlk.

Victor, finding a resistance that endangered the safety of his whole force, instead of exposing the Russians to the issue proposed by the attack under Berthier's instructions, desisted from further action, and left the field of battle by a lateral movement on his right to the road of Bechenkowiczi, with the loss of above three thousand men, including nine hundred prisoners. The Russians had lost altogether as many, including the loss sustained by Alexsief on his retreat the preceding evening.

On the 15th Victor quitted his position and filed his force on Sienno, within view of the Russians, and undisturbed by them, which occasioned some surprise, as Wittgenstein was a chief who had throughout manifested the most active audacity and perseverance.

The Russians reoccupied the former position of Tchasniki.

On the 17th Victor, having secured his communication with Oudinot and Napoleon's army, re-advanced to Oulianowiczi, and on the 20th to Czereia.

On the 22nd, receiving notice that "Napoleon had

reached Bobr, that a Russian corps was marching by Babinowiczi on Sienno, and that Platow had passed Toloczin," he retired on Kholopeniczi.

In this retrograde movement his rear guard, under Parthonneaux, supported by a Dutch regiment, was attacked near Batury by Wlastoff, and suffered severely, the whole of the Dutch regiment being either killed or wounded.

On the 25th Victor reached Ratuliczi, and there formed the rear guard of Napoleon's army.

On the same day Wittgenstein arrived at Kholopeniczi, and on the 26th at Baran.

Having thus traced the operations and movements of the different corps converging on the line of the Beresina, to assist in the rescue or be present at the destruction of Napoleon and the Moscow army, before opening the concluding scenes of the grand tragic drama it will not be an unprofitable expenditure of time to carry back attention to the principal incidents of the campaign, as they affected the fortune and issue of the main contest; and especially to note those over which skill and bravery on the one hand, or on the other error or accident, perversity of judgment, or causes beyond the reach of human vision presided and ruled.

The consequence of an advanced defensive system on such an extensive frontier, penetrated at various points by an overwhelming invading force, naturally and unavoidably subjected the remotely posted corps to hazardous retrograde and flank movements.

Doctorow's corps, stationed at Lida, when the enemy passed the Niemen at Kowno, found itself in this predicament; and having to run the gauntlet along the front of various columns seeking to pierce and intercept its route of retreat, extricated itself from those dangers by an extraordinary activity and under judicious direction which merited the greatest commendation. Dorokoff's successful conduct of his detachment was equally praiseworthy; but the amount of his force was not sufficient to exercise any influence on the campaign.

The whole retrograde movement of the second army under Bagrathion, from Wolkowich to Smolensk, was a series of perils growing out of a confusion of orders ill calculated as to time and obstacles, as well as distance from the appointed rendezvous. From these perils he ably and bravely disengaged himself; opposing energetic resistance whenever he had a reasonable hope of checking the enemy's progress, and foiling by his indefatigable vigilance the plans projected for his own entanglement and circumvention; but Bagrathion, it must be stated without any intention of detracting from his merit, had the auxiliary benefit of local knowledge in an area of wide range for the further security of his movements, and for aiding his evasion from hostile toils, which were neither skilfully set nor vigorously drawn.

The retreat of the first army from Drissa on Witepsk without molestation from the enemy, already in advance to that point, was a felicitous chance, arising from the incident of a partial affair that made Napoleon hesitate, under the idea that Barclay was about to assume the offensive on the Wilna line; but this idea was a very important misapprehension: it repaired the error of the original dispositions by assuring the connection and concentration of the first and second armies " to cover the Muscovite capital."

Amongst the most prominent instances of the rejected favours of fortune, Junot's conduct in the affair of Loubino—or, as the enemy called it, Waloutina Gora—must ever be considered the chief. It was in fact utterly incomprehensible. Having passed the Dnieper, he had only to march on the high road three or four miles and establish himself on an eminence that commanded the outlet of the defile in which Barclay's column, with its immense artillery and material, was wending its slow way along almost impassable roads. That eminence could have been held, and that outlet closed, against every sallying effort of despair.

Individuals might have saved themselves, but the troops who composed that column, which a few days afterwards disputed the position of Borodino with such obstinate valour and bloody onslaught, instead of being preserved for that occasion to signalize their devotion, and render the enemy's success tributary to their own fame, would have been unable to fight or fall with honour, and must ingloriously have laid down their arms.

The denial of support to Ney in his want of strength to force the gallant screen under the orders of Touchkoff, aggravates the charge of prejudicial and most unaccountable inertness against this always heretofore intrepid and energetic general. Counsel and courage could have availed the Russians nought against the controlling circumstances of position. They were fettered victims, compressed within a space that permitted only an impotent struggle; and yet they eluded their fate by their adversaries contumaciously declining to grasp the tendered disposal of their destiny.

Russia, again, owed the preservation of the glorious remains of the army of Borodino, which was the basis of her subsequent triumph, to the supineness of the enemy's pursuit after the evacuation of Moscow, which supineness allowed the wheel to be completed from the Kolomna to the Kalouga road—a movement that changed instantaneously the relative condition of the two armies—converting the threatened into the threatener, and throwing the enemy upon a defensive that could not be maintained.

Well would it have been for Napoleon if, recognising the jeopardy of his situation, he had attended only to military measures of protection, instead of harbouring expectations from political intrigues, that delayed the execution of those measures until they were too late to secure his safety.

Napoleon entered Moscow on the 14th of September, and the evacuation did not commence till the 18th of October—thirty-four days of delay, in which his force was daily deteriorating whilst the Russians were gathering strength; but had he been satisfied with a fortnight's, or even a three weeks' repose, no wintry ferocity, none of the disasters which occasioned the loss of the Viceroy at the Vop, and of the bridges over the Beresina, would have occurred to oppose impediments; and the Russian army under Kutusow, who was always unwilling to act, offensively or defensively, would have been really in a comparatively inefficient state to embarrass and seriously distress his retreat. Had Napoleon so wished, he could have established and maintained his winter quarters on the Dnieper, and he might then have boasted of a succession of splendid achievements that had carried his standard to the central seat of the Russian empire—that had occasioned the destruction of its capital, the great emporium of the national wealth, and the desolation of some of its richest provinces—boasts painful to humanity, but which in all times have been made; while the facts upon which they are founded have been celebrated as accessories to the martial fame of the invader.

He might then, in defiance of Austria querulous for Gallicia, have proclaimed the restoration of Poland, and rendered the position of Russia as an European power dependent on his own will. But here his pride was stayed; and though many a ray of glory was permitted to beam on his further career, that star which had so long led him to the acquisition of dominion never again, from the lingering hour in which he left Moscow, shed its guiding and protecting light upon his course.

Kutusow at the Czernicznia, by counteracting his own orders, by his veto on Beningsen's support of Orloff Denisoff already in possession of Kasplia, and by his curb on the columns that had been disposed to pursue and press on the enemy, gave life, liberty, and credit to the corps of Murat and Poniatowski, whose preservation was essential for the defensive efficiency of the Moscow army, about to commence its retiring movements.

At Malo-Jaroslavets Napoleon unwisely and rashly rejected the opportunity presented by Kutusow for a mitigatory reparation of the error which he had committed by his too long sojourn in Moscow. He suffered himself to be scared by his own imagination of the power which his adversary possessed from a free transit by the routes of Kalouga or Medynsk, either of which routes would have furnished all the requisite supplies, and conducted him with ease and safety to his destination. It would have been well for his fortunes and fame if on the morning of the 25th of October he had, like Germanicus, as Tacitus records, "when behind the barbarians lay a morass, and in rear of the Romans a river and desolation, determined *that valour was his only hope, and victory his only safety.*"

At Wiazma, where Kutusow might have arrived before Napoleon with his Guards had passed, Kutusow granted a pont d'or to the three corps of Davoust, of Poniatowski, and of the Viceroy and Ney; they could have found no line for retreat except under his guns, even if they could have effected a passage of the river at Wiazma (whose bridges he might have destroyed) under Milaradowitch's fire: one of these corps, Davoust's, was, according to Ney's despatch, "already in a state of fearful disorganization."

In fact no human means could have saved them except Kutusow's wilful absence and fiat.

At Krasnoi, where Napoleon was, in spite of Kutusow's wishes and devious ways, not *chased*, but *stalked down*—where he stood like the stag "panting for life, and butting with his antlers at the worrying hounds, feeding their hungry nostrils with the scent, and bellowing for the huntsman's signal to spring on their prey "—at Krasnoi, where Kutusow might have concluded the war with a loss of less than five thousand men at the most extravagant calculation of the most desperate throes of resistance, Kutusow again charged his conscience and his reputation with the responsibility of the escape; and as Alexander wrote, after the evacuation of Moscow, "posterity will severely judge the act."

The detention of the whole army from the 17th to the 20th at Krasnoi, on pretext "of intercepting the shattered corps of Ney," reduced to seven thousand combatants, which service was after all but imperfectly executed, with all the dilatory and discursive marches subsequently made to avoid harassing Napoleon in his flight over the Dnieper, and increasing his danger in the passage of the Beresina—these were but consistent sequences of a predetermination " to make the victor weep, to see the vanquished fly!"

The Beresina.

Napoleon quitted Orsza on the evening of the 20th for Barany, twelve miles on the road to Borisow. The next day he moved to Kokhanowo.

On the 22nd to Toloczin.

On the 23rd to Bobr.

On the 21st his rear-guard quitted Orsza, burning the two bridges.

His force had been strengthened by the garrison of Orsza and that of Mohilew, twelve hundred strong, which he met on march to Bobr; also by a depôt of cavalry from Gorki en route to Mstislaw; and the whole proceeded towards the Beresina in the following order:—

> Advanced Guard, Junot.
> Zajonizek.
> Gerard.
> Ney.
> Viceroy.
> Rear Guard, Davoust.

Berthier, on the 22nd, wrote from Toloczin to Oudinot that he must "find out a proper point of passage over the Beresina, construct two bridges at it, and cover them by redoubts." "This passage must be secured by to-morrow the 23rd, or at latest by the 24th. We must know the direction, for if in the neighbourhood of Beresino, we must quit the road of Bobr to Borisow. The Emperor in this crisis trusts to your zeal and affection."

In a short time afterwards Napoleon determined to abandon the intention of moving on Beresino, about forty miles below Borisow, and thence gaining Minsk by the road of Igumen. That movement would have thrown him into the line of Kutusow's march, whilst Tchichagow could have opposed his passage of the river.

No reasonable hope could be entertained of forcing a passage at Borisow; for though the town had been recovered, the bridge had been cut and burnt, and the Russians occupied the tête du pont and the ground that dominated over the only points which might still have permitted the attempt to cross.

Napoleon therefore resolved to select a ford in the neighbourhood of Wesselowo, about thirty miles above Borisow, which was marked in his map as practicable, and thence, if necessary, to gain the road to Wilna.

In another letter to Oudinot, dated Toloczin, 23rd of November, 11 A.M., Berthier again wrote: "Try to make yourself master of the ford of Wesselowo as soon as possible: having passed, we can fall upon the enemy in the tête du pont of Borisow, and then march on Minsk, or proceed by Wileika, which road you found practicable; *but the first great and chief object is to secure a passage across the Beresina.*"

An order was sent at the same time to Victor "to occupy the road which leads from Lepel to Wesselowo and Borisow, that he might cover the right and rear of the army during the passage, against Wittgenstein;" but Victor had already commenced his movement to the left by Batury and Ratuliczi on Borisow.

Generals Eblé, Chasseloup, and Jomini, with all the sappers, miners, and pontoniers, were sent off to aid Oudinot in the construction of the bridges: unfortunately for that service, two complete sets of pontoons amounting to sixty, had been abandoned and burnt at Orsza for want of horses.

Orders were again issued "for all the useless carriages, tumbrils, &c., to be burnt; for all draught-horses to be given up to the artillery; for the baggage not indispensably necessary to be destroyed; and for the mounted officers to be formed into two troops or companies under Grouchy and Sebastiani."

Every provident measure was taken that could relieve the exigency.

Napoleon put forth all the strength and resources of

his mind to master again the adverse circumstances that had combined to replace him in the jeopardy from which he had been before, and that so recently, delivered.

Oudinot lost no time in executing his instructions according to their spirit, but selected Studenki,* twelve miles from Borisow and about three nearer than Wesselowo, to construct his bridges.

General Corbineau, with a brigade of cavalry, coming from Polotzk after its evacuation to rejoin Victor, had passed, on the 21st of November, at the ford at this point, to avoid Tchichagow's army; and made his report, "that the ford was then only three feet and a half deep, and that a great marsh lay on the right bank, which, when frozen, would bear artillery; that a little hill about half a mile from the river, and on which the village of Brill stood, commanded the marsh; and that about half a mile beyond ran the high-road from Zembin to Borisow."

Russian bivouac fires were now seen at Brill and beyond, but there being a line of heights on the left bank from which the marsh could be swept with the guns, this site was considered the most eligible; and this notwithstanding that General Aubry of the artillery, who had been sent to inspect, found that the ford had deepened to five feet of water, instead of three and a half, its depth at the time Corbineau passed it, and that the river was above eighty yards wide.

Preparations were therefore directed to be made forthwith. Trees were cut, and the wood of the hamlets and of the village supplied some materials; but

* Or Studzianka.

when Generals Eblé and Chasseloup arrived on the evening of the 25th, they found that nothing in fact was advanced; for the timbers and trestles (or supporters) were too fragile and weak, and the pontoniers, sappers, and miners whom they brought with them had to commence the work anew.

The destruction of the pontoons at Orsza was now practically felt to be a sensible loss; for if only fifteen of the sixty had been preserved, a bridge might have been constructed in two or three hours.

Two bridges were forthwith begun, and placed about two hundred yards distant from each other: that on the right was appointed for the passage of cavalry and infantry; that on the left, which was broader and stronger as some remains of an old bridge were found there, for the artillery, tumbrils, and carriages.

The frost had recommenced with violence on the 24th.

The river was full of floating ice. In many parts the ford was six feet deep, and its breadth, probably by the intervening thaw, had been increased to a hundred and ten yards.

This frost was "a mingled yarn of good and ill" for Napoleon; good, as it hardened the surface of the marsh beyond, and assured practicable transit when reached—bad, as it augmented the general distress, and added intensely to the labour and suffering of the workmen toiling day and night in the ice-binding stream.

In order to distract the attention of the Russians from the Studenki ford, demonstrations were made at different points of the river, and especially at Borisow, on which town the whole mob of followers, non-combatants of the army amounting to many thousands, was directed, as well as a considerable body of troops.

Napoleon reached Borisow in the evening of the 25th with his Guard.

The second corps marched direct on Studenki.

Ney was between Lochnitza and Nemonitza.

The Viceroy at Nacza.

Davoust between Nacza and Kroupki.

Victor at Ratuliczi.

The Admiral continued stationed on the right bank of the Beresina before Borisow and Studenki and Wesselowo, with posts at Stakhow and in front of Oukoloda.

Wittgenstein was at Baran, but six thousand of his troops were detached in pursuit of Victor.

Kutusow at Kopys, on the Dnieper; Milaradowitch with his advanced guard at Staroselie.

On this same day, the 25th, the Admiral received notice from Kutusow "that Napoleon intended to pass the Beresina at Beresino," and an imperative order "to move on that menaced point with sufficient force to oppose the attempt."

The Admiral and his officers doubted the accuracy of this information; nevertheless the Admiral, not choosing to take upon himself the responsibility of leaving open that passage after such positive admonition and instruction, marched immediately with the division Woinoff to Chabachewiczi, and pushed on a detachment of cavalry to Beresino.

Langeron remained before Borisow. Tchaplitz, in obedience to his orders from the Admiral, quitted

Studenki to unite with Langeron, after leaving only a regiment of infantry, one of hussars, some Cossacks, and twelve guns, to watch the ford. Before finally removing, however, he advised the Admiral "that he was satisfied that the enemy were throwing bridges across at that point;" but the order of Kutusow was so precise that even then no deviation was thought advisable.

Kutusow, designedly or undesignedly, was thus again the preserver of Napoleon; for error, if error it were, might have been avoided by a closer pursuit, which would have kept Napoleon in view, instead of maintaining systematically an interval of four marches behind, and thus allowing him full latitude for the selection of the route he might deem most expedient after reaching Bobr, which formed the point of the triangle with Borisow and Beresino, from which it was nearly equidistant.

The Admiral's whole disposable force did not amount to thirty-two thousand men, of which twelve thousand were cavalry: with this force he had a line not only to watch, but to defend (being left by the Marshal's absence isolated), of at least sixty miles, in weather the most unfavourable for vigilance and movement.

The enemy's force at this period has been variously estimated. Including every description of persons approaching the Beresina who depended for their safety on a passage being effected by Napoleon, the grand total might amount to seventy or eighty thousand souls, of which the combatants did not exceed forty thousand.

			Infantry.	Cavalry.
Old Guard		Lefebvre	4,000	..
Young Guard		Mortier	3,000	..
Cavalry of the Guard		Bessières	..	1,500
1st Corps		Davoust	1,500	..
2nd Corps with Dombrowski, and Minsk Garrison		Oudinot	6,000	1,800
4th Corps		The Viceroy	1,600	..
3rd and 5th Corps, Division Claparède, Mohilew Garrison		Ney	3,000	400
8th Corps		Junot	..	..
9th Corps		Victor	12,000	1,200
4th Corps of reserve Cavalry		Latour Maubourg	..	150
	Total		31,100	5,050

To this force may be added about four thousand armed artillerymen, escorts, head-quarter guard, &c., and the rest must come under the denomination of non-combatants and men who did not fall into the ranks—useless hands, and worse than useless mouths.

Two roads led from Borisow to Studenki, one direct on Wesselowo, the other a cross road running along the bank of the Beresina, but avoiding its bends and sinuosities.

Napoleon quitted Borisow at night, stopped at Staroi Borisow, two miles off, and reached Studenki early on the morning of the 26th, where he met Oudinot. The delay in the construction of the bridge caused him much disappointment, but he immediately crowned the hill of Studenki with sixty pieces of cannon (his whole park of artillery now again consisted, by the junction of Oudinot and Victor, of two hundred and sixty pieces tolerably horsed) to command the opposite marsh-land, and sent some horsemen through the river, whom he soon supported by four hundred infantry, passed on two rafts each of which held ten men.

This forlorn hope then advanced on Brill and took possession.

Some Cossacks with two pieces of light artillery fired a couple of shots and then retired, as they could not sustain the superior fire from Studenki; but noise, not execution, ought to have been the object of the Russian officer in charge of this post, to convey in the most rapid way the intelligence of the passage to the Admiral.

At one o'clock in the afternoon the bridge on the right was reported passable through the extraordinary diligence and exertions of General Eblé and his coadjutors.

Napoleon, who had never quitted the spot, instantly ordered the corps of Oudinot "to file by him and across." Spectators affirm that "the corps presented a very regular body, and manifested the best spirit." A detachment of the corps moved on Stakhow in the direction of Borisow, and kept the Russians in check, whilst another detachment proceeded by the right to secure the Zembin road, on the possession of which depended the safety of the army for its march on Wilna by Molodeczno.

About five miles from Studenki the road to Zembin lay through a boggy wood which the little river Gama intersected; over this river there were three wooden bridges, each two hundred yards long, and separated from each other by about as many yards. Had the Russians burnt or destroyed these bridges, the route would have been irreparably closed against the enemy's progress; but their detachment found them uninjured, and entered Zembin without any opposition.

It was near five o'clock before the left bridge at Studenki was ready for the transit of carriages. The artillery of the 2nd corps of the Guard immediately commenced their march across it. Ney, arriving, followed during the night; but the bridge for the carriages breaking twice, great delay occurred, and much confusion ensued from the irregularity of the drivers choking up the entrance.

The pioneers and their fellow-workmen indefatigably exerted powers of endurance and labour which entitled them to a high meed of praise: the Beresina was for them a monument of reputation.

The passage was continued all the 27th, by the corps successively arriving at Studenki.

Parthonneaux, with his brigade, had been left by Victor at Borisow as a rear guard, to march when order was received for his departure; but Wittgenstein, who had reached Kostritsa on the 26th, found himself nearer to the point of passage at Studenki than the enemy's rear guard left at Borisow.

Napoleon, who had passed the night in one of the hamlets at Studenki, and since daybreak had been superintending the passage across the bridges, where his remaining authority as well as patience were severely tested by the disorders that required his continual interference, at one o'clock crossed on horseback to the right bank of the Beresina, and took up his quarters in the hamlet of Zanewki, located in the middle of the wood, about three miles from the bridges, and near the road to Borisow.

At four o'clock the left bridge broke down for the third time, and required three hours for its repair; during this pause the multitude began to swarm around the bridges and over the whole ground between them, and Studenki was covered with carriages and the remaining incumbrances of an original army of above four hundred thousand men. All directing control was lost; the wildest disorder and violence prevailed; despair made savages of those who had strength enough left to contend; and the helpless throng, unable to advance, still perversely barred the approaches to the bridges, as if resolved on making the ruin of all inevitable.

During the night, the Viceroy, Davoust, and Latour Maubourg, collecting some armed detachments, forced a passage through this mass with great difficulty; but there yet remained on the left bank, exclusive of the division of Parthonneaux, the division of Gerard with two brigades of light cavalry.

Wittgenstein, who had reached Kostritsa, and whose detachment of six thousand men under Wlastoff had arrived at Giskowo, was informed on the 26th in the evening, " that Victor was at Borisow, and that the passage of the army was being effected at Studenki."

There being no practicable route for artillery from Kostritsa to Studenki, Wittgenstein began his march on Staroi Borisow to intercept Victor, or pursue him if he already had passed to gain Studenki.

Platow, who was at Kholopeniczi, was directed "to march on Borisow;" but Yermolow, who was at Kroupki with his detachment, and Milaradowitch at Maliawka near Bobr, were both too distant to take any part in the projected operation.

Wlastoff, with Wittgenstein's advanced corps, at three o'clock in the afternoon of the 27th reached the farm of Staroi Borisow.

Victor with two divisions of his corps had already passed, but a body of French on retreat from Borisow was fallen in with, attacked, broken, and pursued, with loss of one gun and some prisoners. From these prisoners it was learnt "that the division Parthonneaux was approaching." Wittgenstein, forming his army, sent a flag of truce to require his surrender. Parthonneaux detained the flag, and continued his advance. When in face of Staroi Borisow and the Russians, he deployed his force and attacked with vigour the Russian columns and batteries; he even carried the farm, but was almost immediately driven out by a charge with the bayonet, in which some of the militia of Nowogorod showed great intrepidity.

Parthonneaux then attempted to fall back on Borisow; but Borisow was already occupied by Platow and Sislavin. Parthonneaux, finding his retreat cut off, demanded "to capitulate:" whilst the parleys were being established he and four hundred of his division gained a wood on his right, in hopes that they might pass behind the Russians and reach Studenki; but the Cossacks of Czernozoukoff falling in with them made all prisoners; and at seven o'clock next morning, on being made acquainted with this capture, the whole division laid down its arms.

The force altogether consisted of Generals Belliard, Camus, and Delaitre, with between six and seven thousand men, including three thousand non-combatants, and a brigade of cavalry composed of a

Saxon and a Berg regiment six hundred strong, in effective condition, with three guns.

In the night of the 27th and 28th Yermolow reached Borisow with his corps; and the Admiral, who on the 27th had retraced his steps upon being finally convinced that the passage at Studenki was not a feint, on regaining the tête du pont of Borisow from Chabachewiczi distant fifteen miles, detached Pahlen to support Tchaplitz, who was still lodged in the woods between Brill and Bolehoi Stakhow.

The Russian guards concerted an attack on both banks of the river. A bridge of pontoons was constructed at Borisow, over which Yermolow passed with his detachment to support the Admiral at Bolehoi Stakhow, where the Admiral, after a march of eight miles, arrived on the morning of the 28th.

Wittgenstein moved on Studenki to force Victor, who was supposed to be covering the passage.

During the night of the 27th and 28th little progress was made by the enemy in the passage of the Beresina. Napoleon, therefore, desired that the bridges might be maintained during the day of the 28th; but as Victor, after Parthonneaux's surrender, had only the division Gerard left to occupy a considerable extent of position necessary for their defence, the division of Daendels was repassed, which gave him a total force of five thousand infantry and four hundred cavalry: still there was a great want of artillery, for he had retained only the guns of his reserve, and on account of the embarrassed state of the bridges no more could be brought back; to remedy, in some measure, this deficiency batteries were established, by

Napoleon's order, on the opposite bank to aid him on his right with a flanking fire.

A rivulet bordered by brushwood covered his front; his right rested on the Beresina; his left was so weak in numbers that it could not be extended to a wood which lay at a short distance, and his four hundred cavalry formed its only appui.

At eight in the morning the Admiral, with eighteen thousand infantry and nine thousand cavalry, but which the ground did not permit him to develop, commenced on the right bank of the Beresina the attack on Oudinot and Ney, who were posted with nine thousand infantry and fifteen hundred cavalry, with their right on the wood bordering the Borisow route, and their left on the Beresina. Oudinot defended the right and centre; Ney the left; Napoleon with his Guard formed the reserve. The extent of the alignment was about a mile and a quarter. The ground was covered with open woods, and a partial cultivation.

Seven regiments of Russian chasseurs were thrown into the wood between Stakhow and Brill, and kept up an active fire. Oudinot being wounded, Ney took the whole command; and about ten o'clock, collecting his cavalry and supporting it with columns of infantry and a considerable artillery, charged on the chasseurs, who were trampled down or swept off before they could reach Stakhow: about twelve hundred were killed or taken.

Continuing their impulse and success, they bore down on eight regiments of infantry, whom Sabinief was conducting to the aid of Tchaplitz from the Admiral at Stakhow, but whom Sabinief, on approaching the wood, had scattered as tirailleurs.

Tchaplitz, at the head of two squadrons of hussars of Pavlograd, opportunely checked their career, and gave time to rally the infantry; but the enemy, by advancing the two corps, had gained the side of the wood nearest Stakhow, whence they could not be dislodged, and where they continued for the remainder of the day.

The action was kept up till eleven at night, and cost both sides a loss of not less than five thousand men.

Oudinot, Legrand, and Zajonizck were amongst the enemy's wounded; Dombrowski had been wounded on the preceding day.

Whilst this bloody and interesting combat had been carrying on by the enemy upon the right bank to afford an increased chance of safety to their more unfortunate comrades still on the left bank, Wlastoff, about ten o'clock in the morning, arrived and formed in front of Victor's position; thence he directed an attack on the enemy's left with the hussars and Cossacks, but this was foiled by Fournier at the head of his cavalry, who was, however, repulsed when pursuing his success, by the Russian reserve.

Diebitch having established a battery of twelve guns against the enemy's right flank, the shot plunging upon the mass gathered round the bridges caused a frightful scene of terror, struggle, and carnage. Overset carriages blocked up the bridges; horses in herds without riders flew wildly about, bearing down all in their way; numbers of men and women who attempted to pass the river perished; numbers were driven into the stream by the pressure of those who were farthest distant; numbers were thrown down, trampled upon, and suffocated. It was a pandemonium of horrors.

Victor and his gallant band, nevertheless, undauntedly continued their resistance, and made repeated sallies on the Russians as they encroached on his position, notwithstanding that the Russian artillery was overwhelmingly superior, and thirty-six guns kept incessantly pouring their fire; nor was it till nightfall (at that season and latitude soon after two in the afternoon) that Victor was forced to make a conversion, and approach his bridges with his host, not conquerors, but ennobled by their valour and entitled to take rank amongst the proudest; for the Russians had also fought with great bravery, and in no way favoured the enemy's success by any want of energy on their own part.

The Russian force in action (Steingell's division being left to disarm and secure Parthonneaux's force) had not exceeded fourteen thousand men, of which five thousand were killed or wounded.

The enemy had lost three guns, and several thousand killed, wounded, and prisoners, including the stragglers of other corps.

As soon as the action ceased the unhappy multitude lighted bivouac fires* on the borders of the river, where they lay exhausted by their agony of anxiety and want of food.

The pontoniers under the direction of General Eblé redoubled their Herculean efforts to clear the

---

* These fires were chiefly made of the wheels and other portions of the abandoned carriages and ammunition tumbrils. Whatever happened to be most contiguous was seized to be burnt on the spot. The frequent explosions which took place during the night proved to be the blowing up of powder tumbrils thoughtlessly ignited, and spreading havoc around.

bridges and open an unencumbered passage to them. Everything that embarrassed was thrown into the river, and a trench was dug to prevent that flood of masses pressing on their flanks which had previously caused much of the disorder.

At nine, Victor with his artillery and all but a rear guard passed. At one the transit was free, but the wearied crowd could not be then awakened to a sense of their danger, and, until some carriages were burnt, refused to move.

The greater part, however, were yet deaf to persuasion, and insensible to consequences.

A torpor seized on their faculties as well as limbs: they thought no longer of the perils past, and were quite reckless of the future.

Fascinated to the fatal spot of destruction, from which they had been recently so eager and so resolute to fly, they would not, or could not, anticipate the renewing horrors of the morning dawn. At five o'clock the last rear guard was withdrawn.

This withdrawal roused them from their apathy: there was a general rush to the bridges, and in a short time the passage was again rendered impracticable. All the dreadful scenes of the former struggles were then renewed.

Eblé had orders to destroy the bridges at eight o'clock, but he protracted the execution for half an hour. The flames then burst forth, and with them ascended a wailing shriek of anguish and despair to the skies. Some sprang forward on the fiery platform, and were ingulfed or consumed; some dashed into the river, and, crushed by massive blocks of ice, rolled down the stream, calling in vain for succour.

It was a commingled herd of men, women, and children, doing they knew not what, flying they knew not whither, and in their delirium adding each to other's calamity. All was madness and indescribable woe.

About nine the Cossacks darted down upon their prey, and several thousands, who were still frantically cleaving to the idea of an escape, found themselves thus for ever cut off from all hope.

Many certainly lost their lives in this ungovernable mêlée, but there was no general massacre.

The booty was immense, and of great value. The spoil of the countries traversed by the invader became the prize of the avengers.

Wittgenstein's regular troops reached the Beresina about half-past nine in the morning, but could not proceed farther for want of means of passage. Wittgenstein, whilst awaiting pontoons which the Admiral undertook to send, directed Major-general Koutousoff, who was at Lepel with three thousand three hundred horse, "to march on Wilna by Dokchitsy," and reinforcing Orloff Denisoff with three regiments of Cossacks, the hussars of Grodno, a battalion of chasseurs mounted on peasants' horses, and a company of horse artillery, "to pass the Beresina at Kriczin, and pursue in the direction of Kamen and Zamostie."

Milaradowitch did not reach Borisow till the 29th, and Koutousoff's advanced guard did not reach Oukoloda on the Beresina until the 30th.

In the night of the 28th and 29th the enemy retired on Zembin.

On the 29th his advanced guard reached Plechenitza, and Napoleon slept at Kamen; on the 30th, at Stuiki.

The Admiral had detached General Lanskoi with twenty squadrons and a regiment of Cossacks "to head the enemy." He entered Plechenitza about mid-day of the 29th, and carried off General Kamenki and some orderlies who were preparing lodgment for head-quarters.

Oudinot, and several generals sick and wounded, with a dozen officers, their servants, and some twenty carabineers, were in one of the houses, but they succeeded in defending it until a column appeared and effected their rescue.

At daybreak on the 29th the Admiral, learning the departure of the enemy, pushed on to Brill, finding on his route seven abandoned guns, and overtaking a great many stragglers.

The Admiral thence despatched Tchaplitz with seven regiments of chasseurs, one of infantry, twenty-four squadrons of regular cavalry, and eight regiments of Cossacks, with three companies of flying artillery, to pursue; but Ney having destroyed the three bridges before referred to, in the wood leading to Zembin, their march was stopped until after the night's excessive frost, which congealed both river and marsh. Lanskoi then pushed on to the cabaret of Kabinskoie Roudnia, taking one gun and two hundred prisoners, amongst whom was a general.

On the 1st of December, Platow, who had joined Tchaplitz, attacked the enemy's rear guard at Khoteniczi, and took five guns and five hundred prisoners.

On the 2nd the rear guard, after an obstinate resistance in a wooded line of route, lost one gun and four hundred prisoners near Starinki.

On the 3rd Napoleon reached Molodeczno. His

rear guard on this day lost, near Latigal, nine guns and fifteen hundred prisoners.

The army was able to procure some little subsistence in the country it was now traversing, but the fierce cold, fatigue, sickness, and disorganization rendered it no longer a military force capable of any operations.

Its daily reduction was fearful. On the 2nd December, according to an official return, "there were but seven thousand infantry and two thousand cavalry under arms;" and in a letter of Berthier's of that day it appears that "Ney reported the following to be the state of his corps:—

Division Claparède	200
Dombrowski	800
2nd Division—5th Corps	525
3rd Division—2nd Corps	500
Total	2,025."

In a postscript he adds that "he had sent the skeletons of the 3rd corps with his eagles to follow the Young Guard."

Napoleon had received some despatches from the Duke of Bassano at Wilna, which announced to him "the arrival of Loison with his division (the German division) at Wilna, which he would send on to meet him at Ochmiani." He added that "there were about seven thousand troops in Wilna on the way to join their respective corps, but that he had detained them there, and an army of fugitives, employés, wounded, and sick."

The Duke also rendered an important service to Napoleon by circulating accounts of imaginary successes, which suppressed defections and insurrections that would have proved fatal to his retreat through Germany, if he could have escaped from them in Lithuania.

Wrede, with his Bavarians forming the 6th corps, who occupied Dokchitzy, was ordered by Napoleon "to retire on Wileika to cover the right flank of Napoleon's column."

On the 2nd of December Major-general Koutousoff, who had been ordered "with his three thousand horse from Lepel to pursue the enemy," overtook Wrede's rear guard at Dolghinow, and made a number of prisoners. Wrede found himself therefore obliged to change his direction, and continued his movement on Wilna, by the route of Narvez, Nestawichki, Swiranki, and Nemenczin.

Napoleon, on reaching Molodeczno, had hoped to gain a few days' repose, but Tchaplitz had crossed the river Oucha, three wersts below the town, and forced him to an immediate retreat, which cost his column twenty-four guns, and nearly three thousand combatants and non-combatants; the Polish remnant had been already despatched from Molodeczno on Olita by cross roads to regain Warsaw, and Junot had marched on Merecz by other cross roads, with all the dismounted horsemen.

The memorable 29th bulletin was also written and despatched from Molodeczno, in which bulletin Napoleon, after describing the effects of the cold, proceeded to state,—"Those whom Nature has not endowed with strength of mind to triumph over the chances of fate and fortune lost their cheerfulness, their good humour, and dreamt only of misfortunes: those whom she created with superior powers preserved their gaiety, their moral disposition, and saw new sources of glory in the difficulties to be surmounted."

Napoleon left Molodeczno on the 4th for Bonitza.

Loison's arrival at Ochmiani had been fixed for the 6th, and garrisons had been established at Smorgoni and Miedniki to secure the communication with Wilna.

On the 5th of December, at eight in the morning, Napoleon proceeded in a carriage to Smorgoni, and there convoking a council, at which were present Murat, Eugène, Berthier, Ney, Davoust, Lefebvre, Mortier, and Bessières, he notified his intention "of departing forthwith for Paris, as his presence in the capital was essential for the interests of the army as well as of the empire."

Having made over the command to Murat, and taken the name of the Duke de Vicenza, at seven in the evening he departed in his carriage, accompanied by one sledge, and by a small escort of Neapolitan cavalry. Caulaincourt sat in the carriage; Duroc and Lobau were in the sledge; his Mameluke, and Captain Wasowicz of the Polish Lancers, acting as interpreter, sat on the box of the carriage.

Napoleon's danger could not but be considered by all to be very great, and yet it was still greater than was supposed; for Sislavin, with his partisan corps, who had been marching on Ochmiani, had actually, during the afternoon, entered the town, not knowing that it was already occupied by Loison's advance, which had arrived at mid-day, and having been driven out by it, was bivouacked at a little distance from the road by which Napoleon had to pass.

At Miedniki Napoleon found the Duke of Bassano, who exchanged places with Caulaincourt, and proceeded to Wilna escorted by fifty Neapolitans commanded by the Duke of Roua Romana, who in this journey lost by the cold several fingers of his left hand. At ten o'clock he reached Wilna, but, not wishing to be recognised, proceeded to an isolated house at the extremity of the Kowno suburb.

All the commentators on this war have charged the different commanders with various errors of disposition and execution in the transactions relating to the passage of the Beresina.

The undeniable faults are: 1st. Kutusow's withdrawal of his force from the pressure of the pursuit and combinations to guard the Beresina line.

2nd. The order "for the Admiral's march on Beresino, under the positive assurance that Napoleon was moving by Beresino to Igumen and Minsk."

3rd. The neglect of the Zembin road.

4th. The loose manner in which the troops at Brill were brought into action without contiguous support.

5th. The over caution of the attack on Victor, whose number and circumstances warranted no such uneasiness for flanks or rear as ought to have checked a concentrated assault of his position and penetration of his feeble screen.

6th. The delay in the order sent by Napoleon from Bobr for Victor's march direct on the point indicated for the construction of the bridges, which delay was the fatal origin of Parthonneaux's disaster.

7th. The delegation to others of the selection of the site for the bridge and superintendence of its construction, when the general safety depended on the operation being executed with a promptitude, capacity, order, and exertion that Napoleon's own presence alone could ensure.

8th. The reinforcement of Victor by the return of Daendels, when the unobstructed immediate retreat of the army was preferable to any sanguinary victory; by which, in its weak and shattered state, subsequent ruin was rendered inevitable.

This fault, however, was one which did not entail any self-reproach. The General may have committed an imprudence, but the Sovereign and the Man cannot be condemned for a generous effort to preserve from abandonment so many helpless beings who as yet remained during the day of the 28th on the left bank, dependent, as all believed, on his power of protection for safety.

The departure of Napoleon from the army (at first by his desire represented as only a journey to Warsaw for the purpose of taking the direction of the Austrians and Saxons under Schwarzenberg and Regnier) caused much depression and dissatisfaction; but the motives were too apparently reasonable and prospectively beneficial not to satisfy every one after a short time that it was not a flight for personal safety, but a measure of paramount necessity for the common welfare.

The enemy quitted Smorgoni on the 6th. At Roudziez the rear guard lost seven guns, and above a thousand prisoners were made by Tchaplitz.

The cold was intense—the thermometer twenty-seven and thirty degrees below freezing point, with sky generally clear, and a subtle, keen, razor-cutting, creeping wind that penetrated skin, muscle, and bone to the very marrow, rendering the surface as white and the whole limb affected as fragile as alabaster: sometimes there was a foudroyant seizure that benumbed at once the whole frame, and stiffened motionlessly the still breathing carcase, from which feet and hands were snapped off at the joints with the slightest degree of wrench, but without any pain.

These ravages were terrifically destructive. A general recklessness confounded all ranks; command ceased, and it became a "sauve qui peut" at a funeral pace.

On the 7th the remnant of the rear guard with twenty-five guns fell into the hands of Tchaplitz.

The same day the Admiral reached Smorgoni.

Wittgenstein halted at Ruhki, and Marshal Kutusow, who had left his column to join and command the Admiral's and Wittgenstein's armies, placed his head quarters at Radochkowiczi.

On the 8th the pursuit was continued vigorously; Tchaplitz taking, or rather overtaking, sixty-one guns and several thousand prisoners of the main body; for a rear guard could no longer be formed till Loison's division arrived from Wilna; but this division, composed of young Germans, whilst on its march to Ochmiani had suffered suddenly more severely than any other. Thirty degrees of frost and upwards had so decimated it in a few hours, that it was rendered almost totally unserviceable; the rapidity and violence of the seizure were unparalleled; the climate seemed to be waging war on human life with an exterminating velocity as well as asperity never before experienced.

On the 9th Tchaplitz, at Miedniki, collected sixteen

more guns and thirteen hundred prisoners, but the flying remains of the enemy succeeded in reaching Wilna, in which there was a fresh division of Neapolitans belonging to the 11th corps. Sislavin, the partisan, attempting to enter the city with the fugitives, was repulsed.

The road to Wilna was strewed with dead and dying, to whom "the greatest act of charity that could be done," as they beseechingly said, "next to their deprivation of life, was the imposition of their comrades' corpses on the living flesh most contiguous to the frozen, that a festering warmth might be produced."

Napoleon, in the conference with Maret, had stated to him "the true condition of the rabble train that represented his late magnificent army," and which he described "as being without force, without clothes, without shoes, and a mere fugitive band." On Maret's assuring him that "Wilna contained ample magazines," he exclaimed, "You give me new life," and directed Maret to enjoin Murat and Berthier "to stop eight days at Wilna to rally the troops, morally as well as physically."

With that flattering hope he entered a traîneau which a Polish proprietor had given him in exchange for his carriage.

On the 10th in the morning he arrived at Warsaw, and alighted at the Hôtel d'Angleterre, where his apartments were long afterwards kept unoccupied by the landlord, in testimony of respect for unfortunate greatness. After seeing some of the authorities, he departed again in a few hours—arrived at Dresden on the 14th of December, where he held a short interview with the King of Saxony, and thence proceeded to

Paris, which he reached on the 19th of December, at half-past eleven at night—two days after the publication of the 29th bulletin.

Napoleon's wishes and instructions left with Maret were incapable of execution.

Wilna, overwhelmed with consternation at the unexpected flood of wretchedness and disease that poured into the city, presented the aspect of a town already stormed ; the shops were shut—supplies were withheld—panic prevented all measures of relief—the magazines were soon pillaged, and want engendered every species of disorder.

In the midst of these scenes of affliction the Russian guns were heard.

Wrede, on the morning of the 9th, had joined, with two thousand men and a few guns, the remains of the division Loison and the Neapolitan cavalry at Rukoni, three leagues from Wilna.

In vain he attempted to resist the Russian column supported by cavalry and a battery of twelve guns placed on sledges, that were thus enabled to move and pour their fire in every requisite direction.

Forced back on Wilna, Ney collected six hundred men, and took post with Wrede on the height that covers and commands the town on the side of Minsk. Thus united, they succeeded in beating off the Russian cavalry that had preceded, whilst a detachment of the Guard also repulsed the Cossacks, who had rounded the city, and menaced the opposite suburb.

Wilna could, however, be no longer held as a post of refuge.

Every moment's delay endangered the retreat by the sole remaining line of Kowno and Troki.

Murat had already left the city and taken up his quarters surrounded by the Guards in bivouac. By his desire Berthier wrote to Ney:—

"Wilna, Dec. the 9th, 1812.

"General Wrede having been forced in his position, and your succour under Gratien" [who had replaced Loison, taken ill] "not having enabled him to repulse the enemy, the King has removed his quarters to the barrier of the gate of Kowno.

"His Majesty's intention is to march to-morrow with the Guard to Kowno, intending to arrive there as quickly as possible, to collect the fugitives and isolated soldiers, and defend that post.

"Continue to form a rear guard with the divisions of Wrede and Loison. Evacuate this night if possible all the artillery, and particularly the treasure.

"Under existing circumstances the King can do nothing but gain Kowno as expeditiously as possible.

"Do the best you can in this painful exigency, where the frost has completed the disorganization of the army.

"The King authorizes you to recommend our sick to the Russian commandant.

(Signed) "BERTHIER."

BERTHIER TO COUNT DARU.

"Wilna, Dec. the 9th, 1812.

"The King is at the barrier of Kowno. Ney will withdraw to-morrow as late as he can. Send off the treasure this night. General Eblé will give you, if necessary, artillery horses. Every effort must be made to send it away. We will escort it, if sent to us this night at the barrier of Kowno.

" Distribute, as abundantly as wished, provisions and clothing, for Wilna cannot be held through to-morrow.

" Employ all your energy to send off towards Kowno all you can.

(Signed)   " BERTHIER."

Murat, through Berthier, then sent off despatches to Schwarzenberg and Macdonald, ordering, in the name of Napoleon, " the retreat of the former on Bialystok to cover Warsaw ; and of the latter on Tilsit to approach the Niemen as the new line of operation, but to fall back as leisurely as possible."

On the 10th of December at four in the afternoon Murat began his march with four thousand five hundred combatants.

	Infantry.	Cavalry.
Old Guard	800	800
Young Guard	100	
Wrede and Loison	2,300	200
1st, 2nd, 3rd, 4th, and 9th Corps	300	
Total	3,500	1,000

At Ponari, five miles from Wilna, was a steep hill, with the ice-covered road bordered on each side by a wood. Here was such a confusion that no carriages could pass forward ; all that remained of artillery and carriages were therefore abandoned, and in them ten millions of francs in money, which the soldiers pillaged ; but a loss still more painful was occasioned by the desertion of a number of brave officers, sick and wounded, who could not be carried on farther, and whose fate was the more deplorable, as they were presumed so nearly to have reached their port of safety. The infantry and cavalry then filed through the wood, and thus avoided the defile obstruction.

Ney had withdrawn at daybreak.

The Cossacks instantly entered Wilna, and found in the city at least twenty thousand, wounded and sick, and helpless through the biting injury of the frost.

On the 10th Murat reached Ewé; on the 11th at seven in the evening, Roumcziki, where the troops halted, but Murat proceeded with an escort to Kowno, which he gained at midnight: there he found a garrison of German new levies, fifteen hundred strong, and forty-two pieces of cannon, twenty-five of which were well horsed, large magazines, and two millions and a half of money; but the Niemen being frozen over, the place could not be held as a tête du pont; for the Russians on arrival could cross the ice and surround the town: he therefore retired on the 13th with the Guard on Gumbinnen, after planting nine guns on a hill near Alexioten that commands Kowno.

Ney had entered Kowno with a thousand combatants, and found everything in the most frightful state of disorder.

The streets were full of dead and drunken men; the magazines, some of them of brandy, having been broken open and pillaged.

In the midst of this direful distress, Platow, with his Cossacks and guns, arrived, and about two in the afternoon opened his fire on the bridge of the Niemen, on that over the Wilia, and on the gate of Wilna, where the heavy guns by some mistake of orders had been spiked. The detachment of recruits at this post fled. Ney and Gerard hastened to the menaced point and saved it by their exemplary exertions as officers and soldiers, for they were armed with muskets. General Marchand then made a sally to dislodge the Cossacks from the height of Alexioten, which was at first successful, but the position could not be maintained.

The valour and exertions of the chiefs would not have preserved the city itself unless night had put an end to the attack.

Ney at half-past nine evacuated the place, setting fire, as he left, to the bridges of the Niemen and of the Wilia. Re-mounting the river some way, he turned to the left that he might traverse the forest of Polwiski to avoid his pursuers; in this forest the last gun of the division Loison was abandoned!

On the 14th of December the central body of that mighty armament which had crossed the Niemen under the immediate orders of Napoleon upon the 24th of June, not six months antecedently, to achieve the reduction of the Russian power and continue for ages the domination of France over Europe, mustered under arms only a force of four hundred infantry and six hundred cavalry! every other portion of this army being represented by a handful of officers and non-commissioned officers forming escort to the eagles that had not been captured or buried!

Out of the more than eight hundred pieces of artillery with which these corps had crossed the Niemen, only nine guns taken from Kowno remained in their possession, with the exception of the Polish guns which had been despatched from Molodeczno on

Olita and Warsaw, which detachment had not been pursued.

The destruction by the wind that raised the sand, and rolled it in such waves that it swallowed up and entombed fifty thousand men of Cambyses' host, was but the overset of "a bauble boat" compared with this giant wreck.

Murat, on the 13th, reached Schrauel, and on the 14th Wirballen, whence Berthier wrote to Napoleon: "It must be stated that four-fifths of the army have feet, hands, or face frozen. Your Majesty can have no idea of the state of suffering into which the rigour of the cold has plunged the army: obliged for the last two months to make incessant forced marches, the remaining combatants scarcely suffice for an escort to protect the King, the generals, and the eagles."

Murat arrived at Gumbinnen on the 17th, and on the 19th at Königsberg.

At Königsberg the fugitives at last enjoyed some repose, without the Cossack "hurrah" ringing in their ears and fevering their rest.

Murat then gave orders to collect the stragglers of the army, multitudes of whom had contrived as isolated individuals to precede the retiring force, and distribute themselves over the Prussian territory. Those of the fifth corps were directed on Warsaw; of the sixth on Plock; first and eighth on Thorn; second and third on Marienberg; fourth and fifth on Marienwerder; Guards on Insterburg, where a new division of the tenth corps under General Henderlet, and composed of fourteen thousand men with twenty guns, was daily expected.

On the 10th the Admiral's advanced guard entered Wilna about mid-day, and measures were immediately taken to suppress every irregularity, but it was a work which required time for its accomplishment.

The Admiral himself arrived on the 11th.

Wittgenstein, who had passed the Beresina on the bridge of boats sent by the Admiral, had reached Kamen on the 4th of December; and, marching by Wileika, Narvcz, and Nestawichki, arrived at Swiranki on the 10th; from thence he moved by Szerwinty, Wilkomir, and Koidany to intercept the retreat of Macdonald, who occupied with the tenth corps a line from Frederickstadt to Mittau.

On the 13th Marshal Kutusow arrived at Wilna from Radochkowiczi, which he had reached on the 6th, and whence he had despatched the fourth, sixth, and eighth corps with the light cavalry of Vasiltchikow on Wologin. Ojarowski had already arrived at Wologin on the 7th to watch Schwarzenberg at Slonim; with Ojarowski, Touchkoff, after displacing Ertel (whose valuable force, consisting of fifteen battalions, fourteen squadrons, two regiments of Cossacks, and two companies of artillery, had been wasted by its non-arrival to assist in the Beresina operations), was directed to reunite.

Marshal Kutusow had fallen in with the advanced guard of Milaradowitch at Radochkowiczi, which moved on the 7th to Molodeczno, on the 8th to Smorgoni, on the 9th to Ochmiani, and on the 13th to Wilna.

Kutusow's march route after passing the Beresina at Joukowitz had been:—

Oucha	..	..	December	1st.
Rowaritsa	..	..	„	2nd.
[Halted on the]	..	..	„	3rd.
Kossin	..	..	„	4th.
Bielorouczie	..	..	„	5th.
Radochkowiczi	..	..	„	6th.
Molodeczno	..	..	„	7th.
Smorgoni	..	..	„	8th.
Ochmiani	..	..	„	9th.
Wilna	..	..	„	13th.

During these last marches the Russian troops, who were moving through a country devastated by the enemy, suffered nearly as much as they did from want of food, fuel, and clothing.

The soldier had no additional covering for the night bivouacs on the frozen snow; and to sleep longer than half an hour at a time was probable death. Officers and men, therefore, were obliged to relieve each other in their snatches of sleep, and to force up the reluctant and frequently resisting slumberers.

Firing could scarcely ever be obtained; and when obtained the fire could only be approached with great caution, as it caused gangrene of the frozen parts; but as water itself froze at only three feet from the largest bivouac fires, it was almost necessary to burn before the sensation of heat could be felt.

Above ninety thousand perished, as the subsequent returns will manifest; and out of ten thousand recruits afterwards marched on Wilna as a reinforcement, only fifteen hundred reached that city: the greater part of these were conveyed to the hospitals as sick or mutilated. One of the chief causes of their losses was that the trowsers becoming worn by the continued marches in the inner part of the thighs exposed the flesh, so that the frost struck into it when chafed, and irritated it with virulent activity.

Continually incidents occurred to verify the relation of suffering by the Romans in one of their Parthian expeditions. "By the inclemency of the season," wrote the Roman historian, "many lost the use of their limbs; and it often happened that the sentinel died on his post. The case of one soldier deserves to be mentioned: he was employed in carrying a load of wood; his hands, nipped by the frost and cleaving to the faggot, dropped from his arms."

On the 14th the Admiral quitted Wilna for Novoi Troki and the Niemen, and on the 18th entered into cantonments at Gezno and Preny.

On the 16th Kutusow's column took up cantonments in and around Wilna.

The return of the effectives of the whole Russian army at this period did not exceed a hundred thousand men, thus distributed:—

Kutusow	35,000
Wittgenstein	15,000
Tchichagow	15,000
Sacken, Ertel, and Essen	25,000
Riga Garrison	10,000
Total	100,000

Such was the result of Kutusow's policy and military dispositions at Taroutino, Wiazma, Krasnoi, and the Beresina.

The Emperor Alexander left S. Petersburg on the 18th of December, and on the 22nd arrived at Wilna.

The advent of this Sovereign was a benefaction of Providence for the remaining survivors of the enemy. Every aid that possibly could be supplied was instantly administered to them, not merely by his orders, but under his own personal superintendence, in which work of benevolence he was zealously seconded by the Grand Duke Constantine. Both braved infection, disease, horrible spectacles, and every accompanying danger and disgust in the discharge of these good offices. Money was given to the officers; and without adulation it might be said of the Emperor, that he came on a mission of exalted charity, and mercy to fallen enemies.

The hospital of S. Bazile presented the most awful and hideous sight:—seven thousand five hundred bodies were piled like pigs of lead over one another in the corridors; carcases were strewed about in every part; and all the broken windows and walls were stuffed with feet, legs, arms, hands, trunks, and heads to fit the apertures, and keep out the air from the yet living.

The putrefaction of the thawing flesh, where the parts touched and the process of decomposition was in action, emitted the most cadaverous smell.

Nevertheless in each of these pestilential and icy répertoires three or four grenadiers of the Guard were posted, inhaling the pestilential effluvia.

On the English General making the Emperor acquainted with this inconsiderate " employment of his finest troops," he went himself to the convent and inspected the chambers, speaking the kindest words to the unfortunate inmates, and giving the requisite directions for their treatment. The Grand Duke followed his example, but caught the epidemy, from which he with difficulty recovered.

When the frozen carcases were removed in sledges twenty or thirty at a time, to be thrown into a pit outside the town, the exhibition of the different attitudes in which death had left them was very remarkable: each seemed to have been transfixed in some moment of muscular effort and active volition of thought.

There was seldom repose in any of the limbs; almost all expressed an action of intent, of pain, or supplication, with which the eyes corresponded.

It was a pictorial history of last agonies, fraught with subjects of most interesting contemplation.

Great fires were kept continually burning in the streets of the city, which was one great charnel receptacle, to prevent the infection and spread of a real plague, but it required weeks and months to effect its purification.

Amongst those who fell victims to their exemplary zeal in the pursuit of the enemy from the Beresina must be noted the Earl of Tyrconnel, aide-de-camp to the Duke of York, and acting aide-de-camp to the English General, Sir Robert Wilson—a young nobleman in the prime of life, only twenty-five years of age, of expectancies to the highest mark; for he was gallant, good, and amiable, to a degree that made him the object of universal praise and affectionate attachment.

On the 20th of December he expired at Wilna, and his country was bereaved of one of the bravest of its officers, and one of the most estimable and engaging of its social ornaments.

The Russians erected a monument to his memory in the churchyard of Wilna, which records that "it was raised to a man who by his conduct in the fields of honour and by the gentleness of his disposition had conciliated general esteem."

On the morning of the 26th of December, the anniversary of the Emperor's birthday, Alexander sent for the English General, and after a few appropriate allusions to the festival said, "General, I have called you into my cabinet to make a painful confession; but I rely on your honour and prudence. I wished to have avoided it, but I could not bear to appear inconsistent in your estimate of my proceedings; which I must be thought if my motives were not explained.

"I must, however, first assure you of my great satisfaction with all your conduct during your residence with my armies; and also thank you for your correspondence, which, in justice to yourself, I have directed to be deposited in my archives.

"The consequences which have flowed from your devotion to my interests, when the conference was proposed at Taroutino, were of great benefit to them, and your communications have enabled me to prevent much other mischief.

"You have always told me *truth*—truth I could not obtain through any other channel.

"I know that the Marshal has done nothing he ought to have done—nothing against the enemy that he could avoid; all his successes have been *forced* upon him. He has been playing some of his old Turkish tricks,* but the nobility of Moscow support him, and insist on his presiding over the national glory of this war. In half an hour I must therefore (and he paused for a minute) decorate this man with the great Order of S. George, and by so doing commit a trespass on its institution; for it is the highest honour, and hitherto the purest, of the empire. But I will not ask you to be present—I should feel too much humiliated if you were; but I have no choice—I must submit to a controlling necessity. I will, however, not again leave my army, and there shall be no opportunity given for additional misdirection by the Marshal.

"He is an old man, and therefore I would have you show him suitable courtesies, and not refuse them when offered on his part.

"I wish to put an end to every appearance of ill will, and to take from this day a new departure, which I mean to make one of gratitude to Providence and of grace to all."

His Imperial Majesty then said that "he should distribute rewards to his generals and brave soldiers, who had done their duty heroically; and that he had signed an act of amnesty and general pardon, so that every one under his rule might participate in the joy he felt at the triumph of his country."

This amnesty was full and complete, "embracing even all his Polish subjects who had joined the enemy."

"The past is condemned to an eternal oblivion and

---

* The Emperor explained to the English General afterwards in private to what he alluded when he used the expression "Turkish tricks."

silence—all are prohibited from reviving any reference to these affairs—those only who continue in the service of the enemy after the expiration of two months shall be allowed no more to return to Russia."

Certainly this Emperor had qualities "of noble pith," and was himself one of those happy accidents of autocracy which he had represented as "fortuitous benefits for a despotic country."

Through unexplained causes, Macdonald with the tenth corps, whose head quarters were at Stalgan on the Aa, did not receive the order from Murat for his retreat till the 18th of December. The force of this corps amounted to twenty-five thousand, of which eighteen thousand were Prussians.

On the 19th Macdonald began his march. The left column, formed by the division Grandjean, with five Prussian squadrons, moved by Neoft on Tilsit. The centre under Massenbach, all Prussians, marched by Chawli and Koltiniany. The right under Yorck, consisting of thirteen battalions and six squadrons, only quitted Mittau on the 20th, and fell in behind the centre column upon the same road. Macdonald marched with the centre column, that reached Zoge Platou on the 19th, Janichki on the 20th, Mechkutz on the 21st, Kurtowiany on the 22nd, Waizow on the 23rd, and Koltiniany on the 24th.

The Marquis Paulucci, Governor of Riga, pursued the enemy in the direction of Mittau, where he arrived on the 20th.

Yorck's rear guard made a slight defence, but quitted early in the morning. Paulucci then marched on Memel, where he arrived on the 27th, making altogether a march of two hundred and twenty-five miles in eight days. The Prussian commandant with seven hundred Prussians offered no resistance to the occupation.

Macdonald on the 25th had reached Pojourzé; and the division Grandjean, Tauroggen.

Yorck's column should have been at Koltiniany, but Diebitch, who had some reason to suppose that Yorck and the Prussians were reluctant auxiliaries of the French, had already established himself with two thousand men at that point, and thus intercepted Yorck's line of march.

Yorck being informed of this incident by Kleist, the commander of his advanced guard, "and that Diebitch had proposed an arrangement," agreed to a conference, when a convention was framed and signed on the 30th.

The first article stipulated that "the Prussian corps should occupy a specified district that was to be considered neutral. The Prussians might pass through the district, but not stop."

Second, that "the corps should remain unmolested until orders from the King of Prussia should arrive. If these orders required the corps to reunite with the French army, the corps was not to resume hostilities for two months from the date of the convention."

Third, "Should the Emperor of Russia not sanction the convention, the corps was to be at liberty to march where ordered by its own sovereign."

Fourth, "All stragglers and everything belonging to the corps should have free passage to join it."

Fifth, "The troops of General Massenbach were to be comprised in the convention."

Sixth, referred wholly to the subsistence of the corps.

The same evening a copy of the convention was sent to Massenbach, who had arrived at Tilsit with the division Grandjean, and dislodged the Cossacks.

On the 31st, at day-break, Massenbach repassed the Niemen with his infantry, " to occupy," as he stated, " the tête du pont," and thence proceeded to join the Russians under Diebitch, who had advanced to give him protection; whilst the Prussian cavalry and artillery, which had reached Raguiteys, passed over to the corps of Koutousoff at Phutgallen.

Macdonald had entertained some suspicion of the defection of the Prussians, but still had remained at Tilsit on the 29th and 30th to aid the retreat of Yorck: when, however, he learnt, on the 31st, that Massenbach had withdrawn, he immediately became sensible of the danger to which the division Grandjean was exposed, and began his march on Königsberg with seven thousand infantry and twenty pieces of cannon, that had assembled at Tilsit on the evening of the 29th.

In the course of the day the following letter was received by Macdonald :—

LIEUT.-GEN. YORCK TO MARSHAL MACDONALD.

"Tauroggen, 30th Dec., 1812.

"Notwithstanding fatiguing marches to join your Excellency, it was impossible for me to avoid compromising my flanks and rear; and I had no alternative but either to sacrifice the greater part of my troops, and all the material on which their subsistence depended, or to save the whole by making a convention which permits me to collect the Prussians in a part of the territory of Prussia now in the power of the

Russians in consequence of the retreat of the French army.

"The Prussian corps will form a neutral body, whose future service will be regulated by the negotiations which are about to commence between the belligerent parties.

"I hasten to inform your Excellency of a transaction which the force of imperative circumstances has rendered inevitable.

"I am at ease as to the judgment which the world may form on my conduct, dictated by the duty I owed my troops, and adopted after the most deliberate reflection. Notwithstanding appearances, the purest motives have guided my actions, and in making your Excellency this declaration I acquit myself of all obligations.

"I am, &c. &c.,

(Signed) "YORCK."

Another letter was addressed to the King of Prussia:—

"SIR, "Tauroggen, 30th Dec., 1812.

"My departure, subsequent to the march of Marshal Macdonald from Mittau on Tilsit, was so arranged that I might cover the retreat of the seventh division; but the bad roads and the most unfavourable weather rendered my position desperate, and I have been compelled to conclude with the Russian Major-general Diebitch the convention of which I have the honour to lay a copy at your Majesty's feet.

"In the full conviction that I should have sacrificed the whole corps, with all its artillery and baggage, as has occurred to the other corps of the grand army, I have thought, as a faithful subject of your Majesty, that I should only consider your Majesty's interests in this instance without attending to those of your Majesty's ally, to whom, in his actual condition, the sacrifice of the corps under my command could have been of no real use.

"I place willingly my head at the feet of your Majesty. Should my conduct be deemed reprehensible, I still shall have the consolation to reflect, in the last moments of my life, that I am dying as a faithful subject—as a true Prussian, and a patriot who only sought the welfare of his country.

(Signed) "YORCK."

Massenbach, through whom Yorck's letter for Macdonald had been transmitted, accompanied it with the following note:—

"The letter of General Yorck will have already informed your Excellency that my course of action is prescribed, and that I can make no change, as the measures of precaution taking by your Excellency lead me to suspect an intention to retain me by force, or to disarm my troops. I have been obliged to adopt the line I have pursued to bring myself under the convention that the Commanding General has signed, who has sent me this morning the notice and instructions for my conduct.

"Your Excellency will pardon my not presenting myself to acquaint you of the proceeding I am directed to execute, for the respect and esteem I shall ever preserve for your Excellency might have prevented me from a discharge of my duty.

(Signed) "MASSENBACH.
"Tilsit, 31st December, 1812."

Macdonald, on the 1st of January, reached Skaisgirren, followed, but not pressed, by Wittgenstein, whom the state of the roads had detained. From thence he passed to Melanken, the four regiments of Cossacks at Schillapicken retiring as he advanced, and the division Henderlet marching out of Königsberg and taking post at Tapiau to favour his movement.

Macdonald, when he reached Labiau, proposed to defend himself in that position; but he was attacked by an overwhelming force and driven on Königsberg, losing nearly two thousand men killed, wounded, and prisoners. The Russians lost above five hundred.

Henderlet's division also fell back on Königsberg.

Wittgenstein's dilatory movements have been censured: it has been observed that he could have reached Tilsit before Macdonald, and at all events might have profited by Macdonald's delay of two days at Tilsit to have established himself on the route to Königsberg, and cut off the enemy from that city. It has also been pretended that Yorck had designedly favoured the operation by not communicating the convention till the 31st of December; although, in fact, the terms were settled several days previously.

The state of Prussian feeling against Napoleon, the outrages and wrongs of which Prussia had been the victim for so long a period, may afford a moral as well as a political, though not a military vindication for that convention; but if Yorck insidiously entered into any preconcerted plan with Diebitch for the destruction of the division Grandjean and capture of Macdonald, it certainly was a most disloyal transaction—too disloyal to be even insinuated without strong evidence; and the reproach directed against Wittgenstein is presumptive proof in Yorck's favour that no such views entered into and regulated his conduct in the arrangement.

The King of Prussia was positively no party to this defection.

His displeasure against Yorck, whom he ordered to be arrested and to be replaced by Kleist, was sincere, though fruitless, for Yorck was out of the reach of official communication.

The Prince de Hatzfeld carried to the Emperor at Paris the King's declaration "of continued resolve to maintain the French alliance;" and it was not till Baron Arnstern, subsequently sent by Alexander to the King at Breslau, after three days' persevering discussion, had frankly told the King that "his continued refusal to join Russia and the Tugend Bund might render a suspension of his regal authority necessary," that the King yielded, with strong expressions of reluctance, to the minatory demands rather than to the solicitations of the Russians.

The King was influenced by principles of probity and honour that made him obstinately inflexible against arguments and considerations of mere selfish interests; but as a sovereign he could not be required to maintain a political fidelity which would have inflicted a revolution on his country, and perhaps a dismemberment, as in the case of Saxony. Napoleon himself never doubted the King's sincere desire to preserve good faith, and justified his proceeding.

Murat had hoped to have maintained his cantonments in Old Prussia behind the Pregel, but the defection of Yorck obliged him to fall back on Posen, where, on the 11th of January, he established his headquarters.

Macdonald entered Dantzic on the 16th, and the city was invested on the 21st by a Russian corps, under the orders of the Duke Alexander of Wurtemberg, to whom the fortress afterwards surrendered.

At the time of the investment the garrison consisted of thirty-six thousand men, (of whom six thousand were in hospital,) and was composed of—

Divisions Grandjean	.. .. ..	5,000
,, Henderlet	.. .. ..	8,000
,, Detrés	.. .. ..	6,000
,, Bochèbe	.. .. ..	
,, Oudinot	.. .. ..	2,400
,, Loison	.. .. ..	
Brigade Cavaignac	.. .. ..	1,600
Artillery, Engineers, isolated sick and stragglers	.. .. ..	13,000
Total	.. .. ..	36,000

There had also been collected at the different stations assigned for the rendezvous of the corps, near three thousand officers and above twelve thousand soldiers, but a great portion was still non-effective.

A greater force, however, than the Russians could have brought to oppose might have been collected from the different garrisons on the Vistula and the

Oder, and the English General asked Murat afterwards "why this measure had not been taken, as a well-directed offensive movement, in all probability, would have compelled the retreat of the Russians to the Niemen?"

Murat said, "That he had once entertained such an intention, but that the morale of the army did not permit its execution; that the Cossack 'hurrah' was ringing in every ear, and that half would have deserted the first night at the thought of bivouacs where no fires could be lighted from fear of their serving as conductors to *that horrid screech*."

When Schwarzenberg, who was at Slonim, became acquainted with the disasters of the grand army, he retired on the 14th of December, and on the 18th entered cantonments in and about Bialystok, with the right at Narewka. Regnier, who had followed the movement, cantoned his corps behind the Lenza, with its right on the Boug, and the left at Kamenetz.

The Emperor Alexander had directed "an armistice" to be proposed to Schwarzenberg, which proposition was referred to Vienna; but Murat, approving the dispositions made by the Prince, wished the armistice to be tacit, and not written.

It being necessary, however, to get possession of Warsaw as soon as possible, the Russians under Milaradowitch made a movement to turn the Austrian left at Ostrolenka; and Sacken, to menace Regnier, occupied on the 23rd of December Brest Litowski, whilst Touchkoff kept the enemy in check along their whole front.

This threatening demonstration decided Schwarzenberg to approach Warsaw, and new cantonments were entered by the Austrians between the Boug and Narew —the right at Nur, the left at Ostrolenka. Regnier cantoned behind the Wingrod river.

From that time an armistice de facto existed, and was continued till the 25th of January, when Schwarzenberg having received orders from Vienna, entered into a capitulation for Warsaw, which it was finally agreed should be evacuated between the 5th and 8th of February. Regnier retired on the 4th by Kalish on Glogau, Poniatowski on the 6th to Cracow; on the 7th the Austrian rear guard withdrew from Warsaw into Gallicia, and on the 8th the Russians entered the city. A Polish garrison had, however, been left at Modlin.

The Austrians in the hospitals of Warsaw amounted to two thousand, and there were four thousand French and Poles, who were made prisoners of war. Schwarzenberg wished to stipulate for their liberty, but it was refused. In an intercepted letter of the Polish President of the Senate, he wrote, "Beauharnois promises to make a movement from Posen to succour us, but it is *now mustard after supper*."

Alexander, with the Russian column under Kutusow, having quitted Wilna, proceeded on the 8th of January to Orany, and thence crossed the Niemen.

On the 9th he advanced to Mercez, and thence by Augustowo and Wittenberg to Polotzk and Kalish, whilst Tchichagow blockaded Thorn, and a detachment seized large magazines at Bromberg.

The command of the enemy's army had been taken by Napoleon from Murat, with expressions of great dissatisfaction that produced the seed of future disaffection. Prince Eugène assumed it on the 16th of

January, but was unable to undertake any active operations. The political relations of Austria, added to the Prussian hostility, threw him indeed on a very difficult defensive.

Thus terminated the severest campaign of six months on record in the annals of the world. The Russians calculate that a hundred and twenty-five thousand of the enemy perished in the different combats; that forty-eight generals, three thousand officers, and a hundred and ninety thousand soldiers were captured, and that a hundred thousand were destroyed by cold, hunger, and disease; that only about eighty thousand, including the Austrians and Prussians, repassed the frontiers; and that they (the Russians) captured seventy-five eagles or stands of colours, and nine hundred and twenty nine cannon, exclusive of those thrown into the rivers or buried; and this calculation as to totals cannot be impugned as exaggerated.

On the 13th of January Alexander published the following declaration to his army:—

" SOLDIERS,   " Merecz, 13th Jan., 1813.

" The year has ended—a year for ever memorable and glorious—one in which you have trampled in the dust the pride of the insolent aggressor.

" The year has passed, but your heroic deeds survive.

" Time will not efface their trace. They are present to your contemporaries—they will live with their posterity.

" You have purchased at the price of your blood the deliverance of your country from the hostile powers leagued against its independence.

"You have acquired rights to the gratitude of Russia, and to the admiration of mankind. You have proved by your fidelity, your valour, and your perseverance, that when hearts are filled with the love of God, and devotion to their Sovereign, the efforts of the most formidable enemies resemble the furious waves of the ocean, which break in impotent lashings against indestructible rocks, and leave behind only confused sounds.

"Soldiers! desirous of distinguishing all those who have participated in these immortal exploits, I have ordered medals of silver to be struck, which have been blessed by our holy Church. They bear the date of the memorable year 1812: suspended to a blue ribbon, they will decorate the warrior breasts which have served as bucklers of the country.

"Each individual of the Russian army is worthy to bear this honourable recompense of valour and constancy.

"You have all shared the same fatigues and dangers; you have had but one heart, one mind; you will all be proud to wear the same distinction; it will proclaim every where that you are the faithful children of Russia,—children on whom God the Father will pour His benedictions.

"Your enemies will tremble on seeing these decorations: they will know that under these medals hearts are beating, animated with unconquerable valour, and imperishable, because it is not based upon ambition or impiety, but on the immutable foundation of patriotism and religion.

(Signed) "ALEXANDER."

It would be most unjust and ungenerous to deny, or attempt to impair, the claims of the invader to acknowledgment of his zeal, energy, and bravery in this mighty and terrific contest. Never were courage, devotion, and all martial qualities more heroically and exemplarily manifested.

Never did officers or men of both antagonist forces exhibit to a greater degree in innumerable instances majestic as well as daring defiance of danger, difficulty, and suffering; but neither invaders nor invaded can arrogate to themselves more than a limited self-glory from the transactions that preceded and consummated the catastrophe.

The enemy can boast that he planted his eagles triumphantly on the towers of the Kremlin, but in making that boast he must feel his pride checked by reflection on the dreadful issue of that transient achievement; whilst the Russians, vaunting, with truth and just pride, the national as well as military fortitude, perseverance, and patriotism displayed under circumstances the most adverse and dismaying, must temper exultation at their victorious rescue with grateful thanksgiving to that Almighty Being "who rode on the whirlwind and directed the storm."

APPENDIX.

APPENDIX.

LETTERS AND DESPATCHES.

No. 1.

The Marquis Wellesley to Sir Robert Wilson.

Sir,   Foreign Office, 29th Nov., 1811.

His Royal Highness the Prince Regent having been pleased to select you to be employed upon His Majesty's special service abroad, under instructions from this department, I have the satisfaction to acquaint you of the same, and to desire that you will hold yourself in readiness to proceed upon the above service as soon as I shall convey to you His Royal Highness's pleasure to that effect.

I have the honour to be, Sir,
Your most obedient, humble servant,
WELLESLEY.

No. 2.

Lord Castlereagh to Sir Robert Wilson.

Sir,   Foreign Office, 26th March, 1812.

His Royal Highness the Prince Regent having been graciously pleased to approve that you should be employed in the mission now proceeding to Constantinople, with the rank and pay of Brigadier-General of His Majesty's Forces, and with an extra allowance of one thousand pounds a year to cover your expenses, upon the recommendation of the Marquis Wellesley, whose intention to employ you therein was signified to you on the 29th of November, 1811, from which time you have held yourself in readiness accordingly; I am to signify to you His Royal Highness's commands that you do prepare to embark with his Excellency Mr. Liston, who has been appointed His Majesty's Ambassador to the Porte, and who will be despatched in a few days.

It is His Royal Highness's pleasure that you are to consider yourself as entirely attached to Mr. Liston's mission, and are to regulate your conduct by his orders, and with him alone to correspond.

It is considered and hoped that your military experience, joined to your particular knowledge of the Russian armies, and of many of the superior officers in that service, will enable you to be of use to Mr. Liston in procuring information as to the disposition and condition of the armies, and the military events in progress.

I have the honour to be, Sir,
Your most obedient, humble servant,
CASTLEREAGH.

No. 3.

SIR ROBERT WILSON TO THE MARQUIS WELLESLEY.

MY LORD, Pera, 19th July, 1812.

Mr. Liston will acquaint your Lordship with the motives that have induced him to apply for a Firman to the Ottoman Porte, that I may proceed without loss of time to His Majesty the Emperor of Russia. I therefore have only to acquaint your Lordship that I propose to have a conference with the Grand Vizir and Admiral Tchichagow on my way to the Imperial headquarters, that I may be fully prepared with such information as may be requisite for the attainment of the objects with which I am specially charged; and that I shall lose no time in expediting to His Majesty's Government such intelligence as may be of interest should I find no other British Envoy entrusted with the official correspondence.

Until I receive further instructions I shall endeavour to act in conformity with Mr. Liston's general instructions; and should circumstances arise to which they do not apply, as I conceive your Lordship would direct; and take every opportunity to promote the success of Russian operations against the common enemy, without committing His Majesty's Government on points that ought to be reserved for its consideration.

I have been much flattered by the urgent application of Mr. Italinsky* and Admiral Greig for my mission to the Emperor, and their assurance of a gracious reception.

I trust your Lordship will not deem me too presumptuous in soliciting permission to continue in an official capacity with the Russian army.

Attachments already formed, the hope of being useful, and the assurance of such an appointment being agreeable to His Majesty the Emperor, prompt me to the request, and will, I hope, obtain for me your Lordship's sanction.

Admiral Greig's proposition for the employment of a corps of troops in Dalmatia will scarcely reach your Lordship before the information which I shall be able to collect and transmit on that subject, and which appears to be necessary for a decision upon the propriety of such an enterprise, if it is to be supported by British armaments and resources.

In the present state of the relations between Turkey and Russia—although I understand that the conditions of peace are at last actually ratified—I cannot think that permission will be on the instant granted for the passage of Admiral Tchichagow's corps; and an attempt to force a passage without the private consent of the Porte, or without a secret understanding with Austria, appears a most hazardous and impolitic adventure, menaced, but I presume not seriously entertained, by the Admiral.

There is no doubt of the insurrectionary spirit being high in the provinces lately occupied by the French, nor of the advantage to be derived from the attention of the enemy being seriously drawn to these quarters; but the introduction to the operation is very delicate, and a favourable initiation can only be assured by British co-operation and authority.

The propriety of re-establishing the Russians on the Adriatic is a question which I do not feel myself competent to determine; but I shall gladly execute the instructions of Mr. Liston to discourage the project at Bucharest and Wilna until the decision of your Lordship, or of the officer commanding in Sicily, is known.

I shall thank your Lordship if I am honoured by your future commands or instructions on the subject of withdrawing Spanish and Portuguese, or other auxiliaries from the French armies, if opportunities offer.

I am provided with an authority from the Duque del Infantado;

but your Lordship's orders with regard to their employment, equipment, &c., will be necessary.

I should also thank your Lordship to acquaint me if any officers from the Quartermaster-general's department might be spared to Russia at her request, as Admiral Greig assures me that there is a strong wish for them, and even for such a supply of British officers in general as would be sufficient to organise a Russian corps of reserve.

I have only to add my assurance of zealous service and anxious desire to promote the interests of my country, with the most disinterested feelings as to any other personal advantage than the honour resulting from the approbation of His Majesty's Government.

I have the honour to be, &c.,

R. T. WILSON.

No. 4.

SIR ROBERT WILSON TO MR. LISTON.

SIR,   Bucharest, 2nd Aug., 1812.

I have the honour to acquaint your Excellency that I reached Shumla on Thursday morning, seventy hours after my departure from Pera.

I had during the course of the day which I passed at Shumla two very long conferences with the Grand Vizir, in which I had the opportunity of introducing all the topics that your Excellency wished me to notice.

The Grand Vizir in the most solemn manner disclaimed any equivocal intentions with regard to the Russian peace, which he said was completed, and desired me to assure the Emperor and Admiral Tchichagow that the Sultan had no further cessions to ask or stipulations to make: that if Russia, in a spirit of amity, chose to improve the conditions of the treaty, whatever was granted would be an act of grace and not a concession to imaginary rights or pretensions.

That the proclamation of peace had been delayed from objects totally distinct from any views of the renewal of hostilities; but that now he had written to desire that it might be published.

He would gladly have induced the Russians to withdraw from Servia, and [permit] the country to be restored earlier than the treaty stipulated; but he should not urge the wish if compliance would be inconvenient to Admiral Tchichagow.

He expressed himself as fully convinced of the hostile designs of France and Austria; but said that it was the interest of Turkey to evade war as long as possible, and to the advantage of the common cause that she should accomplish this object: that Turkey could certainly resist any aggression, but that she was desirous of gaining time, that a new organisation of the empire might take effect.

That this preparation would assist Russia, and therefore, he foresaw, would probably be a pretext for the hostility of France; but that war so produced would not expose him to a charge of inconsistency, for he had stated that peace was indispensably necessary; whereas if he immediately entered into an offensive and defensive alliance with Russia, he would have been exchanging only one war for another, and a second war more to be deprecated at the moment than the former.

That it would be impossible for Turkey to admit of the passage of Russian troops to Dalmatia upon the preceding system of policy.

That the Sultan considered England as the stay of his empire, and that her influence must predominate if she continued to show that a real interest in the welfare of Turkey regulated all her propositions and advice.

The Grand Vizir expressed great contempt for the Caimacan's opinion on the subject of the treaty, and repeatedly insisted that the Sultan had delegated to himself alone the option of war or peace, and the arrangement of the conditions.

That peace was very desirable with Russia, not only on account of the state of the Turkish armies, but that had France now found Turkey at war with Russia, very embarrassing propositions would have been made, which would have left Turkey only the alternative of war with France or England, in addition to her Russian war.

I intimated a hope that he would shortly go to Constantinople; but he gave me to understand that he possessed more authority at the head of his troops, and could more effectually at Shumla support the execution of the Sultan's plans for the improvement of the different establishments of the State.

That he had about sixty thousand men, who required discipline, but that they were well disposed.

That he had made the necessary dispositions for the occupation of the Servian fortresses when Russia ceded them, and had anticipated possible resistance from the Servians; but he hoped that Russia would feel an interest in discouraging any connection with Austria.

That he anxiously attended to the Russian war with France, as the success of the latter power would be fatal to Turkey—an opinion that would induce him to recommend avowed co-operation when the alliance could be useful.

I found the Grand Vizir a very strong-minded man, possessing statesmanlike qualities.

On military subjects he seemed to entertain very just notions, and to know that mere personal courage does not constitute the worth of armies.

After nine hours' delay at Shumla, chiefly passed with the Vizir, I again proceeded and reached the ruins of Rudschuk, where I completed my journey of four hundred and twenty-five miles on horseback early on the fourth day.

I crossed the Danube immediately, and at Giurgewo received from Colonel Kutusow, the Commandant, and all ranks, the most flattering attentions and cordial welcome as a member of the British empire.

Early on the morning of the 1st of August I reached Bucharest and waited on Admiral Tchichagow, who has done me the honour to enter into very confidential communications on every subject.

Mr. Italinsky's despatches caused him some uneasiness; but I re-assured him by the language of the Grand Vizir, so that he would not stop the troops now on march to the Dniester, where the first corps will arrive on the 24th of August, and the last on the 20th of September.

He seemed to regret much the failure of his Dalmatian enterprise, for which he would have renewed the Turkish war and forced a passage to the Adriatic, collecting *en route* the Christians of Servia, Bosnia, &c.

I however consoled him by the report which I made of the want of food in the Mediterranean, and by a statement of the military inconveniences and impediments that would have prevented early operation.

Political considerations he did not much respect.

He will now move with an army of fifty thousand men in the highest order, according to every report and my own observation; and fortune must be very unkind if such a reinforcement cannot be turned to good account.

He has promised me to evacuate Servia, &c., in a way that will conciliate the Turkish Government and dispose to confidence; although he does not attach much importance to Turkish friendship, or rather co-operation, under present circumstances.

On military details he discoursed so well that I only lament he had not an earlier command; for I think he would have corrected many abuses that still exist in the economy of the army. But how far he is capacitated for an important command in the field I cannot judge.

He does not seem very sanguine; but an officer has this day arrived from S. Petersburg, who met with no troops in the direction in which the enemy were supposed to have been seen; and a letter from the Emperor, dated the 17th of July, at Paulosk, contains this remark, "Everything, as yet, has gone as I wished."

I enclose to your Excellency a copy of an official report of the various movements drawn out for me by the General, Count Langeron; but we hear that Prince Bagrathion has subsequently effected his junction.

Buonaparte proclaims that he has two hundred thousand French and two hundred and twenty thousand confederates. The Russian army is composed of ninety thousand men under General Barclay de Tolly, sixty thousand under Prince Bagrathion, fifty thousand under General Tormanssow, and as many under Admiral Tchichagow. A new levy of one man in a hundred has been ordered throughout the Russian empire, which will produce a further supply of three hundred thousand men, exclusive of vast bodies of militia, which the nobles are organizing, and several thousand additional Cossacks.

Admiral Tchichagow has charged me with some important

military communications to the Emperor, and has entreated me to meet him on the Dniester; but of course that measure must be regulated by the Emperor's wish and other circumstances.

I have seen his Excellency Ghalib Effendi: Prince Morusis was the interpreter. Your Excellency will hear at Constantinople if I have acquitted myself in these several conferences on delicate subjects with advantage to British interests, and according to your instructions; but apparently I obtained confidence and founded a favourable opinion of our policy.

I leave this place early to-morrow morning, directing my route upon Jassy, Kiew, and Mohilew, unless I am obliged to deviate from new circumstances.

I understand that the Poles are partially in insurrection; but of course I shall take the necessary precautions when I pass through any revolted district, if I should be obliged to do so.

I have the honour to be
Your Excellency's most obedient and humble servant,
R. T. WILSON.

No. 5.

MR. LISTON TO SIR ROBERT WILSON.

SIR, Constantinople, 13th Aug., 1812.

I have had the pleasure of receiving your despatch of the 2nd instant from Bucharest, and cannot but feel a very high satisfaction in observing the able manner in which you have executed the commission I had ventured to entrust to your charge; while, on the other hand, I have reason to congratulate you on the important good effect produced, and likely to be produced, both at Bucharest and at the Porte, by the line of conduct since adopted by the Emperor of Russia. I am far from daring to predict success; but as I have ventured to observe to Mr. de Tchichagow (who does not seem to be impressed with all the respect possible for our diplomatic manœuvres), it is important to have prevented mischief; and it is cheering for zealous and active labourers to meet with a field open to their industry.

I have had too short notice of the departure of Mr. Italinsky's messenger to enter into detail to-day, but I will take an early opportunity of writing more at large.

I have the honour to be, with great truth and regard, Sir,

Your most obedient humble servant,

ROBERT LISTON.

P. S.—Do you think there would be an inclination where you now are to purchase alliance and co-operation at the price of complete restitution—that is, of a return to the *status quo ante bellum*?

No. 6.
MR. LISTON TO SIR ROBERT WILSON.

SIR, Constantinople, 20th Sept., 1812.

I hope you received my letter, No. 1, of the 13th of August, acknowledging the arrival of yours of the 2nd of that month from Bucharest, and at the same time expressing the high satisfaction I had felt at the manner in which you had executed your commission, and at the important advantages that had resulted from it here.

Your second letter, written at Tchernigow, was also delivered to me by the Chevalier d'Italinsky in due time; and the intelligence it contained was of a nature to do real service to the good cause. It is a regular practice among the members and dependents of the French and Austrian Embassies to endeavour to blind and seduce the people of Constantinople by fabricated accounts of victories obtained by Buonaparte. The Russian mission, of course, exert themselves to contradict and refute these falsehoods, but they are sometimes suspected by the Turkish Ministers of being apt to exaggerate their own advantages. So that an extract of a report made by you as an eye-witness, and presented by one whom they have hitherto had reason to consider as an impartial man and a friend, is a document of no inconsiderable value. And I beg you will furnish me with such as often as you possibly can.

ROBERT LISTON.

No. 7.

SIR ROBERT WILSON TO EARL CATHCART.

MY LORD,   Smolensk, 14th Aug., 1812.

I have the honour to acquaint your Lordship that I arrived here this day; and I transmit with the copies of my correspondence with Mr. Liston (according to his instructions) the copy of a letter which I was recommended by Mr. Novosiltzoff, General Beningsen, General Armfeldt, and others, to address to His Imperial Majesty, instead of repairing to S. Petersburg at the instant, as it is hoped that His Majesty may be leaving S. Petersburg, which will afford me better opportunities of communicating personally with His Majesty than at the capital.

I am also very anxious to see the armies of Prince Bagrathion and General Barclay, and to have the opportunity of hearing the sentiments of their Chiefs, so that I may be able to transmit to His Majesty's Government or Ambassador at S. Petersburg, not only the report of the military state of those armies, which, I hear from all persons, are pre-eminent in composition and spirit, but an accurate and impartial statement of those dissensions which I am sorry to say menace the most serious ill-consequences to the safety of the Empire.

The exaltation of General Barclay to the supreme command was originally an unpopular measure; but the conduct of the campaign, which commenced by the sacrifice of six fertile provinces, magazines, &c., has excited a most general discontent against General Barclay and General Foule, who is supposed to have counselled the operations.

The sudden departure of the Emperor from the army, and his impenetrable silence, have increased the mischief; and the strongest representations have been sent to His Majesty for an early attention to the situation of affairs, so that he may regulate the jarring parties.

The removal of Mr. Romanzow is also a point that seems universally required. From Bucharest, I may say from Constantinople to this place, there is but one opinion of the necessity of that measure.

It is my intention to go to-morrow to General Barclay de Tolly's army, who will be under arms early, as it is Buonaparte's birth-day, and an attack is not thought improbable to celebrate the anniversary.

The next day I shall repair to Prince Bagrathion, and then, if I find that the Emperor has expressed an intention to remain any time at S. Petersburg, I shall proceed there without delay.

General Beningsen has assured me that the French army, opposed to Generals Barclay and Prince Bagrathion, exceeds one hundred and seventy thousand men, and in total amounts to two hundred and eighty thousand, and that General Barclay has about eighty thousand effectives, Prince Bagrathion near fifty thousand, Wittgenstein thirty-five thousand. That, including the Moldavian army, General Tormanssow can operate with a force of not less than sixty thousand men upon the Vistula, and that there are one hundred thousand recruits ready to fill up casualties in the first line, exclusive of militia, &c.

I have had opportunity to certify this statement, and have no doubt of Russia having at this moment, by an extraordinary national energy, arrayed a force far more than sufficient for the contest, if its direction be but worthy the character of the soldiers.

I have in my correspondence with Mr. Liston more than once noticed the importance of General Tormanssow's command; and I find General Beningsen is entirely of the same opinion, but he does not esteem General Tormanssow's abilities to bear any proportion to his zeal and courage.

Mr. Novosiltzoff, who has lately returned from Vienna, gives a very favourable account of the feelings of the Austrian nation and army in general; and various accounts from that quarter excite reasonable hopes of forbearance from hostile action, if not of an avowed neutrality.

At present the Russian armies experience no want, and I passed numerous convoys on my road hither. The French, however, it is said, are not so well supplied, and the horses taken from them are generally in wretched condition, with ulcerated backs.

It is estimated that since the campaign has commenced eight thousand French prisoners have altogether been made, including four hundred and fifty taken by the Cossacks the day before yesterday.

I will send your Lordship an accurate statement of the

several movements and marches made by the different armies since the commencement of the campaign, and such other particulars as I conceive may be interesting to your Lordship as soon as I can collect them.

I have the honour to be

Your Lordship's obedient and humble servant,

R. T. WILSON.

No. 8.

SIR ROBERT WILSON TO EARL CATHCART.

[Copy—Commencement missing.]

27th Aug., 1812.

GENERAL BARCLAY.

It must be stated that General Barclay does not possess the confidence of the army. I should be very repugnant to make any report detrimental to his interests if public ones of the greatest magnitude did not depend upon a just knowledge of his capacity and motives of action.

It is a duty therefore, but it is a painful duty, to state that I consider General Barclay as terrorised (if I may use the expression) by the reputation of his enemy. That I am certain he is not making a war of manœuvre upon any fixed and pre-arranged military system, but a war of marches without sufficient arrangement and method to avoid serious misfortune, if the enemy should press with more energy than they have hitherto done.

In the moment of battle I have seen him brave, active, and capable; but these qualities exerted in battle alone are not sufficient, especially for the command of a Russian army. His troops want general direction, and the crisis an ability which shall embrace all the duties of a great captain.

I should hope that a sense of this necessity, and of his inability to recover the confidence of his officers and soldiers, will induce him to resign, and yet serve his country as a meritorious officer in a less responsible station.

The state of affairs is too desperate to admit of any attempt to enforce the maintenance of his authority.

I cannot give your Lordship a stronger specimen of the degree of opposition to the proceedings that have occurred than by citing the words of General Platow, in my presence, to General Barclay, after the evacuation of Smolensk: "You see, Sir, I wear only a cloak. I will no longer put on a Russian uniform; I consider it as a dishonour!"

I have had occasion to ascertain that great improvements have been made in the Russian commissariat department, and that the medical department is also in rapid progress to a respectable system; but I have seen with regret that the interior economy of this army is still very distant from necessary method and order.

The columns of march, notwithstanding General Barclay's commands and, I may add, example—considering his station, are still encumbered with immense numbers of private carriages; and I verily believe several thousand Cossacks are employed in the service of officers.

The duties of our divisionary assistant Quartermasters-general are not known, or never performed.

No ground is ever previously reconnoitred by the junior staff, no roads examined, no reports made of the local conveniences or inconveniences of the proposed post, camp, or quarters.

The pioneers' duty is equally neglected. No bridges are ever repaired to anticipate the necessity; no additional passages are made over the numerous little marshy rivulets that intersect the road, so that the line of march unnecessarily extends for miles, is frequently interrupted for hours, confusion daily prevails, and ruin would ensue if the enemy were enterprising.

I have seen moments when one thousand five hundred daring men would have accomplished that which Buonaparte, with one hundred and fifty thousand, will not achieve when the Russian army is arrayed in order of battle.

I have mentioned to your Lordship that the Russian ammunition-waggons were not calculated to descend hilly ground without great delay and much risk.

General Kutaisow, who commands the artillery, has now, however, accepted my suggestion, and I am to order, at the S. Petersburg arsenal, staples to fix on the shafts, and straps to connect the breechings with that support.

Until this arrangement, the top of the collar affords the only resistance, for there is no breast-strap to connect the lower part of the collar with the belly-bands; consequently, as the horse leans back, the collar flies forward and upward to the end of the shafts.

It is true that iron shoes, to lock or fix the wheels, ought to have been with each waggon, but these have been long broken away; and if they remained, the driver must always have dismounted to set and to unloosen them.

I have also General Kutaisow's request to procure drag-ropes, after the English fashion, for the guns. At present the Russians use cords that wound the hands and afford no purchase.

I have been thus particular in making your Lordship acquainted with the result of my observations and my impressions, that your Lordship may be enabled to form an opinion of the character and temper of the force which is engaged in this awful contest. Its excellences are manifold, and its means are equal to final success. Its defects and imperfections are of a nature to be corrected as soon as qualified persons are charged with the superintendence of its interior arrangements.

Before I left the army, which I quitted with regret at this interesting epoch,—especially as General Barclay, and every officer in command, had done me the honour to invite me to remain with him,—I distributed several hundred proclamations of the Duque del Infantado, which gave me full powers to treat with Spanish officers and soldiers; and by which, as Regent, His Highness pledged himself to ratify my engagements; and General Barclay agreed to leave several wounded Spaniards on the march with the proclamations sewed in their clothes, and with such verbal encouragement as, I hope, will produce a considerable defection from the enemy, if any Spaniards and Portuguese survive his prodigal expenditure of them, as he seems systematically to employ them on all forlorn enterprises.

The English name stands so high in the enemy's army, that numbers of the confederates would flock to a British standard if His Majesty's Government thought it expedient; but I have confined myself, until I receive further orders, to negotiation with the countrymen of our allies.

I have the honour to be, &c.,

R. T. WILSON.

No. 9.

SIR ROBERT WILSON TO HIS IMPERIAL MAJESTY THE EMPEROR OF ALL THE RUSSIAS.

SIRE,   S. Petersburg, 12th Sept., 1812.

A sense of the duty which I owe your Majesty, animated by an affectionate attachment for your Majesty's person, induces me thus to submit the subject which formed the principal feature of my mission to Russia from Constantinople, and which I should have officially pursued, if I had not found here a British Ambassador, to whom I have been required to surrender my instructions from the British Ambassador at Constantinople, that a double diplomacy might not exist.

The communication which I now make by your Majesty's desire is perhaps a trespass on regular diplomatic forms, but I am too jealous of your Majesty's personal glory and interests to suffer any opportunity to elapse which may promote them.

Your Majesty is aware that the proclamation of the Turkish Peace was delayed for a considerable time after the ratifications had been exchanged at Bucharest.

The delay excited great uneasiness in Count Italinsky and Mr. Liston, and the hostile language of the Reis Effendi induced them to apprehend that advantage might be taken of the war in which Russia was engaged, to advance pretensions beyond even the *status quo ante bellum.*

In a conference with the Reis Effendi and Mr. Liston, the former even intimated that Georgia was rather a Turkish than a Russian appendage, and he stated that Georgian Deputies had already come to solicit Turkish protection and incorporation.

The tacit withdrawal of the Servian article, and the secret article relative to the establishment on the Phasis, was in that conference declared to be insufficient, and an explicit declaration of their dereliction was insisted upon, as a *sine qua non* of peace.

It was, however, evident not only on that occasion, but on

various others, and from multiplied sources of intelligence, that the Reis Effendi and a very powerful party in the Divan, being aware of the French and Austrian Treaty that guaranteed the integrity of the Turkish dominions, and of the exigencies which would oblige a diminution of the Russian Imperial forces on the Danube, considered the Peace *in toto* as most disadvantageous and discreditable to the interests and honour of the Ottomans.

The Grand Vizir himself expressed to me afterwards similar sentiments, and told me that only the fear of a war with England had induced him to terminate the negotiations with the expedition that he had done. That he could only maintain the Peace by remaining at Shumla at the head of a powerful force, but that he should profit by the respite he might have from any war by regenerating the military establishment of the Empire, a measure that I most sincerely do believe will be effected with hostile intentions to Russia (if the Turks should not be immediately involved in hostilities with France), and which, being effected, will give the Turkish power a very formidable character.

The Sultan is a man of very extraordinary mind and energy. The Vizir has eminent qualities, with all the wisdom that experience dearly bought can afford.

The Turkish nation in Asia and Europe has already abandoned many of its prejudices. The chiefs are all convinced of the necessity of adopting the European military systems, and the memory of Selim, who perished on account of his spirit of reform, is now held in a sacred estimation by the great majority of the Ottomans,—a fact that I can prove to your Majesty by a variety of incidents which came under my observation in Asiatic and European Turkey.

Under these circumstances alone I humbly submit to your Majesty whether that Peace can be advantageous to Russia which leaves a festering sore in the Turkish mind, a canker that extends as the vigour of the Turkish power acquires force?

If Russia by the line of the Pruth and the Danube had acquired a military line of defence that would prove a barrier to the hostility of the Turks, and if security had been gained by the Peace of Bucharest, then the maintenance of its stipulations (although they checked the advantages of a cordial union with Turkey) might be a plausible measure; it might also be insisted upon,—notwithstanding that, in my humble opinion, any arrangement at the present crisis which neutralizes support for the common cause, and tends to prevent the diminution of the French power, is an erroneous policy: but when security is not acquired, and only an imperfect military line is obtained, a line that cannot in any case be *offensively* useful and must *defensively* produce disaster, then the terms of such a Peace are at the moment mischievous, and, as regards the *future*, most prejudicial.

In these points of view, therefore, I respectfully express an opinion that the conditions of the Peace of Bucharest have not been beneficial, and ought not to be maintained.

Another important inconvenience has also been the consequence. By this Peace so framed, the war of Austria has acquired a national character.

There is not a man in that Empire who does not feel an imaginary interest in dislodging Russia from the embouchure of the Danube. The Austrian interest may not, indeed, be really affected by the establishment of Russia on that river; but jealousies are excited, and the ill-disposed operate on the passions to support a war which otherwise would be most unpopular, and which could only find adherents amongst the most inconsiderate of the Germans.

If your Majesty, influenced by a generous policy congenial to your own feelings, would take advantage of the moment when the superiority of your arms on the Danube is established, when every concession must be accepted by the proudest Ottoman as a grace and voluntary act—if your Majesty, profiting by the moment, would annul all *objectionable articles of the Peace of Bucharest, and re-establish the status quo ante bellum* with some provisional clauses that might even prescribe the demolition of the fortresses south of the Pruth and the Danube, suspicion would be converted into confidence, and a restless enmity into admiration and gratitude and perhaps assistance.

The affection of a Prince (the Sultan) endowed with splendid qualities could be assured. The esteem of a brave and high minded people would be won for ever by such a trait of generous policy. The national inquietude of Austria would be eradicated, and at least forty battalions now required to guard the Turkish frontier might march to act in a quarter where such a reinforcement, at such a time, would be of the most important value.

Europe would resound with praises of the magnanimity and disinterestedness of the sacrifice, and the restoration of a territory that produces an insignificant revenue and no resources of population, that is replete with immediate inconvenience and no very distant ills of indeterminable extent, that may, as your Majesty already knows is my opinion on the subject, be recovered in any future war, with a far less exertion than has hitherto been made, would nevertheless be hailed as evidence of a system that has long been needed, but which no other state in Europe has yet undeviatingly pursued.

The great object of contest is the destruction of Buonaparte's iron sceptre; all other objects, however legitimate and generally desirable, which may retard the principal success, are now of minor and prejudicial character, whereas their accomplishment is assured when the exorbitant power of France is reduced.

Your Majesty must not be deceived by the report of your minister, whose opinion I indirectly elicited, that Turkey has neither the intention nor the means to disturb the Peace of Bucharest.

I pledge myself to your Majesty that Turkey is in rapid growth to an improvement that, with the temper of the nation, will ere long occasion more than vague apprehension.

It is for your Majesty to consider whether it be not better to cement a bond of union with honour and advantage, than to have to prepare against the efforts of a dissatisfied Empire, stimulated to hostility by the temptations of opportunity, of French influence, and Austrian support.

I could urge many more arguments, but I will not trespass any longer on your Majesty's time and attention than to state, that even the influence of Russia in Moldavia would be improved by the restoration of the acquired country, as the division of Moldavia with the obligation of the nobles to sell their property within eighteen months on one side or other of the

Pruth, is a clause ruinous to their interests, since no person will give an equivalent for property under present circumstances.

I have thus, from the anxiety I have for your Majesty's fame and welfare, submitted my opinions. Your Majesty will, I am confident, pardon their freedom from the motives.

&c., &c., &c.

R. T. WILSON.

This memorandum was given by the Emperor's desire as a note of what had passed at the verbal conference. The Emperor admitted the utility of the proposed modification of the treaty of Bucharest, and was disposed to accede to it, when I left S. Petersburg, but the moment of pressure was lost from scruples of delicacy, and as the exigency passed, the conciliatory feeling died away.

No. 10.

LORD CASTLEREAGH TO SIR ROBERT WILSON.

SIR,   Foreign Office, 10th Oct., 1812.

I am to acknowledge the receipt of your letters of the dates stated in the margin. *19th July. 2nd Aug. 11th Aug.*

As you appear to have received the permission and direction of Mr. Liston for proceeding to the Russian armies, you have my full approbation for that conduct; and your interesting account of the battles at Smolensk has given satisfaction. *14th Aug. 22nd Aug.*

Lord Cathcart has since expressed to me his opinion that your continuance with the Russian armies may be of use from your intimacy with their general officers, and the opinion which is entertained of your esteem for the Russian character.

I am therefore to signify to you His Royal Highness the Prince Regent's pleasure, that you do place yourself under the command of General Lord Cathcart, so long as you continue with the Russian armies, and that you do report to him. You will also not fail to take every due means of informing Mr. Liston with respect to every event which may be useful to his embassy.

I am, with great truth and regard,

Sir, your most obedient humble servant,

CASTLEREAGH.

No. 11.

EARL CATHCART TO SIR ROBERT WILSON.

[Extract.]

S. Petersburg, 2nd Jan., 1813.

Under the circumstances, moral and political, which attended the invasion, the presence of a superior officer of a friendly power had many evident advantages, and it was so considered here as well as at home.

* * * *

On my part setting former acquaintance and private friendship out of the question, you will find me ever ready and willing to bear testimony not only to your zeal, but to the service which it has by good fortune fallen to your lot to render during this campaign.

When I say 'to your good fortune,' I do not mean to detract from your merit which placed you in a situation to be of the service in question. Your having seen the Emperor repeatedly and your being employed under me, enabled you at an anxious moment to add great confidence to what was felt in the army concerning the Emperor's determination to persevere to the last extremity in this contest. Your presence at head-quarters during the attempted negotiations by the enemy was satisfactory to every body, as well as to Marshal Kutusow, and your testimony on that occasion was most valuable.

Your reports in whatever manner they fell under the Emperor's view, as His Imperial Majesty permitted them to do, suggested to his consideration such observations as you thought it right to make, and certainly enabled him to compare opinions of yours with those of his own servants.

I mention these for your satisfaction, as instances of the grounds of commendation which I shall not fail to ascribe to your service.

No. 12.

EARL CATHCART TO SIR ROBERT WILSON.

MY DEAR SIR ROBERT WILSON,

Cathcart House by Glasgow, 10th Jan., 1836.

The moment I heard that the King's most gracious appointment of you to be Colonel of the 15th Hussars was gazetted, I was most impatient to write to congratulate you on a mark of His Majesty's favour, which must be in all respects so agreeable to your feelings, and which is an event so honourable to you in the history of your military career. But I was prevented by an occasional indisposition.

I am very greatly obliged to you for your letter of the 10th this moment received; and now take the earliest opportunity of expressing to you my most cordial felicitations, and my wishes that you may see the return of many happy years in the enjoyment of your honours.

I have never changed my opinion of the character of your military services; and the manner in which I appreciated them has always been represented both officially and privately in terms certainly not unfavourable to you.

Neither have I forgot the pleasure and advantage I have had in serving with you on the Continent of Europe.

Believe me ever, my dear Sir Robert Wilson, with very affectionate regard,

Your faithful humble servant,

CATHCART.

No. 13.

SIR ROBERT WILSON TO H. R. H. THE DUKE OF GLOUCESTER.

SIR, *Yurky, 40 wersts from Kalouga, 27th Oct., 1812.*

I have had considerable regret in not being able to communicate with your Royal Highness more frequently, but a variety of circumstances has prevented me from profiting by your Royal Highness's indulgence.

I trust, however, that you have not been ignorant of passing events, or my opinions, through other channels.

The inability of Buonaparte to ruin the Russian army and force a peace was evident to him before the battle of Borodino; but he still calculated that the occupation of Moscow would terrify the Emperor or enable him to revolutionise the country. He erred in every calculation.

The flames of the capital proved the animosity of the nation, and his agents at S. Petersburg soon informed him that he had not acquired an accurate knowledge of the Emperor's character.

The destruction of the magazines, the ravage of the surrounding country, and the movement upon the Kalouga road, instead of the Wladimir road, which movement the world (for the world's interests were deeply concerned in it) owes to General Beningsen, convinced him of the military fault he had committed, which was irreparable in the position in which he had placed himself. Obliged to throw forward a considerable force to cover Moscow, he hourly saw his strength diminished by he successful enterprises of the light troops of the Russians, oy bad nourishment, and an almost total want of forage.

He still flattered himself that the Russians would be awed behind the Oka ; but the combat in front of the Nakra baffled that expectation, and assured him that the Russian army was reinforced to an offensive power of action.

Confiding in Marshal Kutusow's diplomatic predilections, he sent Lauriston to conciliate, and he might have succeeded so far as an armistice if the instructions upon the powers granted to the Marshal had not been notorious, and the *non volo* of the army had not been very decisively expressed.

The injudicious arrangement of the troops under Murat procured the Russians an easy but important success ; and Buonaparte found by the forces they displayed, unfortunately not used, that he had not a moment's time for a painful but necessary measure.

An army of not less than one hundred and thirty thousand men, when united, hovered over him, of which above forty thousand were efficient cavalry. His line of communication was daily attacked ; a great army threatened to establish itself solidly in Poland ; reinforcements expected were necessarily marched to recover Courland and check Wittgenstein's force, which, from a corps, had increased to near fifty thousand men ; and winter was approaching with all its ills to augment the terrors of famine.

The evacuation of Moscow was rapidly executed. The *Gazette* will announce to your Royal Highness the subsequent occurrences that have cost him seven thousand men in one combat, sixteen cannon, and many prisoners taken in every direction, with equipages, stores, and treasures ; and which have as yet foiled his design of subsisting in a route not quite laid waste.

We are now marching towards Yukno, that we may throw him upon his baggage line, moving on the Mojaisk road ; and if we succeed, *as we ought*, I think the greater part of his army will sue to be marched to Siberia.

Those whom we take actually rejoice, and an officer whose exchange I offered to obtain, refused to incur again the distress he had experienced and the augmented sufferings which menaced.

Buonaparte himself could scarcely escape, but he has the peculiar good fortune to have this powerful, brave, and zealous army commanded by the most incapable of chiefs, and in using that term I apply the mildest that I can find to express in any degree the general estimation in which he is held.

He has shattered our nerves more than the enemy ever could; but Russian courage and a special Providence have hitherto preserved honour and success. I trust, however, that the command will soon be in more worthy hands, and that your Royal Highness will only have to wish that wisdom may direct the general councils of Europe.

According to our last advices from Admiral Tchichagow he was at Slonim, General Lambert occupied Minsk, and the blockade of Bobruisk was raised.

The Admiral had resolved to attack Warsaw, but I rather think that he will now move by Minsk upon Borisow.

I shall, however, have more certain advices in a few days, as Lord Tyrconnel will have joined him.

What Buonaparte will do after all his military sins of omission and commission I cannot pretend to determine; but I conceive that he will endeavour to reach the Niemen, and make Warsaw his head-quarters.

This nation has now solidly established its independence—by great sacrifices, assuredly, but they have produced an energy that advances the growth of Russia a century at least.

*No person had previously to this war a just knowledge of the power and resources of the Russian empire, not in its whole extent, but in the circle of a few provinces round Moscow.

At this moment one offers gratuitously forty thousand horses. The more distant governments are no less eager to contribute their aid, and there is one universal emulation of patriotism, one general spirit of vengeance.

In all the late affairs the rude peasants charged *en masse* with the veteran troops, and the pike in their hands is no less formidable to the enemy than the bayonet in those of the regular Russian soldier.

---

* The French, in their intercepted letters and on all occasions, expressed great surprise at finding unexpectedly in Russia a cultivated country, a dense population, good roads, a nobility eager to place their all at the disposition of the sovereign, and serfs emulous of their lords' patriotism.

Firearms, however, have effect under all circumstances; therefore I hope England will liberally supply them, and in so doing she will not only be sure of good service from them against the enemy, but of much increased goodwill in Russia.

If the smallest corps of British could also be landed, such co-operation would have a most advantageous moral influence, and still more because of our notorious exertions in the Peninsula.

Upon such a corps we might form a German army to any extent we chose. I am sure that I could have enlisted ten thousand men from the enemy alone, without a shilling bounty. Russia cannot recruit with any success amongst the foreigners. Language, prejudice, Siberian tales, form a rampart of separation which cannot be removed in one campaign, and the finances of Russia cannot support the expense.

Russia may, and I think will, reach the Vistula before New Year's day, but Austria or England, with the auxiliaries, must then bear the great burden of the war. I think that Russia cannot for a year maintain more than eighty thousand men effective beyond the Oder, and that Europe should not require more, for she needs interior organisation after such a costly struggle.

If, however, all is done that may be done, the war will not last another year.

We must consider the value of an early success, and provide the necessary means for its accomplishment. I believe the whole Continent is ready to meet our propositions, but there must not only be the inclination on our part, we must profit by the moment and apply a suitable activity.

Every impediment must be stormed, and the centripetal force which Jove urged against Danaë's scruples will penetrate all barriers of form and connection. To some we must give the bowels, to others the surface of earth, but all will prove a gift to enrich the giver.

The army with which I am marching, exclusive of its remote detachments, amounts to ninety thousand effective men, of which about fifteen thousand are unarmed.

The regular cavalry does not exceed ten thousand, but is in very good order. The Cossacks are in the highest condition, and the greater part of the twenty-six regiments which have lately joined are veterans, who, according to the privileges of their nation, had retired, but now voluntarily take the field.

We have seven hundred pieces of cannon actually marching with us in superb order, and their service is pre-eminently skilful and gallant.

I had the good fortune to open the ball at Malo-Jaroslavets with some horse pieces, which did considerable execution upon the enemy's principal column, and retarded his attack an hour; a finer opportunity for the effect of grape was never presented.

The army is fed abundantly, and has spirits regularly issued. The hospitals are greatly improved. The wounded are dressed in the field, but the severely wounded too often perish in the flames.

This occurred at Moscow and at Malo-Jaroslavets, when the town commenced to burn at seven in the evening. Some, indeed, must have been dreadfully mangled before death, for the grape poured through the flames as the dark shadows of the combatants appeared beyond.

The horrors of war have certainly raged here. "I could many a savage tale record," but the relation would be bad taste and worse policy.

The weather hitherto has greatly favoured the enemy, but winter's fleecy aid is now in sight.

It will be a rude campaign for us all, but I would not have a degree less cold, or a foot less of snow, for all the comforts and luxuries that a more congenial climate could provide.

I have only one regret—that I never hear from England. Since I went away in April I have never had but one letter from any part of my family or friends, and that letter was dated a fortnight after my departure.

I am also unfortunate in never having had an English aide-de-camp. The Emperor has given me an officer of his Hussar Guards, but he cannot assist me in the extensive correspondence with which I am charged.

Obliged to see every thing with my own eyes, and not to be a *mere* spectator, I assure your Royal Highness that I have been obliged to toil assiduously and sacrifice many an hour of very needed repose; but, thank God, I keep my health, and if friends and foes at the conclusion admit that I have usefully served my country, I shall obtain the object of my ambition, and feel that all is well that ends well.

I would, for the sake of my country, that I were responsible to other masters, and I hope the day is not remote.

I shall request of your Royal Highness to let those who will ever have my allegiance know that I am well, and that you will communicate whatever you may think interesting in this *précis* of what is past and passing.

With sentiments of affectionate duty to your Royal Highness, I have the honour to remain

Your Royal Highness's most obedient

and attached servant,

R. T. WILSON.

The Prince of Oldenburg happening to hear that I was writing, has requested to be put in your Royal Highness's remembrance. He is a very gallant officer, with the best political sentiments, and does much good by his correspondence with his brother married to the Grand Duchess.

I trust all your Royal Highness's staff are well, and that I may be permitted to be remembered to them through your Royal Highness.

No. 14.

SIR ROBERT WILSON TO H. R. H. THE DUKE OF GLOUCESTER.

SIR,   Willenburg, 30th Jan., 1813.

I have the honour to execute His Imperial Majesty's commands in acquainting your Royal Highness that His Imperial Majesty felt very sensibly obliged by the interest which your Royal Highness expressed for his welfare.

Since I last had the pleasure of addressing your Royal Highness, most important events have occurred; but the conclusion of the campaign, however favourable, was more inauspicious to Europe by the escape of Buonaparte than it ought to have been, considering the relative situation and power of both armies. The 29th Bulletin will justify every opinion I adventured at the time, and the present state of the Russian force will afford a severe comment on the policy of those who considered that the evasion of resistance would economise the Russian strength. The march has certainly not cost less to the Russian armies than eighty thousand, and every day the effects extend with alarming violence. Few of our battalions muster more than two hundred men under arms; and all the armies now moving on the Vistula cannot bring into the field more than seventy thousand effectives.

We are taught to expect great reinforcements in the spring, equal to two hundred thousand men; but the whole line of march is a pest lazaretto, so bad, that of ten thousand men who marched from Rayan, only two thousand five hundred entered Wilna a fortnight since, and the greater portion of that number has remained there in the hospitals where eight thousand bodies still remain unburied.

We might have finished the war. We have suffered the principal artisan to escape, and I think we shall find that he has resources in his manufactory which he moves by that great engine, activity, that sooner or later, but always eventually, turns the wheel of fortune in the desired track. How will that Chief who was scared at the shadow of a mutilated trunk, when his force was superior in numbers and composition, when famine, 25 degrees of cold, insubordination, and terror were his allies—dare to meet a renovated frame, with a morale excited by vengeance, and against whom nature no longer arrays her irresistible hostility?

We are now moving to pass the Vistula, and oblige the Saxons, &c., to evacuate Warsaw. The Austrians, who did not make the war as principals, are retiring within their own frontier. I presume this operation will succeed.

The French will, however, assemble their forces at Posen; and, if they can muster any cavalry, we shall with difficulty dislodge them. If they cannot, or if they fear Prussia's politics, they will fall back to the Oder. That will be the moment to gain some solid acquisition—to possess ourselves of Dantzic, which is justly deemed by Berthier, in one of his intercepted letters, "the most important fortress belonging to France," as she fears Russia more than any other power. It is, however, unfortunate that two thousand French have got into Dantzic from Stettin, and that three thousand Russian prisoners have been withdrawn. General Rapp can muster above ten thousand men, and is relieved from a source of just inquietude by this negligent observation of the route from the Oder.

The Prussian policy is still enveloped in indecision. Neither General Yorck nor General Kleist obey the King's published command, but this I believe they have private authority not to do. Still the King seems rather inclined to attach himself to Austria than Russia; and I shall, after all I know, be much surprised if he draws the sword against France without Austrian sanction, or some act of violence committed by Buonaparte. The corps of Kleist or Yorck is near twenty thousand strong, including two thousand five hundred cavalry. Under General Bülow, near Colberg, there are ten thousand. In Silesia thirty thousand, including five thousand four hundred cavalry. It is calculated that thirty thousand additional men may be raised.

R. T. WILSON.

No. 15.

MR. LISTON TO SIR ROBERT WILSON.

SIR,   Constantinople, 12th Feb., 1813.

In my last, which was of the 5th of January, by Mr. Ephemovich, I mentioned that I had had no letter from you of a later date than that of the 26th November from Kopis; and it was not till about a week ago that I had the pleasure of receiving those of the 4th of January from Wilna. Those of the 12th of that month from Merecz, and of the 20th from Lyk in Russia, reached me after I had laid my paper before me to acknowledge the receipt of the others.

None of the packets you entrusted to Lord Walpole or to Mr. Venner have ever been heard of; and the interruption in your correspondence, besides depriving us of your interesting and satisfactory accounts of the events of the war at the moments of the greatest anxiety, occasioned very serious uneasiness on account of your health, of which we have all along been apprehensive you did not take sufficient care.

It will give you satisfaction to learn that the intelligence you have communicated to me, when it has arrived in regular time, has been considered by competent judges as being of a nature to render service to the great cause in which we are engaged. Lord William Bentinck, to whom I had conveyed the substance of your early despatches from the neighbourhood of Moscow, writes to me on the 15th of December in the following terms:—

"I return you my best thanks for your letters of the 3rd of November, which I received on the 8th of December. It is the only intelligence of the affairs of Russia, excepting in the French papers, that has been received in Sicily. It is much to be regretted that such accounts could not come oftener and quicker to counteract the impressions made by the French."

The short notice I have had of the departure of the present courier . . . . . prevents me from writing to-day at the length I could have wished. But no material change has taken place in the state of politics in this place. You have nothing to hope for that is better, and nothing to fear that is worse, than a cold and surly neutrality. . . . . . .

I am shocked to inform you that you are never likely to receive the duplicates of my letters of the 28th and 30th of November. Poor Mr. Levy, to whom they were entrusted, we have every reason to think was shipwrecked on the Asiatic coast of the Black Sea, after having in vain attempted to reach Varna.

I have the honour to be,
With perfect truth and regard, Sir,
Your most obedient, humble servant,
ROBERT LISTON.

No. 16.

MR. LISTON TO SIR ROBERT WILSON.

[Extract from a Letter containing matter having reference to occurrences of later date.]

DEAR SIR,   Constantinople, 17th May, 1813.

It appears to me that, whether diplomatically employed or not, you may always give me intelligence of what is passing in the army where you happen to be stationed. My receiving *early* information is a matter of some consequence to the public service, and there is even an additional advantage in *your* transmitting it to this place, as I find the Reis Effendi inquiring anxiously after your news, and more apt to give credit to it than even to the *Bulletins officiels*.

Everything looks well at present; but I hope it will not be forgotten that late events of invaluable interest to the cause have been brought about by the wisdom and moderation of the Emperor's measures, and that they must be persevered in.

Forgive the haste in which I am obliged to write, and be assured of the sincere and affectionate attachment of

Your most faithful, humble servant,

ROBERT LISTON.

Then a Postscript. * * * . *

Then Postscript second. I have this moment learnt that the Reis Effendi has been dismissed, but I know nothing either of the cause or the consequences. I own I am inclined to be sorry for it, because he was a *good Turk*, and not a Frenchman, though Heaven knows he was not a good Englishman.

8 o'clock in the evening.

Postscript third. The disgrace of the Reis Effendi was a singular *quid pro quo*. A message was sent to him by the Caimacan to inform him that a certain business had taken a favourable turn, and that he might *be at his ease* on the subject. The messenger by mistake told him he might *take his ease* or *his rest*, using a Turkish word that is used when a man is desired to resign. The poor Reis took the hint, and walked off, and the office was vacant for a considerable part of the day.

No. 17.

THE DUKE OF WURTEMBERG TO SIR ROBERT WILSON.

[Copy. Translation. Original in the handwriting of the Duke.]

Head-Quarters at Lüben, in Silesia,
April, 1813.

MY DEAR AND RESPECTED FRIEND,

Our dear Emperor having conferred on me the command of the blockade and siege of Dantzic, I hasten to announce it to you, and I hope that you will come to me as soon as possible to share with your friend the cares and the glories of the enterprise. I have no need to add how much your counsels and experience are necessary for my aid.

Adieu! my dear General. Preserve in your remembrance

and friendship him who will remain all his life the most devoted and most attached servant and friend of your Excellency.

ALEXANDRE DE WURTEMBERG.
[" Uncle to the Emperor."] *

P.S. I leave tomorrow, early in the morning, for my new destination.

No. 18.
Count Woronzow to Sir Robert Wilson.

MONSIEUR LE CHEVALIER,   Londres, ce 25 Novembre (7 Décembre), 1803.

S. M. l'Empereur ayant reçu votre ouvrage, m'a chargé de vous communiquer, Monsieur le Chevalier, sa satisfaction et sa reconnoissance, et combien il était charmé de l'avoir eû. C'est avec le plus grand plaisir que je remplis les ordres de l'Empereur pour exprimer ses sentimens à votre égard, et pour y ajouter les miens. Je vous prie de croire à l'estime et à la considération les plus particulières avec lesquelles j'ai l'honneur d'être,

Monsieur le Chevalier,
Votre très humble et très obéissant serviteur,

S. C. WORONZOW.

Memorandum from the Emperor to Sir Robert Wilson.

Je vous rends grace, Général, pour l'exactitude avec laquelle vous me tenez informé de ce qui se passe à l'armée. Vos notions me sont souvent très utiles. Continuez, je vous prie, de faire de même, et recevez l'assurance de l'estime que je vous porte.   ALEXANDRE.

No. 19.
H. R. H. the Duke of York to Sir Robert Wilson.

DEAR SIR,   Windsor, 17th Dec., 1810.

I have to acknowledge the receipt of your letter of the 12th instant, and I request you will be assured that I am very sensible of your attention in dedicating to me the interesting work which you have lately published, and that I shall have great pleasure in an early perusal of it.

* In Sir Robert Wilson's handwriting.

I am by no means inclined to differ with you in regard to the military prowess of the Russian army, nor would the experience of their services in Holland in 1799 justify my forming any opinion unfavourable to their acknowledged character for bravery. I consider the Russian soldiers to be excellent machines, and capable, under able direction, of overcoming any obstacle; but the Russian troops appeared to me to be, with few exceptions, miserably deficient in officers of all ranks possessing sufficient knowledge or intelligence to take due advantage of the excellent qualities of the soldier. The experience which the army in Poland had acquired in Italy, &c., had probably in some degree removed that objection.

I am, dear Sir,

Yours very sincerely,

FREDERICK.

No. 20.

SIR ROBERT WILSON TO H. I. M. THE EMPEROR OF RUSSIA.

London, 7th Sept., 1841.

May it please your Imperial Majesty,

SIRE,

I presume to lay at the feet of your Imperial Majesty the accompanying work.

However imperfect, I nevertheless trust that your Imperial Majesty will recognize the loyalty of the motives which dictated its publication, and condescend to receive it as a record of attachment and gratitude to your Majesty and the illustrious nation over which your Majesty reigns.

I conceived it to be a paramount duty to vindicate the virtues and honour of a most generous and estimable people, and render the homage of truth and admiration to the heroic fortitude and glorious exploits of your Majesty's army in a most arduous and unequal contest.

I owe to your Majesty great—very great—personal obligations, but I know that your Majesty would never approve of the sacrifice of truth or the language of flattery.

That your Majesty may long continue to reign for the glory and prosperity of the Russian empire and for the interests of Europe, and that it may be my fortune to have repeated occa-

sions of proving my grateful sentiments towards your Majesty, your Imperial house, and brave people, is the earnest prayer and ambition
     of your Majesty's
       Most respectful servant,
          R. T. WILSON.

No. 21.

J. ABERCROMBY (LORD DUNFERMLINE) TO SIR ROBERT WILSON.

MY DEAR SIR ROBERT,   6, New Street, Spring Gardens, 13th Jan., 1813.

Having been applied to by a friend of Mr. ―――― to request that Lord Hutchinson would be the medium of communication, and knowing that our friend Hutchinson was in Ireland, I suggested that I might take the liberty of transmitting Mr. ――――'s letter, and I did so the rather as I conceived that no time should be lost in making the application to you. Mr. ―――― only speaks the common language and feeling of the country when he expresses a confident hope that you will give to the world a detailed and faithful account of the most interesting campaign of modern times.

The last campaign in Russia has not only been the most interesting of any in modern times, but it happens also to be the one of which the public are the most ignorant. After all, the French bulletins are the best reports that we have received, and no one can be ignorant that they are full of the grossest falsehoods and the most abominable misrepresentations. Of the Russian accounts I cannot speak more favourably, and partiality for a Scotchman forbids that I should say anything of Lord Cathcart's despatches.

In this state of affairs you cannot doubt that a faithful and copious detail of these important transactions would be eagerly read by the public, and who so fit to give them as yourself? You have not only had better means of information than any other person, but your experience, both as a soldier and as an author, would recommend any work of yours in the most effectual manner.

There is nothing in the late campaign that is to us more unaccountable than Buonaparte's long delay at Moscow. Was he preparing for his retreat? if so, he has not been very successful. Was he negotiating with the Emperor? if so, he was tempting fortune beyond what it has been her practice to do and beyond what prudence would justify. We are also entirely ignorant of the real cause of the burning of Moscow, and by whom the deed was done. At this time we have no account of the remnant of the French army later than the 29th Bulletin.

Whether you may think it prudent to accede to this proposal, I cannot tell; but I can only again express my sanguine hope that, in some way, you will gratify the wishes and expectations of the public. Excuse the liberty I have taken in troubling you with so long a letter, and believe me to be,

Dear Sir Robert,
Yours very faithfully and sincerely,
J. ABERCROMBY.

No. 22.

ADMIRAL TCHICHAGOW TO SIR ROBERT WILSON.*

MY DEAR SIR, The 23rd Januar., O. S., Strasburg.

It was a very agreeable surprise to me to see H$^{ble.}$ C$^{in.}$ Dawson arrive with your letters. It brought, whoever, poor Tyrconnel to my recollection and dampt my pleasure. Nevertheless I am sincerely thankfull for them, and particularly for the repeated promise to come and see me. I think we would find great many things to say which must not be written, for much of the things written in our corrupt age are the reverse of what ought to be sayd.

In my way of thinking I would always write the truth, and I think it would get the better of the lie at last. I saw for instance in the London Gazette which was given to me by your desire that Lord Cathcart's account of several affairs is such as it has been written in our army, not as you have seen the business done, &c. &c. I was rather surprised that our prince has been so indulgent as to mention G$^{l.}$ Canopka's capture by my army, for in general he keeps very great secret about what passes there in the way of success. I never saw in our

* It has been thought desirable to print this characteristic letter, as well as the French documents which follow, exactly as they were written.

papers a word of what we have done after leaving Brest Litowsky. Neither the destruction of G¹· Krassinsky's corps nor that of Dombrowsky have never been mentioned. But we know both who we have to deal with, and that is enough.

We are blocading Thorn at this moment. The French amuse themselves in spreading all sorts of news about their great force comming to relieve that place; for my part I would not be surprised if they surrender should I threaten them, which I mean to try. But the most desperate thing is our inaction. Enstead of being upon the Oder by this time, and having perhaps got holde of all those wandering kings, marshals, and generals, we are here, doing nothing or doing the most vulgar things that can be most improperly done in the present time. We think of collecting soldiers from Russia, or waiting for them, when armed and enthousiastic people by thousands expect only our appearance forward to form at one blow a formidable army, and throw the ennemy many hundred miles back. Every body is tired of the French, and wait only for a point d'appui. The first man who will be able to inspire confidence enough as to counterbalance the so much weakened sentiment of terror for Buonaparte will unite human kind round him and give a new face to the world.

Just at this instant I have the pleasure of receiving your letter of the 2d accompanied by the newspapers. I thank you most sincerely, and will use them as you desire. It has been said and with reason, that diversions were not proper tho first year of the war, but the second. Now the second is come and I dare say no body will think of them. My opinion is that in our present situation it would almost be enough to send the cadres of regiments and of an army abroad with a sufficient quantity of money, and it would be completed and forme a much better thing than we have an idea of. Most of our partizans are disapointed by what we say, and provoked by what we are doing. I did not understand what you mean by going to Warsaw before you come to see me. Is that town occupied by our troops? I have heard nothing about it.

I am also at a loss to know, as I found by A^d· Greig's letter, that several of our ships under their admirals are arrived to England, what for God's sake are they gone to do there? I cannot imagine because I know them.

Captn. Dawson wishes to stay with me for some time. If we find something to do I shall send him forward to C^t Woronzoft.

I repeat my most sincere gratitude for all what you have done in consequence of my application to you on account of my brother-in-law. I am not less obliged to Lord Cathcart for his kind reception of my request and his disposition to render me that kind of service, to which alone I can be sensible in this, for me, so wretched world.

I am, my dear Sir,
Your most faithful and affectionate
T. C.
[TCHICHAGOW.] *

No. 23.

LORD HOLLAND TO SIR ROBERT WILSON.

DEAR WILSON,   Holland House, 26th July, 1825.

I never read anything with greater interest and delight than your Memoranda. They were new as well as instructive to me, for though they were not necessary to convince me of your zeal, courage, and generosity, yet till I had read them I had no notion of your having had such opportunities of performing such great services, of your having so successfully performed them, and having forborne so frequently and so nobly to taunt both our own and foreign governments with the base ingratitude with which they have treated you. Do you mean to print the MS. or any part of it; and if not, would you allow me to take a copy of it? I keep it till you answer.

Yours ever truly,
VASSALL HOLLAND.

No. 24.

COUNT LUDOLF TO SIR ROBERT WILSON.

MON CHER GENERAL,   Constantinople, 27 9bre, 1812.

Je ne puis laisser partir Mr. Levy sans prendre l'occasion de me rapeller a votre souvenir, en vous remerciant de celui que

---

* Added here in Sir R. Wilson's handwriting.

vous me conservés au milieu de vos *bruiantes* occupations. Je n'attendois pas moins de votre infatigable activité que les relations importantes et frequentes, que vous avéz envoié a Mr. Liston des operations de cette campagne: les dernieres surtout apportés par Mr. Fenchaw nous ont mis à même de voir dans l'avenir avec moins d'inquietude, si surtout on acheve un ouvrage aussi bien en train, que celui de la destruction finale de l'enemi de l'humanité.

Je me fie a vos talents, a votre activité, et je ne doute pas, que partout ou vous pourrai influer a faire le plus de mal possible a nos enemis, vous le ferés.

Je desire que l'example que donne la maison Russe et Espagnole soit suivie par toutes les autres, c'est le moment de profiter de la circonstance unique que la Providence offre, et je ne doute pas, qu'on ne s'empresse de faire conoitre partout, l'etat auquel est reduit Napoleon; de mon coté je n'ai pas manqué de faire passer en Allemagne, et Italie, toutes les notions qui pouront assurer un resultat heureux.

Ici les evenements de la Russie font une grande sensation, et si la Porte desire *in petto* la destruction de Bonaparte, je ne sçais si elle la desire exclusivement par les mains de la Russie: mais dans tous les cas je doute qu'elle veuille y contribuer par ses propres mains.

Vous sentéz bien que nous sommes dans la derniere impatience d'aprendre les suites de la retraite de Bonaparte, et je me flate que vous ne nous laisseréz pas languir.

Soiés assuré mon general de la part que je prendrai toujours a vos exploits personels, et de l'estime et consideration que je vous ai voué, et avec laquelle j'ai l'honneur d'etre,

   Mon general,
    Votre tres humble tres obt. S.
      COMTE DE LUDOLF.*

No. 25.

TRADUCTION DE L'ORDRE DU JOUR DU $\frac{12}{24}$ OCTOBRE, 1812.

Il est ordonné à tous les commandans de corps, aux chefs des regimens de Cosaques, ainsi qu'a tous les partisans qui volti-

---

* Sicilian envoy to Constantinople.

gent autour des restes de la grande armée Françoise commandée par l'Empereur Napoléon en personne, de redoubler d'activité et d'attention dans l'exécution de ce qui leur est enjoint afin que rien ne puisse échapper des débris de cette armée. Après les pertes immenses qu'elle a faite depuis plus de six semaines, que nos troupes légères lui ont enlevé journellement de 100 jusqu'à 1000 hommes, après avoir vu exterminer une grande partie de sa cavalerie et surtout après la journée glorieuse du 1ᵉʳ de ce mois, où le Général Bennigsen a battu complettement le Roi de Naples, qui a perdu une partie de son artillerie, et dont la cavalerie a tellement été abimée qu'elle n'ose plus se presenter devant la notre, il seroit honteux à notre armée et à nos troupes légères si un seul homme de l'armée ennemie parvenoit à retourner en France et ne payoit point de sa vie ou par la captivité l'audace criminelle d'avoir osé suivre dans le cœur des provinces Russes le coupable agresseur qui se fait un jeu du sang de ses peuples. Les renforts de Cavalerie qui nous sont arrivés depuis peu se montent à 20,000 chevaux, au nombre desquels il y a 26 régimens de Cosaques du Don qui enlèvent journellement des dixaines de pièces de canons sur les derrières de l'enemi, qui affaibli, harassé, extenué, se trouve dans l'état le plus déplorable, et employe toutes ses ressources pour tromper notre vigilance et échapper à nos coups. Avec ces avantages décidés, on le répète, aucun Français ne doit revoir sa patrie, mais on met principalement sur la responsabilité des commandans et chefs des régimens de Cosaques, ainsi qu'à tous les détachemens en parti, d'entourer tellement l'armée françoise que l'Empereur Napoléon ne puisse pas échapper de sa personne. On joint pour cela son signalement à cet Ordre du jour.

Le signalement doit servir également à tous les chefs des districts, à toutes les autorités civiles ou armées, à tous les maîtres de postes etc. . . . . Si cet ordre est fidellement exécuté, artillerie, munitions, équipages, tout tombe en notre pouvoir. Nous reprendrons de même comme nous l'avons déja fais en partie, les dépouilles sacrées qu'un profanateur sacrilége a enlévé dans nos temples; renouvellant ainsi les scènes du Vandalisme revolutionnaire.

Signalement de Sa Majesté l'Empereur Napoléon.

La taille epaisse et ramassée. Les cheveux noirs, plats, et courts. La barbe noire et forte, rasée jusqu'au dessus de l'oreille. Des sourcils bien arcqués, mais froncés vers le nez, le regard attrabilaire ou fougueux. Le nez aquilain avec des traces continuelles de tabac. Le menton très saillant. Toujours en petit uniforme sans appareil et le plus souvent enveloppé d'un petit surtout gris pour n'être point remarqué, et sans cesse accompagné d'un Mameluc.

No. 26.
COUNT ITALINSKY TO SIR ROBERT WILSON.

MONSIEUR LE CHEVALIER, Buyukdere, le 3 Decembre, st. n. 1812.

Mr. Levy me remit la lettre, qu'à son depart pour ce pays-ci vous lui avez confiée pour moi, et je puis vous assurer, que j'ai reçu cette marque de votre souvenir avec autant de plaisir que de reconnoissance. Les nouvelles que par la même occasion vous nous avés communiquées, étoient les premières que nous eumes sur le véritable état des choses. Elles nous ont mis à même de prévoir, que l'ennemi ne pouvoit pas rester longtemps à Moskwa, et ce présentiment avoit adouci beaucoup la douleur, que nous a fait éprouver Andreossi par le grand appareil avec lequel il a célébré l'occupation de la dite capitale, et par l'impression facheuse qu'il avoit produit sur l'esprit du ministère turc. La défaite de Murat, que par vos soins nous apprimes bientôt après, annonça comme chose prochaine l'événement qui a occasionné l'expédition de Mr. Fenchow, et qui nous a comblé de joie. Dieu soit loué! nous voici dans l'acheminement de recueillir les fruits les plus glorieux de notre patriotisme, et des immenses sacrifices, dont le noble sentiment a été accompagné. Les François sont au désespoir, sont enragés, et surtout ceux qui composent l'ambassade du *grand Napoléon, l'ami de ses alliés, la terreur de ses ennemis, la Providence du monde.* (C'est le toast qu'Andreossi proposa à diner le jour qu'il célébroit la prise de Moskwa!) Les Turcs sont surpris, et ne savent pas se rendre compte, comment l'Invincible a pu être batu, et être réduit à la nécessité de se sauver par une fuite aussi honteuse qu'elle est désastreuse; ils commencent à baisser du ton et à être plus traitables ; mais ils sont encore bien loin de sentir la justesse et l'importance des observations que vous m'avés faites dans la lettre, dont Mr. Fogassiera étoit porteur, et que j'ai communiquée en entier au Reiss-Effendi. Continués, je vous supplie, à nous tenir au courant de ce qui se passe chés vous, la bonne cause y gagnera beaucoup.

Veuillés bien agréer les sentimens du plus sincère attachement et de la consideration la plus distinguée avec lesquels j'ai l'honneur d'être,

    Monsieur le Chevalier,
  Votre très humble et très obéissant serviteur,
        A. D'ITALINSKY.

www.ingramcontent.com/pod-product-compliance
Lightning Source LLC
Chambersburg PA
CBHW051724300426
44115CB00007B/449